THE CHASM

THE CHASM

*The Life and Death
of a Great Experiment
in Ghetto Education*

ROBERT CAMPBELL

With an Introduction
by James Baldwin

HOUGHTON MIFFLIN COMPANY BOSTON

1974

The author gratefully acknowledges permission to reprint from the following:

"Dream Deferred." Copyright 1951 by Langston Hughes. Reprinted from *The Panther and the Lash*, by Langston Hughes, by permission of Alfred A. Knopf, Inc., and Harold Ober Associates Incorporated.

"The Foolish Frog" by Charles Seeger and Pete Seeger. © Copyright 1955 by Stormking Music Inc. All rights reserved. Used by permission.

"Over the Rainbow," words by E. Y. Harburg, music by Harold Arlen. Copyright © 1938, renewed 1966 Metro-Goldwyn-Mayer Inc. Rights controlled by Leo Feist Inc. Used by permission.

"Peter Cottontail," by Steve Nelson and Jack Rollins. Copyright 1950 by Hill and Range Songs, Inc., New York, New York. Used by permission.

"Living for the City," by Stevie Wonder.

First Printing V

Library of Congress Cataloging in Publication Data

Campbell, Robert, 1922–
    The chasm; the life and death of a great experiment
in ghetto education.

    1. Negroes — Education — New York (City)   2. Socially handicapped children — Education — New York (City)
3. Education — Experimental methods.   I. Title.
LC2803.N5C35   370'.9747'1   74-3077
ISBN 0-395-18502-5

Printed in the United States of America

To Nancy —

who steadfastly sustained
my belief that the earth
was flat
and who cheerfully endured
the hardships of a three-year
voyage to prove it —

and
for Tom and Stephen

Contents

Introduction
by James Baldwin

Her brother's smart, he's got more sense than many.
His patience's long, but soon he won't have any.

STEVIE WONDER, "Living for the City"

A BLACK CHILD is able to relate, though somewhat painfully, to what black people see, but he is utterly at a loss as to what it is white people see. As a black man who was once a black child, I must confess that this bewilderment does not necessarily diminish with time — for example:

Not so many years ago, I was working in a small New England town, an old, very handsome, and well-to-do town, where some very pleasant people lived. I was not, however, working for anyone in the town, and I had not brought my family with me, and the social life of the town was not so irresistible as to cause me to feel left out of it. In short, I was no problem.

There was a bomb scare during that time; that is, we were once again, monotonously, on the brink of war, and the villagers in the drugstore where I was having breakfast one morning were being very plucky. The owner, a big, good-natured man, was describing to a rapt audience what to do when the alert sounded. Relief stations had been, or were being, set up along all the roads leading out of town — stations for gas, food, milk, first aid, et cetera — and each citizen was to leap into his car, with his family, of course, and take the road to which he had already been assigned. Each citizen was to take as little as possible with him. I listened with an altogether intelligent wonder and did not increase my popularity in that town by asking, during a charged, patriotic pause: "What makes you think there'll be any roads?"

Or: a girl I knew, who lived on East 72nd Street, had a bomb shelter in her basement — a private one, her family had built it — and it was stocked with goodies from here to eternity, and it could hold fifty people. She and her father had made up a list of the people who should be saved, and I was one of them. When the siren sounded, I was to leave my Horatio Street apartment immediately, with the overnight bag I was always to have in readiness, leap into the nearest taxi, and drive straight to her house where drink and good food and good company would be awaiting me — like, forever. I told her I didn't know the other forty-nine people.

I am not trying to be outrageous. I am edging myself obliquely into Mr. Campbell's book by forcing on my own attention, again, the fact that Americans are, among other things, ridiculous, and this quality proves that they have some of the more endearing human qualities. Well, this is not quite enough for love, just as the fact that they are blind is not enough for forgiveness. It is not always easy for a black man to remember that Americans are human. Many a black child never finds this out, or when he finds it out, it merely increases his hatred. A twenty-three-year-old black sailor went berserk somewhere in America not long ago, killed a couple of people, and got wasted himself; the news report I read said that this had come about because this one-time honor student, after having joined the navy, *"somehow"* (italics mine) began to hate white people. (His mother, to no avail, attempted to bring light into this darkness: her son, she said, just wanted to be a man.) There was a photograph of the boy from high school, when he was about eighteen, bright, smiling, eager, ready to embrace the world. By the time I saw the photograph, he was twenty-three, and dead.

Many of our children are mowed down very much sooner — even before they have "somehow" learned to hate. And this destruction is not accidental. It is deliberate. I will not go so far as to say that this destruction is accomplished by wicked people, for that is much too easy. But, for the victim, certainly — and to go no further than that — the distinction between a wicked person and a wicked result is not worth making. If one's son, or brother, for example, is a junkie, and one knows that this is a result of the demoralization he encountered in the ghetto school, it does not matter that this result was accomplished by upright Jews and Christians, good white Americans all, who meant the child no harm. The harm is done. And once the harm is done, it is very hard to believe that the harm was not intended. The harm done to black children in the ghetto schools operates, in any event, to reinforce the power held by white people in this country. The ghetto operates to guarantee that very few black children — certainly not the bulk of them — will ever gain the authority or the means to challenge this power.

It is the school that makes vivid to the child his helpless inferiority. It does this by having no respect whatever for the child's experience. Until the child gets to school, his circumstances, however wretched in appearance, however hard in fact, are coherent: in school he discovers that these circumstances are also shameful, so shameful that no one wishes to hear anything about them. He talks the way he has talked since he learned to talk, the way everyone around him talks: suddenly it is all wrong. He wonders what his aunt would think of his teacher; then he wonders what his teacher would think of his aunt. She would think the same thing that she thinks of him. He is colored, that is why he is so lazy. Or he is lazy, that is why he is so colored? The school assures him, anyway, that he deserves his condition. It is in school that he learns that if he had not been brought to America, he would still be a savage, in Africa. (Savage? Africa?) He learns that — in spite of his journey to

America — he has never been a poet or an inventor or a composer or a statesman. He will learn nothing of black artisans, architects, clockmakers, or inventors. He may be given a dim sketch of Matt Henson as a kind of polar Gunga Din, but he will learn nothing, or worse than nothing, of Frederick Douglass, or of his involvement with John Brown; indeed, if he hears of John Brown at all, he will be told that he was a fanatic, who deserved to hang — the proof being that the slaves have been set free. (*He*, the child, is proof of that!) He will learn nothing of Aleksander Pushkin or Alexandre Dumas or Ira Aldridge or Bert Williams or Paul Robeson. He will be told something about Booker T. Washington, who will not attract him, and George Washington Carver, who will attract him even less.

He will not be told that the wealth of Mississippi, as well as the wealth of Massachusetts, was created by his labor, that his forefathers lined the railroad track and then stoked the train engines and drove the trains over these same tracks, to carry the fruit of *their* labor to market. Neither will he be told that the millions of dollars amassed by Tin Pan Alley were almost all stolen from black people, hence stolen from him. (He will learn nothing about Bessie Smith.) *He* never had anything worth stealing — that is what he learns in school. He is told that he was born without any inheritance at all, and now he can never have one, unless and until he makes himself ready. Ready? How? For what? When the school is finished with him — or he with the school, which comes to the same thing — he is ready for the streets, the needle, the jail, the army, the garment center, ready to be used in nearly any way whatever, always assuming that white people — for that is absolutely all that Americans are to him by now: white people — have any use for him at all.

There is a brutal efficiency in the means, to say nothing of the speed, with which this debasement is accomplished: such miracles of efficiency cannot be accomplished by people who do not know what they are doing. They can, however, blind themselves to what they are doing, and to such an extent, indeed,

that many of those most responsible for this devastation are per-
petually suggesting ways of aiding the "disadvantaged": "I
weep for you," the Walrus said: "I deeply sympathize."

This liberal sympathy — for I have never met a Northern
school teacher who did not claim to be a liberal — is rarely
equal to the dry-eyed task of teaching. I know that a good
teacher is rare. I also know that they are not as rare as all
that — I am a survivor of the ghetto school — and that their rar-
ity is not the problem. The problem is that they are deliberately made rare and relentlessly weeded out. This process is
also efficient, and it, too, operates on a level which absolves any
particular individual of personal responsibility.

Children are probably the toughest and the most fragile
human beings in the world, and, bar none, the most important.
They are also the most exasperating, cunning, devious, self-centered, ruthless, unpredictable, and exhausting people in the
world; a hard day's work in the mines can be less grueling than
walking a child through the park. The reason, for me anyway,
that a child is so difficult and so valuable — sacred, really — is
that while it is virtually impossible to fool a child, it is very easy
to betray him.

Children, for example, do not believe in Santa Claus for very
long, and without our testimony, neither could nor would have
believed in him at all. The belief in Santa Claus is nothing
more than an opportunity for the child to exercise his imagination, an opportunity, in fact, to play games with us. The child
lets go of Santa Claus without a qualm since, after all, *we* are
Santa Claus, and he knew that all along. He is very smug and
happy to have so shrewdly seen through his elders — one of the
complex of reasons that he does not immediately make public
his discovery. He waits, as it were, to see if *we* are as smart as
he is. The point is, however, that *we* are there, and as long as
we are there, who needs Santa Claus?

And if we are *not* there, Who needs Santa Claus? For, on the other hand, if you promise a child that you will see him at a certain hour, on a certain day, everything in the child concentrates and hurls itself forward into that day and hour: if you do not keep your promise, the child begins to get lost. If you tell a child that he need only pray to God for something he deeply desires and that God will answer his prayer, the child will believe you; he will take you at your word. And if the child prays and his prayer is not answered, it is not God whom he will reproach, for it is not God who has betrayed him. He can live without God, as he can live without Santa Claus; a child can live on astoundingly little, but he cannot live without love.

It is very difficult to avoid making the child the vehicle, if not the extension, of our fantasies and terrors: many of us, after all, are very poorly equipped to give love, partly because so many of us did not, at our beginnings, receive it. One must always attempt to tell a child the truth. But one cannot do this without telling oneself the truth. A child imagines that there is such a thing as the truth, as palpable as the hand he is holding, but we know better and must attempt to prepare him for that threshold. We know, too, as he does not, that there *is* such a thing as a lie. But, in a child's world, a lie is absolute and his imagination has no defense against it. He would rather that the hand had struck him, for a blow, at least, is real.

Most adults, including you and me, can be fooled very easily. We really prefer to be fooled a great deal of the time because we wish to be reassured as to where the boundaries of reality are to be found. *Nowhere* is the only real answer; reality is shifting and changing all the time, and the word itself is a desperate makeshift. But no adult can live consciously under this pressure from day to day, because he has an adult's responsibilities. His primary responsibility involves making decisions, and these decisions can be made only in the context of a given reality. In order to live, an adult must take a great deal for granted — the trick, of course, is not to take too much for granted. An adult is, by definition, a fixed, a limited form, and while great adventures, let us hope, continue to occur within this form, the form itself is unlikely to change. For example, if one has been a magazine editor for twenty years, it is unlikely that one will suddenly so transform oneself as to embark on the discovery of a new solar system.

But the child may discover a new solar system: the child may do, become, anything, anything at all. And when I say a child is sacred, I mean that we have a sacred responsibility toward the child: to protect without stifling him, to guide without tyrannizing him, to correct without terrifying him, to punish without demoralizing him. To show him where the boundaries of reality are to be found, and to suggest, once he has mastered these, that these boundaries are, after all, quite new: men pushed these boundaries to where they are now. Well, if men could push these boundaries to where they are now, perhaps *he* can push them further. But the price for this is to respect and examine the present boundaries — or, in other words, discipline is the key to freedom.

The above may sound like an outrageously abstract concept for a child's mind, particularly in a ghetto school. But I do not think so: particularly in a ghetto school. In my experience, the difficulty is almost always to be found in quite the opposite direction, that is, in the mind of the adult. In any case, teaching is not lecturing. Teaching is a two-way street, for a genuine teacher also learns from the child. If this two-way street can be kept relatively uncluttered, or if the child knows, in spite of everything, merely that the street is there, that the street is real, the child can find his feet on it. We say that he is *learning:* he feels that he is *living.* He cannot feel that unless he also feels that *he has a right to be here.* If you, the teacher, feel that he is valuable, that he has a right to be here, he will — very slowly sometimes, and by putting you through many a grueling test — respond to that. And if you feel that he is worthless, or if you pity him, or if you fear him, or condescend to him, he will feel that, and he will feel it no matter what you say or what you do or how you smile. He will never trust you; you will never be able to reach him, and he will never learn anything from you. He has learned quite enough already: that you doubt his value. His value is all he has, and you have hurt him, at the very threshold of his life, as deeply as any human being can be hurt.

Now, this is a racist country. It was born that way and has grown up, or has failed to grow up, that way. It is impossible to be an American and not be infected in some fashion, and to some extent, with this disease; the most dangerous carriers of all are those who imagine themselves to be immune to it. Unlike the author of this remarkable book (who, by no means incidentally, is a Southerner), they have never located this virus in themselves, have never been forced to recognize to what extent this foul disease corrupts and constricts their lives, have never been forced, so to speak, to confess it, to wrestle with it, to kick the habit, to sweat it out. That their freedom, then, is a delusion and their ability to teach virtually nonexistent is proved not merely by the ghetto schools, but by nearly *all* schools, and the bulk of their alumni, all over this nation.

It is from all these schools, it is from all over America, that the people who teach black children come; from all these schools, from all over America, come the people who constitute the boards of education; come governors of states, mayors of cities; come heads of unions, and the rank and file. Quiet as it's kept, children, not that it's kept that quiet, this spells power, the main chance, and power is allied with money: one forgets that Education is a billion-dollar business. No one thought of this, for example, when, a few light years back, one watched the brutality with which white Southerners (proving how well they had been educated) treated black children during the Southern school crisis. It was very hard to believe that grown men and women could treat any child that way. But black people knew that when the Northern hour struck, as it inevitably would, though the details of brutality would be different, the principle would be exactly the same, and the results even more devastat-

ing — as they had been already, in the North, for many a gener-
ation. When the experimental schools began, only a handful of
people, outside of the people directly involved, believed that
the experiment could possibly succeed. And the experiment
was discontinued after three years, not because it failed, but
because it did not fail. An energy was tapped in the ghetto that
had never been tapped on such a level before. I have nieces
and nephews in school; I know a few teachers, and I have made
a few visits. I grew up in Harlem; I was a school boy there. It
is quite impossible to describe that particular version of *Pilgrim's Progress*, in which the pilgrim — oneself — moved inexorably from one level of despair to another. One's sense of self,
one's dream of living, receded, blurred, dimmed. One's actual
future encroached, was literally present; one saw it and heard it
everywhere: it could not be escaped. There was only one out,
or, at most, two — the civil service or the army. Otherwise, one
had to find a way to make it on these mean streets. One wanted
more than that. One had more to give than that. But nobody
wanted what one had to give. This accumulating sense of one's
own worthlessness is the climate in which most of us grew up.

But there was a new climate in the halls and classrooms of the
experimental schools. For example, the children who wanted
to paint, painted, and their work was on view. All of it was
alive, however awkward — a child's awkwardness, anyway,
contains a very moving grace — and some of it was astounding.
And this was not so much because one was confronted with
what a child sees, but because one was confronted with reality.
I remember watching one child painting, and thinking to myself
that *I* would never have seen a fire escape *that* way: but it was,
incontestably, a fire escape, something between a trap and a
leap. And the children moved and rang with purpose. They
looked you in the eye, instead of at the door or the floor. When
they spoke, they spoke as though they wanted you to hear them
and not as though they wished to God you'd go away. This
climate was contagious. The children carried it home with

them. The parents carried it into the streets with them and to their jobs. The message was: We aren't helpless. We're coming through.

This is subversion. Not only does this make for a future scarcity of decent maids and porters — a statement neither facile nor malicious, merely blunt — it attacks an unspoken order of things involving rewards and punishments. Rewards and punishments are administered within a specific context, and this context is the received, the given morality, a particular carrot and a particular stick, and this context is not to be questioned. An ex-junkie friend of mine was working with ex-junkies in a city hospital, and these men, attempting rehabilitation, asked me to visit, which I did, along with one of my brothers. These rejects were very remarkable men, far clearer, more honest, and stronger than many of the people I meet outside. We rapped and laughed; some of the men painted and some of them wrote, and they showed me their work. We were having a great time, all of us, and then the supervisor, a hideously hysterical white chick, came and threw me and my brother out. It was a terrible thing to do to the men, an act of real vindictiveness, and there was absolutely no reason for it; we had not broken any rules. But the men were happy and at ease, and this cannot be allowed. If you think I am exaggerating, visit one of our institutions and try it yourself or check with any survivor.

It was on the rock of this terror that the experimental schools crashed. In the first place, and I speak now as someone born and bred in the ghetto, it was neither intended nor expected that the experiment would succeed. Though it came about in seeming response to the parents' demands for community control, it was not understood how passionate was this demand. It was not foreseen, either, that the parents would actually enter the schools and work in them. It was not imagined that the teachers would actually evolve new ways of teaching children, so that the children actually learned. This immediately brought into question, of course, traditional ways of teaching and traditional ways of judging a child's progress, and mightily displeased the Board of Education. But what broke the camel's back was the effrontery of the community in daring to pass on the qualifications of some of the teachers to teach their children. Rhody McCoy transferred several teachers out of his district, and this opened the saddest, most acrid, and most revealing chapter of the entire struggle.

McCoy's dismissal of the unsatisfactory teachers was not intended to be an attack on the United Federation of Teachers. McCoy was the head of his district, responsible for and devoted to the well-being of the district, and there was no particular reason for him to have thought of the union at all. But his dismissal of the teachers meant that he thought he had the *right* to dismiss them. (McCoy felt that he had the *duty* to dismiss them.) That he *had* no such right had to be made immediately and abundantly clear, not only to protect the power of the United Federation of Teachers, but also to prevent any of the billions of dollars involved in the Education business from being controlled by black and Puerto Rican communities. Therefore, the head of the United Federation of Teachers, Albert Shanker, called a city-wide strike. This was to put McCoy in his place and to make certain that his exercise of authority would not constitute a precedent. The strike was to have devastating repercussions: it is to be hoped that Mr. Shanker loves his own children, if he has any, for he certainly has no love for any others.

Mr. Campbell gives a nobly restrained account of this disaster, which injected into the school struggle (which scarcely needed such an ancient red herring) the question of anti-Semitism. This question was injected arbitrarily and with no justification whatever, and I have no hesitation about accusing the people who thus attempted to defend their conduct of the most ignoble cowardice. In the first place, the dismissal of the teachers had had nothing whatever to do with their ancestry, whatever, indeed, their ancestry may have been; nor was anyone in the ghetto so deluded as to imagine that the strike had been called for the special benefit of Jews. The very supposition is an insult, for blacks did not arrive here yesterday and know far more about America than that. They took it for what it was, a power ploy, more proof of the American determination to keep the nigger in his place. Jews were helping them to do this (but Jews are Americans), which was certainly nothing new, and in this context, the Jew might as well have been a Swede. If no one scrawled "dirty Swede" on the walls, it is because Swedes, as Swedes, have never operated in the ghetto, don't arrive to collect the rent, and don't run the pawnshop. Jews do, and have for generations, and there is no point in pretending that this isn't so. Jews may often be inconvenienced in this country because they are Jews, but they do not suffer here as a black man does, and they know this very well. They also know that, even if black people hated them, black people certainly do not have the power to destroy them. And it *is* cowardly, and indeed a betrayal of whatever it means to be a Jew, to act as a white man, benefit as a white man, treat black people as white men do, and then accuse the victim, when the victim reacts, of being an anti-Semite.

The man who wrote this book is very honest, very loving, and his children are lucky: he must be a beautiful cat.

St. Paul de Vence
January 30, 1974

Prologue

What happens to a dream deferred?

Does it dry up
like a raisin in the sun?
Or fester like a sore —
And then run?
Does it stink like rotten meat?
Or crust and sugar over —
like a syrupy sweet?

Maybe it just sags
like a heavy load.

Or does it explode?

Langston Hughes

I N THE HOT summers of 1967 and 1968 the dream did indeed explode — in Harlem and Watts, in Detroit and the Hough area of Cleveland, in other big-city ghettos as well. These explosions, violent as they appeared, were but the mild surface ripples of a catastrophic social disaster that unfolded virtually unnoticed by mid-Americans like myself in the decades following World War II. Had the calamity been an actual geological event, like the uplifting of the Rocky Mountain range, the air would have been filled with a deafening rumble mingled with an excruciatingly high-pitched scream as the earth was torn apart in an epic, Biblical convulsion stretching out over more than a quarter of a century. In fact, however, these fearful events occurred within the American soul in utter silence, in a slow-motion rending of the mind the very quietude of which made the growing and widening and ultimately yawning chasm in America a disaster which was truly frightening. When the whole psychological upheaval ended, the ghetto dwellers found themselves stuck "out here," a somewhat unnerving term they use to refer to where they live (as in: "Life's pretty hard out here," as opposed to "in there," or "downtown," where the power and the money and the opportunities are), stranded in the slums of the cities protesting a disaster of the mind represented by the obvious failure of poverty children in school.

The calamity began with an agricultural revolution in the South which uprooted and displaced hundreds of thousands of poor and ignorant blacks — sharecroppers and tenant farmers mostly. Wave after wave of immigrants migrated to the big cities of the North, seeking the "Promised Land" as Claude Brown so eloquently and bitterly named it in *Manchild in the Promised Land*. So did multitudes of Puerto Ricans, leaving their island habitat for the land of opportunity. A third part of the migrant population was composed of poor whites from Appalachia. Unhappily for virtually all these pilgrims the trail to the Promised Land came to a dead end in a teeming, squabbling tenement. The dream had not only been deferred; it had quite literally evaporated. Our big-city ghettos were not the egress to opportunity the new arrivals had expected and that earlier bands of immigrants had successfully negotiated. Instead they proved to be prisons which turned into steaming pressure cookers of despair, cauldrons that occasionally blew a lid during one hot summer or another, reflecting the terrible forces beneath the surface phenomenon.

Our electronically gifted news media, normally so adept at filtering out "noise," seemed completely incapable of getting a clear channel from the ghetto as to what it was all about. One

caught glimpses of an accusing and threatening Malcolm X.
There were cries of "We going to get Whitey." During those
hot summers several storekeepers in our local shopping center
in rural New Jersey became convinced that bands of marauding
blacks would appear any day, any minute, from Newark or Elizabeth to burn and plunder and perhaps rape our cozy community. In more rational moments such people were simply bewildered. This bafflement took the form of an apparently
reasonable question: "We made it; why can't *they?*" It was a
good question, even if there was an implication of inferiority in
asking it to begin with. The problem with the question is that
the old "melting pot" idea of "us" making it is an American
myth. And like so many other myths people cling to and continue to live by, it is simply not true. Yet eliminating obsolete
ideas from the American mythology is difficult, for this is a
mythological country, established upon some grand myths
about human nature and human rights long ago, ideas about
freedom and opportunity, equality and happiness. Unfortunately these basic myths have been largely eclipsed by later
and more questionable ones which have seriously beclouded
the American issue — to the point where one wonders whether
America is a genuine country at all, whether it has any real and
fundamental character, or whether it is only a dilly-dally flap-
doodle, a flimflam, a humbug operation.

Humbug. What a marvelous and original word! The perfect
word for these latter-day notions of what America means! As
Stephen Decatur said: ". . . our country, right or wrong!" A
lot of fellows charged over the top to that one, at least in some
wars when the country seemed reasonably right. Yet, as G. K.
Chesterton commented on this particular bit of idealism:
"That's like saying 'My Mother, drunk or sober.' "

A country capable of enjoying such a word and of coming up
with variations on the theme as the occasion arises cannot be all
bad — as W. C. Fields might say.

The humbug about "us" making it in school in some ancestral

fashion was put to rest by Colin Greer of Columbia Teachers College in New York. He did a survey of big-city school children going all the way back to the turn of the century. The survey revealed that poverty children never did "make it" in our urban schools — whether they were Irish, Italian, Polish, German, English or whatever (some Jewish groups excepted due to strong family pressure to succeed despite "the system."). The survey included New York, Boston, Philadelphia, Minneapolis, Washington, D.C., Pittsburgh, and most other major cities. Instead in the old days those kids, the big kids who always sat in the back of the classroom, could get work permits at the age of fourteen, fifteen, or sixteen, depending on the availability of jobs for "hands" (Hands Wanted, signs said in factory windows some generations ago), and so could go to work and get out of the ghetto. The Irish built railroads, became hod carriers on construction projects, and unmarried sisters upgraded both themselves and their marriage prospects by becoming teachers in the public school system — to be followed at a later date by Jewish girls who now dominate the school scene, at least in New York City. Polish and Italian stonemasons escaped to build structures like the Jersey City waterworks. Germans and Scandinavians moved west to the farm regions of Pennsylvania, Minnesota, and elsewhere. All this was possible because there was ample work available outside the ghetto, starting at the unskilled level and progressing upward.

After World War II, however, this traditional work picture simply disappeared. There was still such work around, of course. But the jobs had largely been sealed off by the white trade unions that had just gotten the scent of money and didn't want anyone else sniffing around the hive. So as an accident of history more than a matter of race, the current ghetto dwellers are struck. The same technical revolution that initially uprooted them also destroyed the dream of opportunity, simple opportunity, they thought lay waiting in the Promised Land. Ironically it also generated a swelling tide of affluence for virtually everyone else in the country, and as the wave grew, blue-collar workers and the middle class took off, increasing even more the distance from those stuck out on the mud flats the tide left behind. To the stranded ones, locked into their dreams, where the wave has gone is apparent enough. Day in and day out it tosses its haughty head and looks back in derision at the unfortunates over television. Across the chasm and into the ghetto come the messages designed to persuade, entice, cajole, and blackmail the "Other America": Get sexy "wheels." "The Dodge rebellion wants YOU!" the squiggly white girl proclaims. (Me?) Fly now and pay later, as though you were a member of the jet set instead of some local car pool. (Car pool?) Easy credit and loans with our instant bank plan. (Credit? Loans?) So a kid sees, amid squalling siblings and a slap in the face if he's uppity, amid roaches and rooftops, and preachments about God and good behavior and mind your manners or I'll belt you one, he sees — what? An unattainable dream contrasted to an unbearable reality. What happens to a kid if you put him on a rack like that? If you met that kid on a dark street some night what would you expect? From you? From him? Particularly if he's older now, wiped out, not caring anymore? What would you say to him?

Resisting the blandishments of the great American commercial hustle is difficult enough for citizens of the Other America. Still, it is not a total flimflam operation, for the bridge to opportunity is there. With prudence a cautious citizen can negotiate the bridge and advance himself, however materialistic its underpinnings may be. On the other hand, if he is too easily beguiled he may discover that instead of making out, he is perilously close to walking the plank. By and large, however, the system permits most people to move along and better their lot in life. But "out here" there is no ramp leading onto the bridge to opportunity. Instead it ends abruptly, a mile high in the air. From the end of the bridge a variety of goods and services is dropped to the stranded ones by an American society that professes some concern for the basic needs of all its citizens. But the operation is a bit like pouring cheap cement at a graft-ridden construction site. And at ground level the goods are readily recognized for what they are — shoddy ghetto goods, stuff that wears out or doesn't work very well, like the schools that are the only way up to the bridge today. Few kids, even if they are agile enough to scale a five-story schoolhouse, can reach the bridge that does not touch down.

So all too many emulate the version of making out which they see in the local streets. And in doing so they are wasted. Day in and day out. Thousands. Tens of thousands. Hundreds of thousands. Year in and year out. Forget it. Drop out of school. Get your own hustle going. Little hustle first; big hustle later on — if you make it. Any way out will do. And when the only legitimate way out is unattainable, what then? The complete wasting of almost all Claude Brown's friends answers the "what then?" Popping. Glue. Then the hard stuff. Drift and dream. When you're nodding the fact that you have nothing and there's no way out isn't important anymore. When you're on your own private trip only you and the trip are real and the reality of where you actually are — stuck — drifts out of consciousness. Drift and dream. Dream and nod. Escape.

"Out here," of course, almost everyone has known this for some time now. In fact, many people even believe there is a Great Heroin Conspiracy between the pushers and the police to cool things off in the ghetto. The logic is absurdly simple: get everyone strung out; let 'em steal TV sets and stuff for their habit; addicts are simply out of it when it comes to any kind of organized rioting. Whatever the reason, the fact is there. By the same token folks know perfectly well that the only legitimate exit from the ghetto today, the only exit that does not end in self-destruction, is labeled "education" — learn, get smart, get with it, and get out. Now that the dust of an unexpected technological revolution has settled, now that the old jobs for "hands" are gone, education is the only way to a decent job

today, the only ramp that doesn't lead to cleaning house for
white people or pushing a cart in the garment district at near-
sweatshop wages. Yet it is just as evident that the ramp doesn't
work. So quite predictably a sense of frustration and rage
builds up against the schools, implanted in the neighborhoods
of the poor like solid bastilles, feudal castle-keeps manned by a
colonialistic and absentee bureaucracy, schools that are not a
way out at all, never were for the poor, never will be. Rather,
they sit there like monolithic weights on top of imaginary man-
holes which, could they be lifted up, might represent an escape
route down into and through the sewers of the old city to a
point, some point, where a kid could come up for air.

"Our children are failing!" ghetto parents cried in despair.
"We know," the school system responded sympathetically. Yet
it could only address the failure with a quizzical query:
"What's wrong with *them?*" Ghetto parents found it hard to
believe there was all that much wrong with their children or
that they were either genetically stupid or socioeconomically
stunted. Like children anywhere these kids, particularly the
little ones, had real human potential. Then, later on, they
seemed to fade and fail. Why?

In New York and other cities steps were taken by the establishment to deal with the so-called "ghetto education problem." In the middle and late 1950s there was a lot of talk about
integrating the schools. The talk persists to this day, bolstered
by the celebrated "Coleman Report" done for the federal government which demonstrated that in schools with a 10% or 12%
black enrollment the minority children could make it by association with their white peers — a racial balance that could easily
be achieved by busing in small communities like Hagerstown,
Maryland; Fayetteville, North Carolina; or Marietta, Ohio. But
in our big cities where the heart of the problem lies such a proposal is logistical nonsense, considering that virtually every
American ghetto is an isolated and impacted slum. Moving
children in or out would end in their spending the whole school

day on a bus hopelessly stalled in traffic. New York took a different tack, conceiving plans for really fine schools on the borders between ghetto and white neighborhoods. One is worth noting because it was so hopeful and grand. It was called Linear City.

An unused railroad right of way was discovered running clear across Brooklyn, separating the ghettos of Bedford-Stuyvesant and Ocean Hill–Brownsville from lower middle-class communities like Flatbush, Canarsie, and other white enclaves. Ambitious plans were conceived for converting this abandoned strip of real estate into a beautiful mall several miles long, with shopping plazas, community colleges, associated low-income housing, and excellently equipped and staffed educational parks to accommodate children from both sides of the tracks. The sunken railroad bed, bridged over to support Linear City, would be used for subway and freeway lanes providing additional access to the mall above. Linear City went down the drain in a single mayoralty election when the white enclaves rejected these inducements to better education, proclaimed their schools were bad enough without integrating them, and made it plain how the voting would go in south Brooklyn if the plan went through.

Another bit of idiocy that arose in New York, back in the days when integration appeared the solution to the ghetto education problem, was Intermediate School 201 in Harlem. When the construction of the school was announced, it was labeled as a part of the overall city plan to integrate the school system. Some years later it materialized at 127th Street in central Harlem, in the shadow of the elevated railroad tracks that carry commuter trains from Grand Central Station to the suburbs north of the city. The new school was windowless and air-conditioned (though the system never worked). Community people were outraged on two counts. One was why, under plans for integration, such a school should be built in the middle of black Harlem to begin with. The other reason was its windowlessness, which people regarded as a turning of the back on the Harlem community. The building had been designed by some architects from New Orleans who felt it was necessary to shut out the noise from the passing trains, but more importantly believed they had drawn up a unique oasis of education. Informed of community objections to the school the architects exclaimed: "They just didn't understand the marvelous conceptual thing we were trying to do."

With attempts at integration proving increasingly absurd, as manifested in anomalies like I.S. 201, the prisoners of the ghetto simply turned their backs on the whole idea. The very evident white backlash provoked one obvious response: who wants to send a child to a school where the child is not wanted and not welcomed? Moreover, long and bitter experience suggested that "being done for" by the big-city school system was rather consistently a euphemism for being done in. A new cry was added to "Our children are failing!" It was: "Give us control of our own schools! You have failed. Let us try. We at least deserve the right to fail ourselves." So the question of community control of the schools came on the agenda. There was some justification for the demand. It had been demonstrated in isolated instances that there was no essential disability in black and Puerto Rican children which blocked the learning process. A number of adventurous and courageous teachers like Jonathan Kozol and Herbert Kohl had managed to get their classes launched on a real learning track by alternately defying, ignoring, or otherwise circumventing traditional schoolhouse procedures and normal teaching materials. They had made their achievements a matter of public record through their now-classic descriptions of the typical big-city wipe-out and how they contended with it as individuals. Unfortunately there is no way for an urban school system to deal with individuals — whether they be teachers, children, or materials for that matter. A bureaucracy can only deal with and handle "norms." By these standards a teacher is qualified or not qualified; a child is at grade level or not at grade level; materials are suitable or not suitable — to the system. Not to the participants in this educational charade. This being so, the system can only function by utilizing what have come to be called "programs" — to be dispensed by norm teachers to norm children in the norm school. Maybe that's why it used to be called "normal school." New York and other big cities managed to avoid the issue of control of the schools to a degree by trying various programs in the hope of coming up with something that worked with ghetto kids.

As a consequence there has been, year in and year out, a continuing discussion of programs. Any accredited edbiz group which can develop a program, along with the suitable materials, stands a good chance of making good money in the edbiz market — provided the program is couched in the right edbiz jargon for sale to school systems. Certainly some are better than others, like the Sullivan reading materials and the new math. The problem with programs, however, is that they do not teach real children in a real community. It was once thought that if only ghetto kids could be given preschool training to acquaint them with books, pencils and such, they could then be funneled into a city school system. The program that arose was known as Head Start. When it became clear that Head Start wasn't sufficient, a lot of hand-wringing resulted and the idea was condemned quite unfairly. Other programs met a similar fate. Year after year new approaches crop up which, it is alleged, can turn the corner with ghetto children. For a time kids light up. But then the light flickers and goes out. Several years ago something called "performance contracting" was all the rage. A well-established research institution undertook to teach children with its own specially developed teaching materials, on contract. That is, the institution would get paid by the school only for each child whose reading and math skills were demonstrably improved. Performance contracting looked good for a time; but it doesn't anymore. The only school that showed con-

sistent results was the Banniker School in Gary, Indiana — and
I would bet my last dollar that this record was due to other factors in that school which have far greater value than any program. Now, even in Banniker, the light appears to be fading.
Today "open classrooms" are the thing. But tomorrow they,
too, will pass, and it will be back to the same old malaise once
again. There are some rather sharp people at the New York
City Board of Education. One is Dr. Nathan Brown, the assistant superintendent. Some time ago he observed: "We have
offered all kinds of solutions, but they are not producing results
and nobody knows why." I believe him.

Since programs per se do not work and, by contrast to this,
since individual teachers have demonstrated that poverty children can learn, what then? When the cry for community control persisted in New York, the city came up with two responses.
One was a broad plan to decentralize the whole school system to
some degree. Under this plan, the proposed Marchi Law (named
for State Senator John Marchi from Staten Island) was introduced
as a bill into the state legislature in Albany, which has ultimate
control over the city schools, to divide New York into a number of
fairly large school districts, each with its own elected school board
which could, among other things, select its district superintendent. In this way people in the new districts would have some
voice in the operation of their schools. The power delegated was
minimal, however, and the central board retained a major share of
control. By the same token so did the United Federation of
Teachers, the union that represents all the city's teachers. The
U.F.T. and its president, Albert Shanker, had no intention of
relinquishing its right to bargain with the central board for the
whole city teaching staff, whatever might happen in the new
districts. There were overtones of both tokenism and cynicism
in the plan. For example, part of the responsibility for the failure of the schools, which had traditionally been laid on the
doorstep at 110 Livingston Street in Brooklyn where the central
board is sequestered, could be conveniently passed along to

local boards, thus equivocating and defusing the disaster to some extent. When the districts finally emerged from the drafting rooms, there were charges of gerrymandering as well. A minority of the new districts drew their students from remarkably homogeneous middle- and upper-class areas. The majority, given the racial balance of the city, were almost pure ghetto.

As these larger plans for the city's schools were being drawn up so were some smaller ones to meet more immediate needs. Given the here-and-now pressure for action, the volatile level of frustration with failure, and the demand for home rule of the schools, it was decided to set up several experiments involving small clusters of schools under direct community control — to see what they might demonstrate for the system at large. Three such "demonstration districts" were established. One came to be known as the "I.S. 201 Complex" in Harlem, consisting of Intermediate School 201 and four elementary schools in the neighborhood that acted as feeder schools to the intermediate school. A second was the "Ocean Hill–Brownsville" demonstration in Brooklyn with two intermediate schools (I.S. 271 and I.S. 55) and six feeder schools. The third experimental district, "Two Bridges" on the lower east side of Manhattan (near the Manhattan and Brooklyn bridges), was quickly engulfed in internecine warfare and conflicts with the city and never got off the ground. The districts elected their own local governing boards which included representatives both from the schools and the community. Since they were quite diminutive by city standards, these districts managed to reflect some communal sense, which is difficult at best in a city like New York. Each governing board selected a unit administrator to be the educational director of the cluster schools. Charles E. Wilson, a black educator who had majored in educational psychology, was named unit administrator of the 201 Complex. Rhody A. McCoy, an acting principal in the city system with an impressive record in schools for particularly difficult children, was selected for Ocean Hill–Brownsville.

The experimental districts were launched with the full blessing of the Board of Education and the United Federation of
Teachers. The Ford Foundation, interested in educational in-
novations, provided seed funds for planning the administration
of the districts so they could be organized and begin to operate.
The districts set up shop with blessings from all quarters. In
retrospect, many things are unclear about this sanction. On one
hand, it can be regarded as a temporizing placebo to cool off a
couple of big-city hot spots to buy time. It can also be looked
upon as a gesture of noblesse oblige on the part of power
brokers who never intended to give away anything or have anything demonstrated to begin with — unless it were an exercise
in how the jungle bunnies might fall on their faces upon receiving such largess from the establishment. Possibly it was assumed that those involved would merely "play the game," accept the grant, not make waves, and so generate another in an
unblemished series of failures. Whatever the mixture of motives, and it probably was just that — some intended, some not,
some merely overlooked — no one foresaw any particular problem. The demonstration was chartered to run for three years, at
which time it was presumed the whole city would be decentral-
ized. Whatever the experiment did or did not demonstrate
would be taken into account and the new school system would
go on from there.

One thing certainly *not* anticipated was a problem the districts would ultimately have to face for themselves. From the
vantage point of a big-city power structure, places like Harlem
and Ocean Hill are seen as if through the wrong end of a telescope, as crowds of people, indistinguishable from one another
at such a distance, mill around in anguish and despair. But it
turned out from the other end of the telescope that both ghettos
contained a considerable amount of latent talent that was eager
to "seize the moment" in a truly Faustian sense. David X.
Spencer, a former elevator operator, emerged as the eloquent
and hardheaded chairman of the 201 Complex Governing

Board. The Reverend C. Herbert Oliver, an ally of Dr. Martin Luther King, Jr., in his Southern Christian Leadership Conference, was now resident in Brooklyn and was chosen to head the Ocean Hill Board. And a fascinating array of teachers, administrators, and community people was attracted to the new districts as if by a magnet because something was "on." The problem posed to Spencer and Oliver, Wilson and McCoy, and the other administrators was what that "something" should be. Though it was apparent that the children could learn under the right circumstances, establishing programs was no real answer. The problem was how to set up an honest-to-God schoolhouse, a schoolhouse largely populated by replicas of Kozol and Kohl throughout the grades, a schoolhouse that would then give a poverty kid a real ladder to climb, so he could actually reach up and grasp the bridge that does not touch down for him.

The issue could have been avoided by conveniently overlooking the essential challenge of the experiment: build a schoolhouse. Taking that route would have required a dissembling soft-shoe Uncle Tom act which, perhaps, the city had expected. But the people concerned were too bright, too proud, too dedicated, and too determined to go that way. Instead they accepted the challenge at face value in a rather deadpan style — or so they hoped. Doing that, however, required committing an unpardonable sin as far as big-city ambiance is concerned. Traditionally the problem had been put in the form of the question: "Why can't the children *learn*?" (i.e., what's wrong with *them*?). Charles Wilson and Rhody McCoy, convinced they *could* learn, felt obliged to turn the question around: "Why can't the teachers *teach*?" They were as diplomatic as possible about this shift of emphasis, to the point of appearing devious and evasive occasionally. Still, the new question had to pop out of the bag sometime.

The bag burst when McCoy, assuming he had the authority in any situation where it had not been stated he didn't, ordered a handful of teachers transferred out of Ocean Hill–Brownsville on the grounds that they were dragging their heels and had become antagonistic to the experiment. Albert Shanker reacted violently to what he regarded as a highhanded act of aggression against the union, an assumption of authority on McCoy's part which he interpreted as a direct threat to his own authority and to that of the union over all teachers in the New York City school system. If one district superintendent could shuffle teachers around, accept some and reject others, what would happen if *all* districts assumed such a prerogative? Would that put the union in the position of negotiating separate teacher contracts with each district in the city? If so, the U.F.T.'s basic clout, a blanket contract with the whole city system, would be seriously weakened. Moreover, there was an implication in McCoy's assumption which Shanker and many others did not take kindly to, to say the least. This was a question of accountability. A teacher goes to teachers' college and acquires a certificate to teach. But what if the teacher cannot deliver what the certificate certifies; i.e., teaching? Is not the teacher accountable, just as a certified doctor would be if he demonstrably botched an operation or prescribed a fatal or near-fatal prescription for a patient, through failure to consider the patient as an individual?

A question of such novelty had never been seriously raised in New York. The union's consistent response to failure in the classroom has been a campaign for better pay, smaller classes, and more "prep" periods for teachers. All of which are clearly desirable. But whether the union's amalgam of mother hens was capable of delivering what the certificates certified could be delivered seems to have been regarded as a nonunion problem. Moreover, since the teachers' union is essentially a big-city bureaucracy as is the Board of Education, questions of individual capability cannot be accommodated anyway. Qualifications must be systematized, and teachers must be made interchangeable according to points, credits, and other ways of classifying large numbers of people. Added to this is the fact that though there are many dedicated and competent teachers in the New York school system, the profession has to a large degree been regarded as a means to an end — a way off the farm, a route to the middle class, a means of meeting a nice young man in the big city. Raising the question of accountability, of whether the goods being delivered were not typically shoddy ghetto goods, laid it on the line.

Albert Shanker responded to the posing of a question forbidden by all standards of big-city accommodation by calling the longest, most acrimonious teachers' strike in New York City history. The strike dragged on for three months. There were charges of "genocide" from the black ghetto. There were charges of "anti-Semitism" from the predominantly Jewish union. Two of the most oppressed peoples in human history became locked into a confrontation neither should have had to experience, let alone endure. The trouble was that a clearly identifiable need had sprouted in a forest of urban education which had been petrified from the very beginning as far as poverty children were concerned. And the clients of the system, almost overnight it seemed, were declaring that the fact of failure was no longer an acceptable fact of life — at least for them. The educational bureaucracy was incapable of responding. If, in the outer world, there exists a crying need, it simply cannot be perceived that way through the spyglass on top of the citadel, if doing something about the need implies a threat to the fortress itself. This being the case, any real recognition of the essential issue by the demonstration districts made a head-on collision inevitable.

The union's strike erupted like a volcano, enveloping the whole city in a mammoth educational calamity. Through the media, one only got brief glimpses of local militants, confrontations, curb-side press conferences, and read pieces about teaching children "studies relevant to blacks and Puerto Ricans" to which colleges later acquiesced with spineless docility, probably because university deans knew little more than anyone else about the real depths of the human disaster which had taken place and so lacked any personal resources to think about it. Ultimately the upheaval subsided, and one did not hear much from the local militants anymore. The smoke of once-popular confrontation blew away, toward where? Occasionally one heard the fading voices of Charles Wilson and Rhody McCoy saying that something had actually happened, that the experimental demonstration in New York had, in fact, demonstrated something. But such assertions were drowned out by a bigger sound indicating that the establishment was safely shored up again. The U.F.T. retained jurisdiction over its brood of teachers. The Board of Education, which had vacillated throughout the storm, was still alive and well. The Ford Foundation seems to have acquired the only bloody nose. During the fracas a question was raised in Congress as to whether foundations should be taxed. Being no expert on the kind of muscle the power brokers of New York can muster in the nation's capital, I can only wonder how this was managed. But I do know that the question came up quite seriously at that time and that foundations all over the place ran for cover, worrying about their tax-exempt status.

Now a sulphurous malaise envelops the city, a stifling stillness, an educational inversion that hangs in there as it always has, an inversion in which no wind blows. Yet suppose that for a time there had indeed been a breath of air, a small wind that breathed some life into a few ghetto schools, before they were blown away? Suppose you had seen that? Suppose Charles Wilson and Rhody McCoy had indeed held the keys to the kingdom? Suppose that the first real revolution in ghetto education in American history had actually occurred — but no one came?

I

*In Search of
the Disadvantaged
Child*

O N A GRAY and drizzling March morning in 1969, I got into a taxi in midtown Manhattan and asked the driver to take me to 125th Street and Park Avenue in central Harlem.
"Are you sure you know where you're going?"
"Yes, I think so."
The driver shook his head dubiously, reached back and rolled up the windows, locked the doors of the cab with a pointed emphasis that could scarcely escape his passenger's attention, and headed uptown. I felt a bit apprehensive about the trip myself, what with all the talk about polarization, genocide, and anti-Semitism that had become an alarmingly steady staple of the television news diet. I didn't take much money with me, and I had left at home my father's gold watch which I normally carry. I was not particularly afraid of my purpose in going to Harlem to begin with, but that I might encounter some junkie who would prove too desperate to understand or care about it.

The driver took the winding roadway north through Central Park and emerged at 110th Street. From there he might have proceeded farther uptown on Lenox Avenue, taken a right on 125th Street, and easily dropped me at my destination — thus confining the trip to the main arteries of Harlem which are generally broad and open and provide the casual visitor with some sense of security. Instead, perhaps through perversity or possibly because of some protective instinct that led him to wish to demonstrate a touch of the danger implied in his opening question to his passenger, he turned right on 110th Street and headed directly for Park Avenue. If ever a street expressed polarity in granite and steel in a big city it is Park Avenue. Downtown, of course, it is a broad and sunlit monument to affluence, if not downright avarice, concealing the commuter tracks of the Penn-Central that run beneath it from Grand Central Station. But uptown, at 97th Street, the tracks emerge from their tunnel to become an overhead elevated line, supported first by a massive granite base punctured periodically by dark, narrow tunnels which permit the passage of crosstown streets, then by steel stanchions a few blocks farther north. Thus, quite abruptly, a broad avenue of wealth and light is transformed into a trough of gloom and poverty by the elevated railroad where Harlem begins. Above the dark level of the streets, morning and evening, rattle the commuter trains which carry so many of the city's free white people, most of them newly rich, to and from the posh suburbs north of the city. From this vantage point they can look into the windows of Harlem tenements and occasionally catch a glimpse of one or another of the newly stuck — the ghetto dwellers, the prisoners of poverty and of many things other than poverty.

East 110th Street was a largely Puerto Rican area. It was littered with an incredible amount of rubbish — bottles and cans, papers and cartons, broken dolls and baby carriages, turned over trash cans, as well as larger debris like discarded iceboxes, pieces of stoves, shells of automobiles with smashed out windows and bashed in doors that had been cannibalized for their tires, wheels, engines, and anything else which might have had some marginal value, perhaps just for a passing game. Children raced about, oblivious to traffic but also apparently immune to it; young men congregated near small, decrepit Mom-'n-Pop stores; older people leaned on the windowsills of decaying buildings. When the taxi stopped for a red light, I felt a bit apprehensive and wondered what kinds of things might possibly then occur, a feeling heightened by no sense of rapport with the street scene itself. The cab probed into one of the dark and narrow granite tunnels supporting the railroad above. It was easy to imagine how, by tipping over a pushcart or shoving a kid out into the street, someone could arrange an ambush there. We headed north beneath the shadow of the "el" accompanied by the same scene of teeming desolation, the same sense of anticipation whenever the light turned red. At 125th Street I unlocked my door, got out, and paid the driver. If he had intended to teach a supposed greenhorn a lesson he could have skipped it, but the trip did remind me of some things I had almost forgotten.

Nestled beside the elevated railroad on 125th Street and Park was a small office building. I took the elevator to the eighth floor and walked into the administrative offices of the I.S. 201 Complex. Inside was a small reception room with a desk and table-top switchboard, a chair, and a bench along one wall. Black people, and a few white people, came and went with some sense of urgency. I told the receptionist I had written a letter to Charles Wilson, had telephoned, and that an appointment had been arranged for me to come and talk with him. She regarded me noncommittally and asked me to take a seat. I got the passing impression I had requested an audience with the frosty soul of Malcolm X. I sat down on the bench and waited.

There was some literature lying about, and I picked up a newspaper obviously published by the Complex titled *Kweli* — the word for "truth" in Swahili as I later learned. The main headline read:

BD. OF ED. LAUNCHES NEW ATTACK
ON I. S. 201 COMPLEX

The whole issue was devoted to what had come to be known in the city as the "seven teachers incident," an outgrowth of the acrimonious city-wide teachers' strike of the previous fall.

During the strike the demonstration districts had remained open, asserting their tenuous autonomy, while all the other schools in New York were shut down. At the I.S. 201 Complex, David X. Spencer, head of the governing board, pleaded with the Complex teachers to remain on the job so that the experiment could continue uninterrupted. Of the several hundred teachers in the little district only nine felt they should follow the union and strike. The rest went along with Mr. Spencer's exhortation, some because of dedication to the experiment and others because they felt they were under the jurisdiction of the district in any case and had no real choice. Of the nine who went out, two later transferred, leaving only seven teachers officially on strike. Since they were also on salary, "the seven" were informed they could pick up their pay at the district office; there was no feeling of ill will at the time because it seemed reasonable to presume the teachers were acting according to conscience.

Then came the Thanksgiving holidays. The Complex schools, open all along, closed down for the normal school vacation. But a shortened holiday had been proclaimed for the rest of the city to make up for teaching time lost during the strike. At the end of this abbreviated period the seven teachers showed up at P.S. 39 in the district, which was, of course, closed. Instead of reporting to the Complex office to see what they should do under the circumstances, the teachers demanded that the police open the school. The police did just that. To the governing board and to many local parents this act appeared as a deliberate effort to cause trouble and promote doubt and confusion in the district, possibly the opening shot of a broader vendetta planned by the powerful teachers' union against the experimental districts for raising "the forbidden question." When the normal holiday ended and P.S. 39 was fully staffed a strange spectacle ensued. Regular teachers returned to their classrooms. "The seven" continued to enter the school as well, under police escort. They were confronted daily by community pickets proclaiming they did not want these teachers working with their children, that people they had formerly regarded as allies of the children were, instead, simply there to demonstrate union clout. So, day after day, parents paraded in protest and just as dutifully the police escorted "the seven" to their respective classrooms. There each teacher sat for the full teaching day accompanied by a police officer, while other policemen patrolled the hallways. Meanwhile, the rest of school resumed the winter's work. But the seven classrooms, with the seven teachers and the seven officers, contained no children due to the parental boycott.

This strange, monotonous, early morning ritual bothered the administrators of the Complex. They interpreted it as a small but quite visible demonstration within the Harlem community of who really ran New York, with implications that the "experiment in progress" being operated by the jungle bunnies "up there" was perhaps just a bit shaky, just a bit flaky, a trifle unprofessional if it could lead to such an absurd and seemingly unreconcilable impasse. Implicit also was another notion: that the experiment existed only through the largess of the power brokers downtown, that the incident was but a small flex of a much larger muscle that could go *pow* if the occasion arose. Their control of the local police made that rather clear. This demonstration of the establishment's power in central Harlem could not help casting a large shadow over the district, a shadow that questioned its strength, validity, durability, commitment, intelligence, and ultimate meaning. Complex officials, reading the challenge in this light, attempted to get the central Board of Education to call off the morning walk. The response was a large amount of vacillating, equivocating, compromising, and otherwise pussyfooting around. Sweet reasonableness emanated from various members of the board, each of whom, however, had his own particular view of the matter. "Let's see if we can work it out *this* way." "No, let's see if we can work it out *that* way." Reasonableness filled the air, clogging it with a suffocating hopelessness.

The union's provocative activity at P.S. 39 dragged on. In the newspapers and on television the eerie charade came over as a minor "confrontation" which erupted spasmodically from time to time. The failure to resolve it produced equivocal feelings on the part of outsiders and many Harlem parents as well, feelings that both parties to the dispute were somehow at fault. (There are two sides to every question, aren't there?) This was certainly the way the matter struck me as I sat reading *Kweli*. Sensing this effect the Complex administration came to regard every maneuver that delayed the resolution of the affair as an attack on the Complex itself. Hence the headline.

Another bit of literature I picked up while waiting was a broadside which proclaimed, in conclusion:

> Charles E. Wilson knows where he's going; and
> the whole United States will be grateful to him.
> Wait and see.

These materials gave me the impression that there must be some sort of black paranoia blowing in the wind. Certainly the media, particularly television, confirmed the notion, what with all the images of anger, outrage, and almost total irrationality — "Bar *Little Black Sambo* from the schools! Throw out *Uncle Remus!*" It sounded almost Hitlerian. I like Joel Chandler Harris, though one has to take his times into account. The idea of destroying history struck me as not far removed from burning the books. The level of irrationality and impatience seemed worse than unreasonable — it appeared dark and dangerous. Reading the Complex literature against such a background led me to wonder if this cluster of schools, having gotten hold of some degree of local power, wasn't being more propagandistic than pedagogic, that maybe this kind of literature was more for bolstering up home-rule egos than for communicating anything substantial — a feeble wind blowing against the educational power structures in Brooklyn and Manhattan. In any event, it did not take long to finish the material, which left me hung up, pretending to study it extensively, for I had to wait over two hours to see Charles Wilson. During that time of feigned reading, I listened to voices come and go, mostly educated, cultured, concerned voices. None of that "Hey, man, hit me five!" kind of jive I was used to on television. Was that what I had expected? I don't know.

A polite young woman appeared and said: "Mr. Campbell? Mr. Wilson will see you now." She ushered me into a large, pleasant office overlooking 125th Street and the elevated railroad tracks and introduced me to Charles Wilson. We shook hands and sat down at a long table. I expressed some "thoughts" I had picked up about the problems of teaching ghetto children and that a number of people had suggested I visit him, and didn't know exactly what else to say. We talked rather aimlessly for a few minutes. Then, somewhat abruptly, he said: "Come, take a walk with me."

We took the elevator down and walked a few short blocks to P.S. 39, where the seven teachers fuss was in progress and where Charles Wilson apparently had some business to attend to. Inside the school, clustered in pairs at strategic points, police officers chatted quietly, available in case of trouble. Quite by accident I caught a passing glimpse of an empty classroom where one of "the seven" was having a cup of coffee with a police protector. The sight of an idle classroom, an idle teacher, and an idle policeman produced one of those quick short-circuits of thought that juxtaposed these images with another set of images of a city beset by a serious educational crisis and an alarming law-enforcement problem to the point where it could ill afford to have these resources immobilized. The building was a typically large, old, city school, five floors tall and massively built to insure its everlasting endurance in the neighborhood as a piece of city property little short of an air raid could seriously damage. One immediate impression of the school as we walked through it was how clean it appeared.

This is normally the responsibility of the custodian and his staff, a separate wing of the educational establishment concerned with "hardware" ("plant and equipment" it would be called in industry) as opposed to "software"; i.e., the teaching staff, teaching materials and, presumably, children. I remarked on the cleanliness of the building. Charles Wilson responded: "Custodians make as much money as principals, you know." (I did not know.) "We got rid of the old custodian," he continued, "and since they were all out during the strike, parents came in to clean up the schools themselves. Because, after all, these are *their* schools. So naturally they got a look at the kind of mess kids can do in a school. And don't you believe a lot of kids didn't catch hell after that."

Clearly there was some concern about this school, some local concern anyway. We took an "up" staircase, enclosed in heavy wire mesh to prevent children from either falling out or breaking in, and stopped at a classroom on one of the upper floors. On the massive oak door hung a full-size ship's life preserver which, I learned later, the teacher had picked up during a vacation. On it was inscribed: "Class 2–5, the best." Mr. Wilson knocked on the door, introduced me to the teacher, a young white man, and said he had some business to attend to down in the office but that he would pick me up in a little while. The teacher explained his class to me. It was organized on three tracks, in separate areas of the room, which the children could follow in terms of their individual interest and progress, even switching back and forth on one day or another depending on what the particular day might suggest. In this way the children were organized like small ensembles, each with an inner mobility of its own. The young man circulated among these groups continuously, lending a thought here, an ear there, a hand elsewhere. The scene was one of quiet chaos but with a substructure holding it together that certainly seemed preferable to the usual arrangement of children locked like twenty- or thirty-odd peas in a square pod with the teacher conducting the class.

After watching for some time and occasionally asking the young man what this or that group was doing, what some of the materials were for (most had been constructed by the class under the teacher's direction) and so on, it struck me that Charles Wilson had failed to come back for me. I felt I was beginning to overstay my visit, said good-bye to the teacher and walked out into the hallway. In the corridor was a long bulletin board displaying posters the children had painted protesting the presence of police in their school. The posters depicted clusters of officers at the ends of hallways, the kind of peek-in view of a policeman and a solitary teacher I had also observed, and street scenes of teachers being escorted into school through groups of protesting parents. A small Puerto Rican boy came wandering down the hallway, stopped, and asked:

"How do you like our posters?"

"I like them very well," I answered.

He walked over to the wall and shyly pointed to one.

"I did that one," he said.

"That's a very good one," I said.

The child smiled and walked away, turning around to smile once more as he entered the caged stairwell at the end of the hall.

Charles Wilson still had not come to retrieve me so I remained standing in the hallway for a long time listening to the school, sensing it, feeling it. Individual children came and went along the corridor. There was a faint background hum of voices. Gradually it dawned on me that this school had a purpose. It felt almost palpable. I sensed somehow the teachers knew it, the parents knew it, and certainly the children knew it. They would be the first to get the message, whatever the message was.

I went downstairs to find Charles Wilson. He was standing on the street with a bearded black man I presumed was David X. Spencer. They were being interviewed by television people, a sidewalk press conference concerning some new devel-

opment in the seven teachers affair. I waited until it was over
and then joined Mr. Wilson to walk back to his office.

"I think I'm beginning to see something here in the Complex," I remarked.

"Good," he said, nodding his head. Inside his office he
turned and looked at me:

"What do you think a child is worth? I mean if you took out
an insurance policy on a kid and just made up a number. Say
ten thousand dollars? Would that be okay? So a teacher has
twenty-five children in her class. That means she's doing a
quarter million dollars' worth of business a year, right? In industry you got someone doing that kind of business for the company, he comes to town, and he sure as hell gets wined and
dined, right?"

From a drawer he pulled out a brochure on a big estate just
north of the city called Tarrytown House, with spreading lawns,
gardens, tennis courts, and a swimming pool. The estate is
rented by big-city corporations like IBM, AT&T, et cetera, for
executive "think tank" sessions and other major management
activities. Wilson said the estate was used by the I.S. 201 Complex, too, for weekend retreats for the teachers and supervisors
of each of the five Complex schools. The idea struck me as a
flamboyant and expensive gesture, and I couldn't see much sub-
stance to it. We talked some more, but I really didn't understand much of what he was saying. This bothered me. I wondered flatfootedly whether or not there were some differences
between the white mind and the black mind — whatever that
might mean. Then I recalled a thought from Saint Augustine
that helped:

> No man knows the things of a man,
> save the spirit of man that is in him.

It was clear to me that the spirit of man inhabited Charles
Wilson. He was an open, humorous, and attractive person with

a flare and language style clearly all his own — medium sized, well built, dark, with a closely cropped head and a mobile, expressive face. Yet there seemed to be a strange wall between us as we tried to talk to one another. And our early conversations reminded me of nothing as much as the supposed exchange between Emerson and Thoreau, with Thoreau in jail and Emerson peering through the bars to ask:

"What are you doing *in there*, Henry?"

And Thoreau responding: "What are you doing *out there*, Waldo?"

Lunchtime came. Since Wilson had many things to attend to, I left the Complex offices with a request to return in a few days and spend more time in the schools to get a better idea of what they were about and to talk some more with him, to get a better idea of what *he* was about.

"Fine," he said. "Come up anytime."

I found myself standing on 125th Street in a hesitant state of mind. Normally I would have gone downtown and sought out one luncheon crony or another. But I didn't feel like doing that now. A strange thing had happened, among many strange things that morning. I had come to Harlem with some sense of fear, aggravated by the word "polarity" that seemed to have been written across the American landscape in huge blood red letters. Yet I had memories of Harlem from many years earlier, back before the "time of troubles," memories of dropping into the bar of the Hotel Theresa for a beer in the afternoon (where Fidel Castro so imaginatively quartered his U.N. delegation at a later date), or an occasional pleasant lunch at a nice restaurant called Frank's. I felt defiant of the current impasse. Why should I not be here? Why should I not be on any street in the whole goddamn world I wished to be on? Like the Algierian section of Paris, down below the Pantheon, Napoleon's tomb, when "they" said you shouldn't go there because even Sorbonne students were being mugged and killed in the place. I had felt free to explore those streets in the middle of the night, because as far as I was concerned those cats were just as free to explore my street, wherever it was, any time they wished. Besides, I now had a curious feeling that I had a reason for being in Harlem, though I could not possibly have explained it at the time. Moreover it seemed to me that if a person became fearful of other human beings, whomever they were, that could only represent a loss of humanness and by the same token a loss of self. I did not want that bell to toll for me. So, I walked slowly west on 125th Street to Frank's to see what that fine old restaurant was like now, with a vague notion that if I were going to spend lunch money, why shouldn't I leave it in Harlem instead of taking it back downtown?

Frank's was the same quiet, conservative establishment it had always been, a congenial meeting place for blacks and whites who had business in Harlem — local politicians, people with an enterprise going, something with a little affluence attached because it was not an inexpensive restaurant. From the black side of the ledger would come, most probably, the bourgeoisie who lived, or might live, on Sugar Hill, the best residential area in Harlem — those whom Malcolm X detested as sellouts to the white man. From the white side, who? Officials from City Hall, the Board of Education, housing contractors? I did not know. I did know that Frank's was only pseudo-Harlem, the accommodating facade of Harlem. Not the real Harlem of Claude Brown or Malcolm X. Ambling across town I had toyed briefly with the idea of finding some restaurant on the byways to eat in. But I had decided against it. I felt such a move would be presumptuous. For now, sitting in Frank's was sufficient. I had a beer and some delicious Maryland crabcakes. As I sipped the beer and picked at the crabcakes, images tumbled through my mind as though two completely different films were being projected simultaneously. One involved scenes in the old ghetto school I had just visited — quiet, clean, purposeful. The other was composed of images of a dozen or more ghetto schools I had explored elsewhere in New York and in other big cities during the past year. Here and there one could find a small oasis of learning, but invariably this was the result of one special project or another involving highly trained and motivated teachers, parents, and assistants. Otherwise, such schools were uniformly dirty, graffiti-ridden, noisy, and chaotic to the point of being little more than custodial institutions for black and Puerto Rican children, with a sprinkling of poor whites.

To one who had become a reasonably experienced school observer, P.S. 39 in central Harlem simply made no sense. It was clearly no special school crammed with all sorts of experimental programs, expert teachers and so on. It seemed to be just another ghetto school, albeit under "community control," whatever that might mean. Yet it felt totally different from any other school I had been in, so much so that I was almost dumbfounded. This bothered me on a number of counts, one very simple: I am a rather thorough reporter and for well over a year now I had been exploring the so-called "ghetto education problem." My investigations began with an assignment to write the script for a film on various ways of improving ghetto schools, new concepts in school design and the like. The film company was a very fine New York documentary group, Larry Madison Productions. I have handled many complex subjects before. But never, after doing so much research, have I encountered a totally unexpected surprise at the end of the line. A few last-minute nuances, perhaps, but nothing suggesting that a completely different ball game might be playing in the same park at the same time. Searching for some clue to this disturbing development, I reflected back to the last time I was in Frank's and shuddered a bit on realizing it had been twenty-five years earlier. It hardly seemed possible.

Back then I was a newly arrived, wide-eyed greenhorn in "the big city," a white manchild from the dear old Southland seeking opportunity in the Promised Land up north. My own odyssey began just after World War II at about the same time as the great black migration out of the South, though I was quite unaware of that movement. And aside from having very little money, there were no similarities anyway. I was not a displaced person; I left the South voluntarily. And in so doing I had some confidence I could get a foothold on the bridge to opportunity. One of my reasons for leaving was negative: I could not tolerate the ingrown, self-satisfied society I grew up in, where good manners, the proper amenities, and superficial small talk — "Glad to see ya!" "How are ya?" followed by a quick aversion of the eyes — was regarded on all sides as representing something like real communication. Though I managed to negotiate that world well enough, I dropped out in my own mind at quite an early age and became a loner, though I still have some very dear personal friends "back home." I must say in defense of the South that since then I have seen no reason to "drop in" as far as the larger American society is concerned, and I have come to believe quite seriously that there are some strange things about the South which may provide the salvation of America in the long run, at least in terms of the old dreams of this mythological nation. In the dreamland that is the South many of them are still very much alive and well, hanging in the warm and heavy wisteria-scented air. Perhaps getting whipped in a dreadful war is a part of that, whereas the Yankee victors remained free to pursue new paths to glory. Perhaps losing in Vietnam will have a similar salubrious effect on America at large.

Another negative reason for leaving the South was the obvious racism I had lived with all my juvenile life. A caste system which placed black people at one level of society and opportunity and white people at a higher and more privileged level could hardly make sense to a child who was beginning to develop his own ideas of what it meant to be a human being. In our home my closest friends, apart from my parents, were our cook, Vera Mayberry, her husband, Thomas, who did odd jobs about the place, my father's chauffeur, Arthur Coffee, and especially my baby sister's nanny, Lucille Yates. Among my fondest childhood memories are the many hours spent sitting in our big kitchen near the large, black stove talking with them. We discussed all kinds of things. And I much preferred these people to the company my parents kept out beyond the butler's pantry and the dining room. Though they chatted and laughed a lot out there over eggnog and beaten biscuits with Virginia ham and all, as far as I could tell, they talked about hardly anything worthwhile. Whereas my friends back in the kitchen had quite a bit to say that interested me mightily. Of course, a true liberal cynic would observe that entertaining me was part of what they got paid for, but I don't want to go into that. In any case, I could not comprehend why the folks I regarded as first-class people were considered by the folks I felt were second-class people as being beneath them. Now, after so long a time, I take pride in recording and commemorating here the names of Vera and Thomas, Arthur and Lucille, albeit far more briefly than they deserve.

Lucille was in many ways my favorite. She was slim, attractive, very bright, and a bit jazzy. I could easily tell it was difficult for her at times to maintain the deferential mien expected of a servant. Her true spirit was evident to me, but now and then it popped out in the presence of white adults, leading them to refer to her as an "uppity nigger," an attitude which sometimes drove me to tears. Lucille took it all in stride without appearing put upon and never suggested any resentment in my presence. I recall discussing an approaching Christmas Eve communion with Lucille. It was to be held in the lovely — and fashionable — local Episcopal church and was considered a social event by the largely hypocritical white upper crust who only turned out at Christmas and Easter. Lucille startled me by remarking that she loved those services, too, and occasionally came to the church and sat way in the back. I was delighted and asked why she didn't come up front and join us in our pew. She turned the question away so deftly I completely forgot I had asked it. Years later, home on college vacation, I wandered about the black part of town inquiring after Lucille. No one seemed to recall the name. In retrospect, I realize such an inquiry could only have aroused suspicion. ("Who knows what he's after?")

The positive reason I left home was a long-standing desire to become a big-city journalist, and New York was *the* big city to me. After a few months in town I got quite a break by landing a job as a baby reporter on *Life* magazine. I was ecstatic that the big magazine would actually pay me the munificent subsistence wage of thirty-five dollars a week to do something I would have done for no pay at all if I could have afforded it. I rented a small room on West 53rd Street for seven dollars a week right across from the Museum of Modern Art — three flights up, bathroom in the hallway. New York was a wonderful city in those days, and one could live quite cheaply. My area of midtown Manhattan, now dominated everywhere by immense office buildings, was then largely a quiet residential zone of rooming houses and small brownstone apartments except for Rockefeller Center, where the Time & Life offices were located. There were also quite a few limousine garages about. The residents were mostly reporters and writers, artists and actors, chauffeurs and storekeepers, and a number of retired people who also required inexpensive quarters. The social focus was naturally the corner saloon, in this case Jerry's 54th Street Tavern, where one could drink beer for ten cents a glass and eat a pleasant dinner for a dollar to a dollar fifty.

In coming to New York I believed the Promised Land to be the haven of liberalism as well. I thought I had left the evils of racism behind me, except for a collection of ugly memories including a few activities in which I had participated myself, despite my sensibilities. I remember vividly one summer Saturday evening cruising around town with a couple of drinking buddies in my father's big black LaSalle, which I had borrowed. We had a case of beer in the back, mostly empties by that time, and were all a bit high if not downright drunk. We drove slowly through "niggertown," let fly a broadside of empty cans at a group of people standing idly on a corner beneath a lamppost, and sped away. It was clearly a peer-inspired deed. I would never have done such a thing alone. But as Saint Augustine remarked about his pear-tree theft: "I was ashamed to be ashamed." As I think about it the act was also absurd. I feel sure that both LaSalle and driver were noted and that the word of such a mindless act went out through the black community overnight. So, several years later, on inquiring as to the whereabouts of one Lucille Yates, a blank response may very well have reflected this lingering intelligence.

One of my early *Life* assignments was a very complicated story on atomic physics which took me uptown to Columbia University for the better part of a year. Columbia is on the fringe of Harlem, so I occasionally wandered about along 125th Street to explore the place, and so discovered Frank's restaurant. Mostly, though, my *Life* activities were confined to midtown and whites. I worked there as a reporter and later a writer for a dozen years, then turned to free-lancing and the film business. I had always been fascinated with that medium and, living across the street from the museum early on, had seen virtually its whole collection of the classic pictures. From *Life*, film was a natural move, though I continued to write pieces for the magazine until it died. It was in this state of midtown and mid-American isolation that I began to hear some "noise" from the ghetto in the late fifties and on through the sixties. Since it was largely unintelligible, I didn't pay much attention. Very occasionally my wife and I went to a cocktail party. Very occasionally one liberal host or another had invited a Godfrey Cambridge "rent-a-Negro plan" black man as well. Very occasionally, as steam built up in the sixties, I talked with one. But I failed to perceive what all the heat was about. If we were free and equal citizens in egalitarian New York, why were people suddenly angry? Later on, after we moved out to the boondocks of New Jersey, my exposure was even further reduced. When the film project began both the Madisons and myself felt that a picture on facilities would make little sense unless the film also came to grips with what was generally known as the "ghetto education problem," the problem of the so-called "disadvantaged child." So I set out in search of some understanding of that child. I did quite a bit of reading, including *Death at an Early Age, 36 Children, Manchild in the Promised Land,* and *Dark Ghetto,* by the black psychologist Kenneth Clark. Verbally, at least, I began to acquire some perception of ghetto schools; what they were like, what happened to children, why they dropped out — some remote understanding anyway — and I could see to some degree the educational disaster that had befallen black and Puerto Rican children. Finally, long after I thought I was through reading and knew something, I discovered *The Autobiography of Malcolm X.* The book stunned me. This was partly because it presented a completely different experience from the glimpses I had had of Malcolm on television or the angry words and proclamations that were printed and made much of in the newspapers, like his "Now the chickens are coming home to roost" on the occasion of John Kennedy's assassination, which had been harped on with considerable indignation, but which I now saw in quite another light. What really got to me, however, was the soul of the man. I rejoiced with Malcolm almost word by word as he described his pilgrimage to human freedom and dignity from out of the ghetto and all the unreal enchantments of one hustle or another, to the point where he could stand up and proclaim in behalf of all black people: "Here I am, everybody, an honest-to-God black MAN!" Boy! That was some proclamation! Some discovery! I never believed a word of all the mythology, the stuff Elijah Muhammed put out about Master W. D. Fard and his messianic message that black people were the original humans and white people were some evil aberration of humanness and so on. But that wasn't important. A good myth need not be true, but it must exhort the pilgrim to seek the truth, to become perhaps better than he might have been in the absence of the myth.

So Brother Malcolm rose up and shook his fist at the world and proclaimed himself a man, a message that scarcely came through on the tube though the bit that did filter out scared Whitey quite a lot. After Malcolm's proclamation, like Martin Luther's nailing a message on the door of the old Catholic church, things happened. Malcolm was a true liberator. Almost overnight the old imitation-white styles of "konked" (dekinked) hair and bleached hair and skin disappeared to be replaced by Afro looks of colorful and rich variety. Suddenly for the first time in the history of this country black people began to look like real people instead of the imitation people most whites had secretly hoped they were, or wished they were, or demanded they be, largely because of Malcolm's dedication to the truth, wherever the chips might fall.

All too soon the chips fell for Malcolm X, because there is something about truth that subhumans cannot tolerate. I remember standing on a street corner years ago in a little town in Tennessee listening to a group of rednecks talking. Not about anything to speak of, just conversation. There was the charm and inventiveness of their language that only flowers in the South. But there was also a clear comfort taken in a shared ignorance and obliviousness, a kind of subhuman expertise about how it really was in their view of the world. As I listened I became cold and afraid of this very ignorance which afforded the conversationalists so much mutual comfort. For the truth-seeker has but a tenuous integrity and a fragile perception that is easily destroyed by mindlessness. I would bet this same kind of mindless exchange went on between other people when it was decided that Brother Malcolm was making waves, that he had to go.

Malcolm X startled, delighted, and illuminated me on several counts. It was almost as though he had grabbed me by the neck and shaken me out of my unintended isolation in white midtown Manhattan and its counterparts elsewhere in white America. He woke me from a dream. For years I had fancied myself another lotus eater in the happy land of liberalism. Now, on blinking my eyes, I realized I had been gulled — engulfed in a conspiratorial and surreptitious nightmare staged by Yankee rednecks whose evil works lay concealed from my view by layers of hypocrisy that would have been marveled at in the simple-minded Southland. From childhood I had known perfectly well that black people were human beings, but I had forgotten. Rather, I had come to believe that the conditions for having such a thought to begin with had long ago evaporated. Now I found myself abruptly brought up short to discover the liberation march was barely beginning. This unexpected revelation infuriated me, and I shared vicariously Malcolm's sense of rage, a portion of which I directed at myself for having been so naive and gullible.

Malcolm's pilgrimage to truth reminded me of other critical events in my own life. Though our backgrounds were completely different, the end result was much the same. Any young person with half a mind is deluged with impressions of the world around him, almost to the point of being suffocated at times. In my case, one particular point of strangulation had been my perception of adults. I detested their attitudes and beliefs so strongly I lived in almost daily fear that one day I would become one of them. Of course, these were private and personal thoughts, and I felt some uncertainty about my evaluations. Then, in prep school, I encountered an adventurous English teacher named Edward Chandler who introduced me to the poetry of T. S. Eliot. The particular poems that really excited me, aside from *The Waste Land*, were *The Hollow Men* and *Prufrock*. In these works by an actual adult I found some objective confirmation of my own perceptions of the grown-up world which until then had been only the private notions of a child. What an experience that was! From then on and throughout college I found further confirmation for emerging feelings, notably in Plato and Saint Augustine. With such memories I could scarcely escape rejoicing with Malcolm X as he found the valid check points on his own personal journey toward becoming a free man.

Malcolm, more than anyone else, convinced me that talented children were being wasted in the ghetto. Yet, despite everything I had read, I felt I did not understand what the supposed disadvantaged child was like. Somehow in my imagination I could not feel like that child, see the world like that child, or react like that child. It seemed to me that if I could not become that child in some reasonably valid though admittedly vicarious way I would never perceive "the problem." I naturally supposed there were people who understood the matter far better than I and that the place to find them would be at the Board of Education at 110 Livingston Street in Brooklyn. So I set out to explore the corridors of learning in that great mausoleum of education.

The first thing I wished to do was merely to wander about the building, look at labels and titles on doors, and get some sense of the whole structure of the organization. I was turned over to a fellow named Eddie, an Irish functionary in one division called the Office of School Planning and Research which was concerned with the building of new schools and the refurbishing of old schools — this because our film was partly about facilities. Eddie was my first encounter with the methodical, orderly civil service mental set. He asked whom and what I wished to see. I said I didn't really know, that I just wanted to prowl around the building for a while and get some feeling for the place. Eddie's service-oriented mind, occupied largely with the precisely defined pigeon holes that specified his duties, prerogatives, and limitations, simply lacked the mechanisms for coming to grips with such a fuzzy request. His whole

world at the Board was a drafting loft where he and about ten
other engineers carefully scrutinized plans and blueprints for
new schools to be sure that certain criteria were met: that all
doors opened out instead of in (a regulation that followed the
terrible Coconut Grove nightclub fire in Boston years ago in
which the inward-opening door was jammed closed by the pan-
icked crowd trying to escape), that electrical wiring was prop-
erly installed, that the kitchens, plumbing, and a million other
details met requirements built up over the years for adequate,
children-proof school buildings, buildings that could be easily
evacuated in case of fire or some other disaster. New York City,
a crowded place at best, is rather sharp about such things.

Confronted with Eddie's procedural bafflement, I sat down in
the drafting loft and looked over a guide book to 110 Livingston
Street to pick out some people who might be worth talking to
because of their various specialties. At precisely 11:59 Eddie
walked over to a hot plate in the big room and put some water
on to boil. Then, forty-five seconds later, he took a paper bag
out of his desk drawer, removed a sandwich and made himself a
cup of instant coffee over at the hot plate. It took a few minutes
for these activities to register on me.

"Oh," I said finally, "you're having a sandwich."

"Yes, I'm on my lunch hour. But I'll be back at one o'clock."

There was no hostility in his remark; it was a simple statement of fact. Eddie's lunch hour was merely one of his many
routines. I got up, a bit embarrassed, and said I would go out
and have a sandwich myself and come back later.

"Fine," said Eddie. "I'll be back at one."

Under Eddie's guidance I met a psychologist on the staff, an
intelligent and dedicated white man who gave me quite a bit of
his time on several occasions. The description of the disadvantaged child which emerged from these conversations goes about
as follows:

The child lives in an overcrowded tenement apartment on
welfare. His father is absent, probably permanently. He has to

compete with his siblings for his mother's attention, to get food, clothing, almost everything. It is highly probable that it is not his real mother the child must demand things of but some relative, perhaps an aunt he has been parked with. The words he hears in the flat are simple and direct: "Shut up. Get out of my way. Go to bed." He quickly comes to see himself as an impediment to the others who are also struggling to survive in the same crowded environment. This may lead him to become overly aggressive at an early age. It could as well have the opposite effect, producing feelings of withdrawal and worthlessness and a retarded sense of his own value, in which case what should be a normally emerging individuality is suppressed. The child arrives at school with an assortment of hang-ups, a low vocabulary, and is possibly tired because his sleep has been disturbed in the crowded bedroom. In all likelihood he is hungry as well.

Out on the street, quickly enough, this same child observes at a very early age who appears to be making out. Contrary to society's accepted standards of achievement, it is the local pusher, the hustler, the big numbers man, "Cadillac Daddy," the cat who drives the big car and sports the fancy suits and monogrammed shirts. Clearly Cadillac Daddy is not his own daddy, or his aunt, or his Mommy, either, who is perhaps hustling downtown. So the child begins to develop his own little hustles — jimmying candy machines, stealing from the grocery store, doing mysterious errands for the "big cats." When that child hits a school system of middle-class values, a system predicated on some perception of goals that are twelve and maybe even twenty years distant, he is confronted with something that is completely contradictory to the here-and-now gratification or maybe-you'll-never-get-it principles which are the everyday operating guidelines on the street where he lives. A kid who is hungry to the point of stealing is hungry today, not tomorrow. This being the situation it seemed to people at the Board that such a child needed some kind of compensatory education,

something that would increase his low vocabulary, reduce his
hang-ups, and prop him up so he could enter the system and
succeed within it.   Quite a few people at Livingston Street
were concerned with how to achieve this, despite Nathan
Brown's observation that all such efforts had failed.   Yet since
the established system was taken for granted, the matter could
only be viewed as a problem posed by the disadvantaged
child.   How such a child might view the matter himself did
not occur to them.   And strangely enough in all the time I spent
in these corridors and rooms of big-city education the one word
that never came up was *teachers*.

  One day I invited Eddie to lunch and suggested we go to
Gage and Tollner's, a famous old Brooklyn sea food restaurant
on Fulton Street I had heard a lot about but had never visited.
The restaurant was only a short walk from the Board of Education and proved to be one of those nice antique wood-paneled
places frequented by local judges, politicians, and businessmen
for the most part.   We had a drink and ordered.   I selected crab
Norfolk and Eddie chose Irish stew.   I am a rather slow eater,
having had it drilled into my head as a child by my extremely
Southern mother that it was bad manners to wolf down food.
As a consequence I am invariably the last to finish a meal with
any of my normal New York companions.   But as this particular
lunch with Eddie drew to a close I realized, with considerable
astonishment, that I was now in the company of an even slower
eater, a Yankee at that.   Since this was the first time in twenty-
five years this had happened I was naturally curious.   I remarked on the fact to Eddie, hoping he might have some observation to offer, but I drew a blank.   There were no pigeonholes
to accommodate a query of this sort.   It struck me that perhaps
his methodical mind had simply made a natural calculation: es-
timate number of bites in portion; divide into time allotted for
lunch (1 hour minus 3 minutes walking time each way from
Board of Education, minus 12 minutes to drink whiskey sour,
minus 10 minutes for coffee); so take one bite every 64 seconds.

Eddie's boss was a gentleman named Ben, a native New York of Puerto Rican descent. I asked Ben to take me on a driving tour of Brooklyn so I could look at some ghetto schools in the area. I had read and read, talked and talked, and now I wanted to go see. Cruising around the ghettos of central Brooklyn and the adjoining area of east New York was an eye-opening experience to one who had been confined largely to central Manhattan for so long. Once I had wandered about Harlem a bit, and the south side of Chicago, too, one of the more depressing pictures of living with nothingness I have ever encountered — in this country at least. But now, after the riotous summers of 1967 and 1968, things looked different. The effects of burning and looting were visible everywhere. Everywhere we went I saw burned-out or boarded-up buildings and abandoned stores. Many blocks were simply demolished and covered by a blanket of rubble to make way for urban renewal projects. Over the whole dismal scene hung a feeling of anger and outrage and despair that had not been there before.

In the Ocean Hill–Brownsville area of the borough we came upon what struck me immediately as a school of quite novel design. It was built of brick with small slit windows and reminded me very much of the old Bastille in Paris. It even had a suggestion of turrets as part of the design. I remarked to Ben that it looked like a rather terrific school for such a dismal neighborhood.

"That's I.S. 55," Ben remarked. "People around here hate it!"

Ben went on at some length about the way schools were treated in such neighborhoods, about vandalism and so on. I suppose this was natural since his main concern was with building and maintaining school facilities. But I had read elsewhere an interesting observation that if a kid threw a rock through a schoolhouse window one ought to be able to conclude there was a message attached. I asked Ben what he thought would happen if they built a pleasant, open school with lawns and picture windows and things like that in such a neighborhood. His instant response was that it would be destroyed; that you have to construct a building as solid and foolproof as possible in a place like this. Ben also had reservations about blacks, expressing the old feeling: "We made it. Why can't they?" He felt blacks just didn't have the stuff to make out whereas his own Puerto Rican stock did. I have heard that distinction in other quarters, that a Puerto Rican family will tend to start up some small enterprise, work at it, and get it going, whereas blacks seem incapable of such communal efforts. But after reading Oscar Lewis's *La Vida* I am not so sure what those Puerto Rican cooperatives add up to except possibly one way of trying to make out as opposed to another and different way of trying to make out in a foreign land known as America.

If there is anything underlying the notion of black shiftlessness, I believe Malcolm X put his finger on the root of it when he proclaimed that the black man had been brainwashed by white Americans into believing he was inferior, into aspiring to become white, an aspiration reflected by the sense of superiority of the old New Orleans Creole musicians who proudly regarded themselves as "light-skinned people," as distinct from the black people from the "back of town" like Louis Armstrong. Anyone who believes himself inferior can't help acting a bit obsequious in the face of such a notion, like certain white Christians in church who shuffle around and grovel and otherwise look rather fawning before a superior god. If Negro aspirations end in a shuffling Uncle Tom act in a Pullman car, what real alternatives to shiftlessness could there be? Any halfway smart kid would sense that, particularly if his parents subscribed to the doctrine to begin with. But Malcolm's proclamations blew all that nonsense away like the trumpet of God.

As Ben and I cruised about the dismal chaos of Brooklyn, we came upon P.S. 158 in East New York. I asked Ben to stop the car.

"Can we look at this school?"

"You want to look at that school?" — eyebrows raised.

"Yes."

P.S. 158 was an old school, but no special antique by city standards. It had the typical fortresslike construction. Its asphalt playground was surrounded by a cyclone fence, and it was littered with broken glass. Here and there lay an unbroken sherry bottle in a wrinkled paper bag, tucked away in a corner by local winoes who had shared its contents and then passed on or passed out. We entered the school. The wire-encased up and down stairwells presented a liberal exhibition of graffiti:

"Kiss me."

"Kiss my ass."

"Susan and Piri — 69."

"Pussy is good for a headache."

"LSD is fuck all."

"Piss."

Since Ben was officially a buildings man we went to the basement first to find the custodian of the school, his logical connection. The custodian was absent. The cavernous basement accommodated a locked-in area which held a large collection of metal drums stenciled with Civil Defense labels. The drums contained rations in the event of a nuclear disaster and were stored in the school because it was by far the most durable structure in the area and was owned by the city. The drums were locked up because, as Ben explained, neighborhood people often pilfered such supplies since they sometimes had nothing else to eat. The sight of these objects in a school infuriated me for they juxtaposed the prospect of nuclear catastrophe with the rightful expectations and budding futures of children. Why the dust-gathering provisions for such an eventuality should be stored in a school where children gathered who would have the least responsibility for it, simply eluded me. It was logical enough; but it was the illogic of the logic that struck me, the thinking downtown that was behind it, or rather the nonthinking: "Hey, we got a real good pillbox in East New York! We got good pillboxes all over the goddamn city if we need 'em." Except, of course, it was not thought out that way, felt that way, conceived that way, or concluded that way. It was simply logical to store these drums which represent an intolerable human calamity in a place that was supposed to deliver some basic human prospects. A small seed of conflict began to germinate in my mind: there was some kind of hiatus between city structure and human needs.

We went upstairs to explore the school; here all my reading and what I was now seeing collided head on. I had thought I had an image of Herbert Kohl's "bean school" in my mind's eye (so named because of the prevalence of beans on the welfare lunch menu in New York ghetto schools), I had empathized with Jonathan Kozol's children and their school. Yet, actually seeing such a school quite confounded me. We walked up and down the five floors of the building along broad, wooden corridors. The massive oak classroom doors had once contained windows so observers — the principal or one of the assistant principals on the staff — could look in. But these had long ago been broken out and the custodian had nailed plywood over the openings. Moving along a corridor past these sealed cells was a bit like listening to a poor transistor radio that gradually went into full, distorted volume as a door approached, then diminished until the next door came along. One door burst open abruptly and a small voice cried out: "Motherfucker!"

A young white female teacher was ejecting a black child from her classroom, holding the boy by both hands. The boy had deliberately let his body go limp to make the expulsion more difficult. The teacher nevertheless managed to get the child out of the room and into the hallway, explaining in an icy voice that only emphasized her rage:

"Nice little boys don't use words like that!"

The door closed and the small boy wandered off down the big, wide corridor. It occurred to me that "motherfucker" was probably the largest word in the small boy's small vocabulary.

It is certainly common enough, even in the best of circles. To the child it was pure street jargon expressing distaste for the teacher, or the school, or life as he saw it or heard about it or lived it. But to the teacher it had represented an affront and so had become the occasion for a status-oriented response. The kid had made use of the word "public" for her. I didn't understand why a child's private world of words should have to become a matter of official posturing. Not that I felt the teacher should have patted the child on the head, exclaimed to the class what a big word it was, and suggested that everyone should get together and parse the expression. Still, I felt her solution of the problem could have been improved.

Eight out of ten classroom doors in this school were closed. Behind them children and teachers could be heard shouting and screaming at each other. But here and there we came upon a few classrooms, some with doors open, some closed, where relative peace prevailed. Finding these small units of positive activity struck me as what it might have been like to stumble across Jonathan Kozol's classroom in Boston or Herbert Kohl's in Harlem. Among the teachers in such rooms were a few young men of obvious draft age who were just as obviously avoiding the Vietnam war by teaching and who, for reasons related to their moral objections, cared about their classes and the children in them. Out of the depths of a dismal and mindless and malevolent war here at least was a small positive spin-off; small because what good would it do for a child to have one good year with a young man who cared, only to be plunged back into the rest of that bean school the next year, and the year after that? Yet the situation could not have been that simple. It seemed reasonable to suppose there were "regular" teachers who cared just as much about what was happening to their charges, in spite of the uproar behind most of the closed doors. So although the experience of walking into a bean school like P.S. 158 was shocking enough, I realized I was only on the fringe of a highly complex social situation and that any conclusions I might draw about New York's ghetto schools from one visit to one building would be hopelessly superficial.

In the gymnasium on the ground floor closed chaos became open bedlam. Among all its other woes this particular school was overcrowded, which meant that a large segment of its student population had to be confined in the gym or out on the playground until classroom space became available on the floors above. In these areas, in a deafening and erratic Brownian motion, children and groups of children shouted and ran about, colliding, bouncing off walls and fences and doors, and generally letting off steam. Teachers and aids, armed with bullhorns, police whistles, and broomsticks, guarded all the doors and exits in an effort to contain and control the situation. The messages from the bullhorns were unintelligible to a visitor, but it was clear that the children, well adapted to if not well pleased with the situation, heard the various messages and obeyed or ignored them as the spirit moved them. The whole spectacle reminded me of those old 1930s films featuring Jimmy Cagney, Barton McLane, Charles Bickford, George Raft, and others about life in prison, with the cons banging their tin cups in the mess hall under the watchful eyes of the well-armed "screws." In this school the teachers were clearly the screws. Perhaps not deliberately, or intentionally, or malevolently. But they were screws nevertheless because of "the situation."

Since the situation, whatever it was, involved mostly black and Puerto Rican children, I felt I should contact some black educators who might have thoughts on how to teach ghetto kids. I paid a visit to an associate of Dr. Kenneth Clark's, Ken Marshall, whom I had met briefly some weeks earlier. I felt nervous and sweated a bit as we talked. I was quite aware that matters had become seriously polarized between blacks and whites, but since I knew so little of the real underpinnings of this polarity or the educational disaster which formed a large part of it (even though I had now seen a pristine example), and since my main source of information had been a large amount of unintelligible noise emanating from the television screen, I must have appeared to him as the ultimate stranger. He did suggest a principle of cooperation: that if blacks and whites could work together on projects of some mutual advantage, why not? As my interest was education he added: "Why don't you go see Charles Wilson up at the 201 Complex?" I knew that the "Complex" was one of the city's demonstration districts, like Rhody McCoy's Ocean Hill–Brownsville schools. I thought at the time I knew something about these experiments because of all the reporting that had boiled up during the big teachers' strike the previous year. Consequently, though I felt it might be interesting to talk with Charles Wilson, I didn't see any imperative reason for doing so. However, I said I might follow up on his suggestion.

The next day I called on another black, Dr. Vera Paster, who headed the Board of Education's Bureau of Child Guidance. I explained I was looking for something that might work with ghetto kids instead of wiping them out — some program, some place, where something positive was being achieved. I had in the back of my mind the quixotic idea that there must be, some-where, a magical formula or program that could succeed with these children and that it would be important for our film to reflect this. I looked at her directly and she looked at me in the same way, as though I had wandered in from the outside world, a strange and optimistic pilgrim seeking truth and hope in a lab-yrinth where those words had long ago been abandoned. Vera Paster was a handsome woman, with a sadness in her eyes which struck me as having behind it a long history of frustration and disappointment I knew nothing about.

"We have pieces of it," she said. "But only pieces. Nothing that goes together yet."

She mentioned schools where I might find some of these pieces: programs to hold the interest of children after school better than the streets; programs which dealt with children in terms of their ethnic background; preschool programs which at-

tempted to prop children up so they could enter the edbiz pipe-
line. And then she, too, mentioned Charles Wilson. As I left I
inexplicably asked her to wish me luck in my search.

"Good luck, Mr. Campbell," she said warmly.

I wrote a letter to Charles Wilson explaining that I was interested in the ghetto education problem and asked to come up
and see him sometime. I got no answer so I phoned the Complex office requesting an appointment. I had difficulty connecting with anyone who had any understanding of why I wished to
see Charles Wilson in the first place. ("Bob Campbell from
New Jersey?") Most of the problem stemmed from the fact that
I didn't know myself what I wanted to see Mr. Wilson about.
It was just a hunch.

Meanwhile I had more pressing matters to attend to. I had
described P.S. 158 to the Madisons, and we agreed that our film
on facilities should start with what a bean school was like by
way of introducing the problem. But one does not cart camera
equipment into a New York school without the consent of the
district superintendent. So I called the lady in charge of this
chaotic school in East New York and tried to explain the film
we were working on and what we wanted to do.

"Are you an expert on education?" she snapped over the
phone.

"No, I'm a writer. But . . ." (At a later date I might have
had the courage to ask: "Are you?" But not at this time.)

"Well I just don't agree with anything you're saying. Not at
all. I have an inexperienced principal in that school who is just
trying to hold things together — and a drunken custodian on top
of that who's absent half the time! And here you call me and
ask to take pictures in it or something!"

I tried to keep the conversation calm but the lady, an old-line
Irish supervisor, was moving rather rapidly from a state of extreme suspicion to one of near hysteria.

"I've just been viciously attacked in the press by Ken Clark,"
she shouted, "and now *you* come along! " (Kenneth Clark had

accused the woman of needlessly expelling a dozen disruptive students from a high school in her district.)

"Thank God I have a little vacation coming up next week, and I'm going away to try and rest up from all this nonsense!"

I contacted the Board of Education and inquired where I might find overcrowded schools elsewhere in the city and, perhaps, a superintendent who might prove more sympathetic to the project. I was provided with a list of six schools in the south Bronx in a district run by Dr. Edythe Gaines, the only black superintendent in the city. I visited Mrs. Gaines and was greeted by a warm, outgoing, and very bright woman, a diminutive dynamo who could, I suspected, also be quite tough and sharp if the occasion arose. With her consent I toured the six schools, talked with their principals, and found they were indeed overcrowded, but were on split shifts and did not give that appearance at all. I could not tell whether I had been deliberately misled by headquarters or whether I was just another victim of a bureaucratic foul-up downtown.

One of the schools proved interesting simply on its own terms, however. It was in an area of the Bronx that had the highest per capita junkie population of the whole city, which I should think would make it the junkie-densest region in the western world. Visiting the principal of a New York school requires following certain established procedures after making an appointment. One first goes to the second floor where the general administrative office is located, a large open room inhabited by clerks and secretaries who are usually white women, getting on in years, slow-moving and for the most part comparatively stodgy, humorless, and unattractive. Inside the door a visitor is faced with a long counter separating him from the open pool of desks, tables, and filing cabinets behind. In this counter are two waist-high gates that can only be opened by an inside latch. Actually an adult accustomed to this entrance can easily reach over one of the gates and let himself in, though doing so would produce considerable consternation if one were not well known in the school. A tall child or one who stood on tiptoe could do the same, but I don't know why a student should want to. Under normal circumstances, any appearance in the office means a child has presented a discipline problem to a teacher and has been sent down to be reprimanded or possibly even suspended by one of the assistant principals or by the principal himself. So the little gates, fragile as they are, indicate well enough where the authority lies. I imagine they make the same point to parents who have some grievance to express.

Off to one side of the general office is a door leading to the principal's office, the spacious quarters provided for the captain of the ship. In the navy that would be just about the appropriate rank, for the average elementary school contains somewhere between 1200 and 2000 children, roughly the crew complement of a battle cruiser if not a full battleship. The captain of a school is a big man: he has the only private toilet in the school, to which he has his own private key. From his office the principal issues orders via the APs who are more visible since they patrol the hallways. Information feeds back to the command post the same way. Now and then the principal is forced to confront an actual child who has been sent down for some discipline problem. Occasionally he must confront the parent of such a child as well. Usually, though, he sticks to his cabin.

The principal of this particular school had done the basic layout one better. He not only had his regular office, but had appropriated two rooms on the floor above and converted them into a private study, to which I was invited for coffee. It was a pleasant sanctuary, its walls lined with bookcases which provided a feeling of "Academe." There were comfortable chairs and several coffee tables as well as coffee-making equipment. Almost no noise penetrated this inner sanctum, except for the occasional muffled jangling of the school bells. I almost felt I had been transplanted to some master's quarters in a posh New England prep school, but this feeling was negated by my trip to the south Bronx to begin with. I had ridden up on the el. Sitting next to me was a black man obviously drunk from the night before who was muttering dark and malevolent threats against someone or something unknown to me. He stumbled off the train several stops before mine and left on the seat a long and very sharp pearl-handled hunting knife which had somehow fallen from his clothes or out of his grasp. I handed it to the conductor when I got off the train.

Over coffee in his study I asked the principal if he had made any effort to involve parents in his school.

"Parents?" he responded sharply. "We hold all kinds of affairs for the neighborhood! We invite them in all the time! We had a whole program arranged just last week with speakers engaged for the occasion, just for parents. You know how many people showed up? Six women, that's what! Look, these parents are busy working for someone. Cleaning, household work, whatever. They don't have time to come to the school. They're too busy making a living."

I asked whether he thought teachers should have any special qualifications for working in a poverty area like this one.

"There's a lot of flak going around these days about teachers in this city. I think it's a lot of nonsense. You go to the doctor, right? Do you ask him if he's a qualified doctor? You certainly don't, because he has a degree right there on his wall that says he has passed his medical exams. Right? Well, these teachers have their certificates, too. They are certified to teach, and I don't see any difference. Nobody questions the qualifications of doctors. Why all of a sudden are a lot of supposedly community-minded people questioning the qualifications of teachers?"

The principal sat back in his comfortable chair. Whether he was concerned about what was happening in the officer's quarters of his ship, let alone the fo'c'sle where the crew of nearly 2000 children was housed, I could not tell. Whether he had any intimation that the ship might be sinking, let alone whether it had ever gotten to sea in the first place, I could not tell. He was simply occupying a colonial outpost as he saw it, as it was defined on the books downtown. Given his rank he had gone to no small lengths to insure that the poop deck was as habitable as possible. Plants and flowers decorated the windowsills of the inner sanctum, bathed in the morning sunlight. I could not resist wondering whether one of them might be a breadfruit tree, though I would not have recognized such a plant.

Stuck with the problem of finding a bean school for the film I returned to Edythe Gaines's office and laid my cards on the table:

"I'm trying to find a real custodial school for the film I'm working on, like the one I described in East New York. We've already shot some good things, few and far between I must say. But I guess I want to ask you for the other side of the coin which I have seen and know about."

"Look, Mr. Campbell, the bean school you describe does not really exist, except rarely. Not as a whole school anyway. I have some menopausal principals, and I have some rotten teachers. You talk about children and teachers climbing the walls? Well, what about the quiet classroom where nothing at all is happening? A classroom where some social reject type of teacher agrees with her class that she will give up what is to her the pointless charade of trying to teach when everyone in the room knows she can't or won't and the children for their part won't bother to try and learn anything. So nobody bugs anybody, okay?"

"Well," I said, after thinking that one over for several long seconds, "that is some silent scene all right. I'm sure you are right that the total disaster is the exception. I suppose any school with twelve hundred or fifteen hundred children and five floors of classrooms can't be homogenized, all bad or all good, but maybe you could direct me to one of your menopausal principals?"

The moment the question slipped out I wished I had swallowed it. I think Dr. Gaines realized this, too, otherwise she would have bitten my head off and that would have been that. Instead she said, somewhat tartly:

"I cannot ethically do anything of the sort. I can direct you to one interesting situation in the district. One of our 'landmarks' is the oldest school in the city; it will be one hundred next year. It's on One Hundred and Sixty-seventh Street off the Old Boston Road and you have there an interesting situation. In fact, I was just by there this morning. That school has been slated for demolition for years, and a new school was built just across the street to take its place. But by the time the new school finally got finished, the neighborhood population — mostly Puerto Rican — had become so dense that both schools were needed. Not only that, but a third corner of the intersection is occupied by temporary huts with classrooms in them to take the overflow. On the fourth corner is a burned-out building where children play as they come to school and leave. It's a very dangerous situation, and I've called Herman Badillo [a Puerto Rican congressman in the Bronx] about the whole thing. I told him if something wasn't done, I'd take pictures of that situation."

I believe she would have, too — personally if need be. Dr. Edythe Gaines struck me as a lady of that kind of determination. Mrs. Gaines thought for a moment:

"If you have the patience to continue looking, Mr. Campbell, I will do one thing for you."

"When I think I have something to find, Mrs. Gaines, I can be a very patient man."

"Good," she said. Dr. Gaines escorted me to her office door and gave a directive to her personal secretary:

"Mr. Campbell has carte blanche in my district."

I thanked her, we shook hands, and I left. My first stop was the crossroads Mrs. Gaines had mentioned. It was indeed an incredible scene, one reflecting the ecology of education in a city which took forever and a day to build a school to the point where, when the damn thing was finally completed, the entire neighborhood had changed so drastically as to make the original plans virtually meaningless. The old school was a towering and foreboding brick structure straight out of a classic horror film like *The Body Snatchers, The Murders in the Rue Morgue* or better still, *The Fall of the House of Usher* — the original, highly impressionistic version. The building loomed above the street with tall, narrow stairwell windows and broader classroom windows capped with brick arches of antique design. When the school first opened its doors, this area of the Bronx had been a rural suburb of the big city to the south; now it was pure teeming tenement. Half the windows of the building were broken and many were covered with pieces of cardboard to keep the cold air out. There was the usual collection of graffiti applied to the walls with chalk, spray-paint cans, and brushes. Its beleaguered appearance was made the more bizarre by two blue lamps glowing just a few doors up the block to mark the local police precinct. I could hardly help admiring the daring of the vandals who had operated right under the noses of the law, though perhaps the police had their hands full with more urgent problems in such a neighborhood and simply had no time to protect property.

There was one jarring note in this otherwise uniformly dismal scene. Many classroom windows had red and green, blue and yellow cutout flowers strung across them, bright colors completely at odds with the muted hues of the ancient and dilapidated building. Obviously the children and teachers had worked to make their homerooms more cheerful, as teachers who come from teachers' colleges are taught to do to get the children involved so they feel at home in their own room. No doubt it is a perfectly valid thing to teach teachers to do; after all it *is* the children's room. It was simply that this strange note of pedagogic cheer, strung onto this particularly antique building in such a rank and crumbling neighborhood, did not, could not, add up. The little patches of color seemed quite out of joint, the work of some celestial con man who, with a touch of thin fingers — *plink, plink* — declared there should be brightness and education in the midst of chaos and disaster in an overcrowded community which barely supported life. It wasn't the antiquity of the building that was incongruous; it could have qualified as a historic landmark in the city. Far from being torn down, it should be preserved for some worthwhile purpose — even education. Rather, it was the obvious antiquity of an educational system which declared in some stereotyped and oblivious way that there should be cheer when in fact there was none anywhere that a child could see. It was the mindlessness incapable of coming to grips with old buildings or new children that was shocking. The sight of the "new" school across the street, now ten years old, only aggravated the impression. It was pure Board of Education design, incredibly dull and monotonous, painted in insipid pastels — a cheap plastic box. The temporary huts on the third corner contributed little to change the impression. Only the burned-out building Edythe Gaines had objected to for safety reasons standing in a pile of rubble on the fourth corner suggested any hope; there at least a group of kids might discover some interesting adventures. So finally the whole idea of adding color to some windows appeared more as a pretense, a hoax, than anything else, and an image began to build in my mind of a monolithic educational establishment that ground along, propelled by its own momentum and other inexorable laws of physics, crushing the minds of countless children who lay in its path, staked out there by law.

I looked at many schools in Mrs. Gaines's district, and I decided to settle down and spend some time in one that seemed better run than most. It was reasonably quiet and under control, and I sensed it might present a far better picture of ghetto education in the city than the total disaster of P.S. 158 in East New York, which had been a purely custodial situation and, as Edythe Gaines had pointed out, not the norm at all. It is easy to get carried away by bedlam — an affliction all too endemic to journalists — but that is a fatal disease if one actually wishes to understand something. P.S. 67, just off Tremont Avenue in the Bronx, was a newer school than most in the district. The principal was a tall, handsome, light-skinned black lady named Mrs. Pollard, a cool, competent, and well-collected person. I felt she had assessed what she could do and what she could not do with her school and her children, within "the system." That she held her position at all was due in large measure to Edythe Gaines. Mrs. Pollard was only qualified as an assistant principal. She could neither be named nor paid as principal so she ran the school on behalf of the actual principal who had left for some reason. Mrs. Gaines could not appoint her to the full role because there is a long waiting list of accredited white candidates that won't be used up for another five years.

I came upon Mrs. Pollard's school more or less aware of the tragic impasse between black and Puerto Rican ghetto dwellers, protesting the failure of poverty children, and a school system whose teachers were mostly Jewish women, the last people in the world to wear the mantle of the oppressor. When Jewish teachers discover they are participants in a system that has historically failed poverty kids, that they are the keepers of a gateway which does not liberate anyone, the realization can only lead to complete consternation. Quite unwittingly I aroused these feelings one day in P.S. 67 when I entered one of the kindergarten rooms as a "visitor to the school" during a lunch hour. Six teachers were congregated around one of the low children's reading tables eating sandwiches. Five of them were women, the majority Jewish. The sixth was a young man. My entrance produced a reflex response of almost instant hysteria. The teachers swarmed over one another and cut each other off to explain all the things they were doing for "the children."

"Look what I am trying with my children here!"

"Look what we're doing in this area over here!"

"No, no! Look over here; over here!"

"No, look *here!* See what we are doing *here!*"

Clearly the teachers cared very deeply. They were trying desperately to teach, and they were just as desperately hoping the children would learn.

It seems incredible that an educational confrontation of such magnitude had not been anticipated years ago, both by Albert Shanker and his United Federation of Teachers and by the Board of Education, especially considering the ethnic groups that were on this catastrophic collision course. But Shanker seems to have looked upon the problem from a purely trade union point of view, pressing for smaller classes, more teachers, stronger contracts, higher pay, more benefits, et cetera. The question of whether the membership was actually delivering "product," i.e., teaching, seems not to have seriously entered his mind. Perhaps he felt he simply had to accept teachers as defined, trained, and spewed out by a multitude of state and city teachers' colleges. Still if Shanker had perceived the core of the developing disaster a decade or more ago (it had certainly been readily observable) and blown the whistle on the whole situation, he would not be stuck today with the posture of maintaining his same old brood, deviously avoiding the question of whether these mother hens are not just clucking about and laying a sterile educational egg. With foresight Mr. Shanker might well have led his Jewish teachers through the Red Sea of big-city bureaucracy and onto the higher ground that has to come. But as *Time* might say: "Al Shanker, no Moses he." Because of that failure his constituents are stranded, caught in an untenable "now" by failure to anticipate "then." Shanker's weekly column in the Sunday *New York Times*, an advertisement paid for by the U.F.T., might have had the felicitous title: "Where We're Going." Instead it is called "Where We Stand."

Since it was still lunchtime I walked with Mrs. Pollard out onto the playground where various classes were enjoying recess. It seemed hardly possible that even a slab of asphalt could support the bedlam there. Children, blacks and Puerto Ricans mostly, rushed this way and that, shouting, yelling, tumbling over one another, screaming, pushing and shoving, tearing at clothes, falling down, bouncing up again. Here and there sporadic fights erupted and just as quickly evaporated. Some boys were hanging from the screen grill work that protected the school's windows, hoping not to be seen in the process. Girls, more docile than boys, skipped rope or played hopscotch, though among them, too, there was an occasional outburst of violence. I had a 35 mm. still camera with me and, tired of carrying it, I laid it down on a sturdy padlocked box in one corner of the playground as I wanted to wander around and take a look out behind a cluster of temporary huts that occupied part of this large fenced-in arena.

"Hey, mister," a boy said, "you better not leave that there. Somebody might steal it."

"I don't believe that children in P.S. 67 steal things, do you?"

I walked away. Back behind the school a ball game was in progress with one of those orange-colored rubber balls that kids everywhere possess, even in the south Bronx — perhaps particularly in the south Bronx. One youngster hit the ball up onto the roof of the school. Another, with no hesitation whatever, promptly scaled a drain pipe all the way up to the gutter along the edge of the roof, retrieved the ball, tossed it down, and then shinnied down the slender metal pipe from five floors up. Unconsciously I had been holding my breath all this time and suddenly realized, as the kid reached the comparative safety of the second floor, that I was dying for air. Returning to the main area again I saw the small boy in his sneakers and tattered jacket sitting on what I imagined was the custodian's hope chest with one hand on my camera. He handed it to me with a smile. I smiled back. "Thank you very much." The boy disappeared. I rejoined Mrs. Pollard, somewhat confounded by all the high-pressure steam being let off in what was just a typical ghetto playground to her.

"You should watch out for the children," she said in her casual and competent way.

"Maybe you should have a sign out, Beware of Flying Children, or something like that."

"Perhaps we should," she replied quietly, appreciating the thought. It later became a small joke between us. Recess was coming to an end and the supervisory people in the playground, mostly middle-aged white and black women, went into action for the big roundup. Bullhorns and police whistles appeared to get the attention of the children. So did a few mop handles. The communications that resulted, so far as I could decipher from the distortions of bullhorns and loud voices to which the children were clearly much better attuned, went about this way:

"No running!"

"First graders! Line up over here!"

"You put that down and get over here, you hear?"

"Get over! Get over!"

"Get on your line! What you looking at? Get over!"

"Line up now! No running!"

"*No running!*"

"What's the matter? Didn't you finish eating? Don't fool me! Don't fool *me!*"

"Fifth graders! On line now!"

"You, there! Wha'cha doing? Get over here!"

"I mean now, *not* tomorrow! You hear me?"

"Give me that stick! What's that? What you doing with that? Give me that stick! Right now! You hear me?"

Gradually the various grades were rounded up and assembled in lines on the playground. Then they were marched into one of the school gyms to be received by their homeroom teachers. Here the second line of staff took over, again with bullhorns and police whistles that contributed to the echoing pandemonium in the big, bare, reverberating room. A pert young Jewish

teacher in a miniskirt was in charge of the occasion and, because of her diminutive size, she hopped onto a chair with a
bullhorn to oversee and organize the manifest chaos:

"Two–four is looking good now! Quiet now. Two–four is
lining up very well!"

"One–three! One–three! Oh no! One–three is not ready yet.
Better get ready, one–three. Line up there nicely now."

"Quiet, three–five! Over here now! Listen, three–five, you'll
never get back to your teacher unless you quiet down and line
up nicely!"

"Good, two–four. Very good. Very quiet and nice! You may
go up now with Miss Kupferman. Thank you."

One by one the classes were lined up, quieted down more or
less, and led away by their teachers to the classrooms on the
floors above. What sense this regimental procedure made to
the children I don't know. What damage it did to them I have
no idea. It obviously made complete sense to a bureaucracy
faced with the problem of processing a thousand or more children in each of a thousand schools in the city. It had all been
worked out through years of experience with large masses of
children, like changing the watch on a battleship. If I had been
treated that way as a child I think I would have felt lost and ter-
rified. Yet the children of P.S. 67 took it all in stride, seemingly
either immune or indifferent. Children are amazingly plastic.
They can be pressed into the most absurd routines, given the
most meaningless things to do (meaningless to them), have all
sorts of senseless and even vicious tasks laid on them by
adults — for the convenience of adults — yet they will try
desperately to identify the game and play it in order to please or
perhaps simply to get along. Dogs respond the same way. If
they are trained with threats and blows they may become un-
trustworthy and vicious, or perhaps just skittish. Trained with
affection they grow to be loving and obedient and yet at the
same time take on a dignity and independence wonderful to
behold. Unfortunately independence is something most adults

find difficult to tolerate, either in children or in animals. As Sherlock Holmes once noted, one can tell quite a bit about a person or a family by the way the family dog behaves. I suspect one can tell a lot about a society, too, by the way its children behave.

After recess I wandered about the school some more and accidentally encountered one of the playground attendants, a big, handsome black woman with a billowing Afro hairdo. She had struck me as one of the more severe participants in that scene and some of the directives I have mentioned were hers. I made a casual remark about the problem of handling so many children, and she agreed it was quite a problem.

"You have to handle these kids the way they are handled at home by their parents. Otherwise they don't understand you."

She said this in a quiet, ordinary voice that was completely contrary to her "public" voice on the playground. It was as though we were both backstage now. We chatted a bit more and it turned out her name was Mrs. Campbell, which somehow gave us the feeling of a mutual connection we did not pursue. Mrs. Campbell was a pleasant, open lady whose seemingly harsh performance had been a complete act by a woman who was a consummate actress when "on stage." It seemed fair to conclude that she was reasonable in her dispensation of justice as it was defined under the precepts of such a school. Certainly the children had responded to her that way. They had not regarded her as a vicious or capricious person, so far as I could tell. She was just a part, probably a rather good and trustworthy part, of the way it was.

One of the interesting things about Mrs. Pollard's school, which she pointed out to me, was the condition of the displays on bulletin boards in the hallways. One presented an exhibit of pictures relating to computers, programming, the space age and so on. The children had all but destroyed the show by ripping pictures off the board, scrawling marks and otherwise defacing the exhibit. Mrs. Pollard in her characteristically quiet way made no comment other than to point out the phenomenon. On another corridor she showed me an exhibit devoted to quite a different subject, paintings and caricatures which the children had done of themselves. The exhibit hung unmolested and undefaced. The children respected the efforts of their peers, but what ghetto prisoner could relate to computers or the space program or "downtown stuff" like that? Did a black face ever appear significantly in all the NASA television coverage? So how could this be read as other than just another put-down by a kid attending P.S. 67 in the south Bronx? This led me to wonder why it had ever gone up to start with. It was certainly not Mrs. Pollard's idea. I felt that the lady, given some freedom and autonomy within the system, would have selected a subject more directly related to her children and consequently more inspirational. Why, then, had she shown this strange contrast to me, one she herself was obviously quite sensitive to? It did not take much effort to figure out the answer. The idea for this exhibit had emanated from the central Board of Education — suggesting that the subject of computers and space travel would be a most suitable one for children at certain grade levels to work up an exhibit about. Display boards of standard construction and standard dimensions are suitably located along the corridors of every school in the city. Naturally the specifications of all available display space would be known downtown, including the total number of bulletin boards for each grade level, their dimensions, construction (plain cork or glass-encased), and so on. Of course, the exact numbers might be some years out of date, given the inertia of the system, but that wouldn't matter. Naturally there would also be many people downtown, perhaps arranged in subgroups each with its specific pedagogic specialty and prerogatives, who would be concerned with the kinds of materials that should appear there and who would have suggestions for grade projects in various subjects. To a central system that can only deal in "norms" and programs, it would seem quite timely to propose that an exhibit on the space age would be an interesting thing for "the children" to do. But what children? Where? In what part of the city? In what environment? Of what background? Of what hopes? Of what knowledge? Of what interest? Of what expectations? How could a middle-class school system do anything *but* come up with middle-class ideas directed at middle-class children?

One afternoon in P.S. 67 I met a young black student teacher named Mr. Cox, a bright man and a former dropout. It was becoming clear to me that many dropouts were in fact the more intelligent kids who simply buzzed off on perceiving the hypocrisy of a system that was not directed at people "out here" at all and was therefore intolerable. Mr. Cox had come under the wing of an older young man who recognized his potential. This "big brother" had said to him:

"Look, you're a bright kid. So why don't you get smart? Get through. Get out. And when you get out look around for another lost young brother like yourself, in the same mess you're making of yourself right now, and help him out in turn."

Mr. Cox's mentor not only offered advice; he pulled strings to help him get through school and into college. Mr. Cox spoke of his big brother with a sense of devotion that showed what being taken under such a wing had meant to him as a human being, which was just about everything in the world. It had helped him change from a person caught in a negative spiral of self-deprecation to an individual who was turned around and moving up, with some confidence, toward becoming his own man. For all intents and purposes it had literally saved his life, as much so as if he had been physically drowning. Now Mr. Cox was in turn fulfilling his part of the bargain through his concern with the children of P.S. 67. I asked him what he thought of the teachers in the school. For the most part he felt rather negative toward them because, as he saw things, very few teachers there had any sense of how to relate to children

from this environment.   At that moment an extremely tall and
lanky white teacher, a young man with a pale face and black
hair, came ambling down the hallway with his class.   He behaved like a martinet as he directed the kids about:
    "Freddie, get over there!"
    "Sally, cut that out *now!*"
    "Wilbur! *Wilbur!* What do you think you're doing? Get over
here! *Get over here!*"
    I looked at Mr. Cox, who obviously knew the young man,
with a questioning expression that asked what kind of a teacher
he was.
    "He sounds tough, doesn't he? Well, he is. That's his style.
But he's also absolutely fair. In fact, he's one of the best damn
teachers in this whole school. Notice one thing: he knows his
class, every one of them, by name. It's never 'Hey, *you* over
there!' or that kind of business. And his kids respond to that.
They've had a bellyful of that 'Hey, *you!*' stuff. The fact that
he's taken the trouble to know all the children in his class,
every one of them, shows he's talked to each one a lot. You
may not know it, but that's a novelty in a ghetto school."
    The observation shunted my mind into one of those thought
processes which leaves a person looking distracted for a moment or two: children to be numbered and processed, the curriculum handed down from the top of the educational mountain,
the teachers the dispensers of the revealed word, with the possibility that the gospel might not get across in a ghetto school a
problem the system was not geared to cope with. The real
focus was on the structure and process, mandated and paid for
by law, how it was set up and administrated efficiently so that
the teacher had her authority in the classroom, went home
promptly at 3 P.M. to wherever she lived, and got the summers
off, satisfied I suppose that she had functioned as the rules
specified, and so could receive the financial rewards and benefits for which her union had fought so hard. This lanky young
man had apparently extended himself from process to people.

"Do you know what it means to his class that he knows the name of each child?" The query came in faintly at first until I could get my attention refocused.

"It means he cares about his kids, and every one of them knows it, in his own way. That's the important thing. If you think his style seems harsh, forget it. The kids couldn't care less, because they know they have a teacher."

A small girl came running down the hall and Mr. Cox grabbed her and spun her around.

"Why are you out of your class?" he demanded. She gave an evasive answer.

"Have you been fighting?" he asked sternly.

"Yes," — sullen, provocative.

"Who you been fighting with?"

"Jimmy and Phillip. They said things about me."

"Now listen, Ellen" (Mr. Cox stared at the small child), "I want you to cool that off, you hear? Do you hear me?"

"Ah," Ellen retorted, turning easily out of his grasp and moving off down the hallway with a little self-centered skip, a small but provocative jig, not enough to offend but enough to say I'm my own kid and I see what I see.

"I see you, Ellen," Mr. Cox called after her.

"I see *you*, Mr. Cox," the girl shot back, lightly but defiantly.

"That's a tough little girl," Mr. Cox remarked, shaking his head. I asked why.

"She's smart, and yet she feels called upon to beat up a couple of boys who've been bugging her. Why? Go and look at her home and maybe you'll see why. Maybe her father, if she has one, comes home and beats her mother up, if she has a mother. Maybe she's playing a role, acting out how she feels her mother should strike back. I don't know."

As we stood there I suddenly became aware of a strange sensation, the effect of which was heightened by the fact that I had been concentrating on Ellen and Mr. Cox and consequently was startled. A small hand had crept into mine and was holding it.

Because of the element of surprise my immediate inclination
was to jerk my hand away and then check on what was happening. For some reason I managed to curb this response before it
occurred. Instead I looked down at the small boy who had appeared out of nowhere. I asked him how he was and he said
"fine." I suggested that maybe he ought to be in his class. He
ran off down the hall, throwing a quick smile over his shoulder
just before he disappeared around a corner. I realized that if I
had jerked my hand away, as instinct had suggested, I might
have ruined his afternoon — or part of it, perhaps. Or I might
have added another small bit of confirmation to a concept that
was already beginning to germinate in his mind.

I left Mr. Cox and walked slowly toward the down staircase at
the far end of the long hallway. Midway something caught my
eye, or maybe it was my ear. Perhaps I had become aware that
I had entered what a sound engineer would call a "dead spot."
I don't know, but somehow I was compelled to stop before the
door of one particular classroom and look in through the small
viewing window. There I saw the "silent scene" Edythe
Gaines had mentioned. A middle-aged white male teacher was
sitting at his desk reading the *Daily News*. The children were
goofing around quietly, playing games, hand wrestling and
things like that. There was the standoff.

"I won't try to teach, and you won't try to learn. So nobody
bugs anybody. Okay?"

"Okay."

I left the school and walked to the nearby subway stop. On
one of the platform walls, neatly printed, appeared the following:

FUCK YOU YOU FUCK FUCK YOU

Arrange the above words in
a common, everyday sentence.*

* Time and neatness count.

It read just that way — asterisk, footnote, and all. Clearly the children of P.S. 67 were perceiving things, could accomplish things, could invent things. It was a question of style, and where you were at.

With Edythe Gaines's consent the Madisons and I filmed a few vignettes of ghetto education in her district, the way it was, not the way it's supposed to be, for the prologue to our film that came to be called *A Child Went Forth*. But the more that film on "the problem" and on good school facilities and things like that came together, the more I found myself personally coming apart. I had spent a year or more in search of the disadvantaged child and I was still completely uncertain as to where I was in that pursuit, other than that I had come to know in a visceral way that ghetto schools as normally mismanaged were an utter disaster to which no one in all that time had been able to suggest more than the barest trace of a solution — more personal attention, more relevant materials, after-school programs, child guidance, smaller classes and similar make-do approaches which clearly would never make it with poverty kids. It seemed to me that a raging and fatal social cancer was being treated as though it were a head cold.

So it was that as I sat toying with my crabcakes in Frank's restaurant on a drizzling spring day in Harlem I had the impression that two movie projectors were running simultaneously in my mind and that the two films were oddly different. One was quite clear and composed of scenes of ghetto schools and of conversations and happenings which I have just described. The other was brief, underexposed, and out of focus; it contained images which were little more than preliminary impressions of P.S. 39 in Harlem, Charles Wilson's school, a school even older than P.S. 158 in East New York but with a completely different feeling about it from all the schools-as-usual which I had been exploring for so long. It was clean, devoid of resentful graffiti and broken windows, a school parents were involved with and concerned about rather than put off by, com-

pletely open and remarkably quiet despite being located in one
of the toughest ghetto areas in the whole city. One film showed
me a boy being ejected from his class shouting "motherfucker!"
in defiance. The other showed a similar boy pointing shyly to
his poster of police in the school. I knew if that child had been
thrown out of class in the usual fashion he would not have discussed his picture with me. Rather, he would have been sullen
or defiant or in search of a dark corner to cry in. I sensed he
had been ejected nevertheless, for classes were in session at the
time I encountered him wandering aimlessly about, but probably with an admonition more like: "Ramón! Go take a walk.
Cool off. Then *come back*, you hear?"

Kenneth Clark, in *Dark Ghetto*, makes a distinction between
what he calls "social fact" and "social truth." At this point I
began to realize how profound his distinction was!

> Statistics (i.e., social facts) may be manipulated and played
> with, analyzed and treated in a way calculated to lead to
> minimum pain or personal involvement. They are "man-
> ageable." Figures on the extent of malnutrition in Southern
> states or rural areas are impersonal and are not especially
> disturbing. Direct encounter with a starving child, on the
> other hand, is a truth which is personal; it remains per-
> sonally disturbing until the child is fed. To face social
> truths seems to require empathy, social sensitivity, and a
> peculiar type of courage.

In my search for some understanding of the disadvantaged
child I had encountered quite a few starving children, dying
from malnutrition of the mind which, as Jonathan Kozol so per-
ceptively pointed out, is as good a definition of death as one
could hope or hate to come upon. Yet now, after so long a time,
I had met one child who seemed at least to be getting some in-
tellectual nourishment, a bit of soul food, in a school which one
could sense was putting out something better than the usual
poorhouse fare. I felt both puzzled and a little foolish that it

had taken me so long to get to Harlem in the first place. What would normally have been a ten-minute subway trip years ago had proved to be, for me at least, a voyage of over a year. I had started out with an accumulation of social facts and had encountered some very negative social truths. Now my voyage was apparently going to be unexpectedly diverted by the appearance of more positive social truth at P.S. 39. The projectors ran out of film in a bewildered mind, confounded by a dim but growing perception of the chasm which had developed in the American social fabric, its vastness, the yawning dimensions that now separated Harlem and the children of Harlem from the world of downtown, how far away "out here" really was. What was Charles Wilson into, or onto, that he could produce a schoolhouse with such a different feeling about it? I certainly did not know. But I was hopelessly hooked on finding out. Another thought from Saint Augustine came to mind:

> There is but a dim light that burns in men. Let them walk; let them walk — lest darkness overtake them.

I left the restaurant and walked slowly east on 125th Street, in no hurry to leave Harlem, looking at storefronts with Afro wares and alligator shoes, listening to music blaring from loudspeakers over the doorways of record shops, looking at posters proclaming that dope peddlers should be run out of Harlem, past the small building that housed the I.S. 201 Complex offices, and on down the block to the Lexington Avenue subway stop. Without thinking about it I took the subway back downtown as I would have years before, determined to return to Harlem and explore Charles Wilson's little cluster of five schools to find out what the I.S. 201 Complex was all about.

II

Soul Food

I CAME TO the city early one morning and took the subway up-town to see Charles Wilson. I was shown into his office right away and we greeted each other. Instantly I experienced one of those curious mental loops that can take over the mind for a second and shift it to some quite unexpected subject: I would not have recognized the man in a different setting from the of-fice where I first met him. I had had virtually no contact with black people since childhood, and it was now difficult for me to distinguish one from another. I have trouble remembering names and faces anyway, but in this instance I would have thought I'd be more perceptive. Later I remembered being in Paris for the first time and thinking what a completely gray city it was. It took some days to discover Paris was made up of every shade and hue and texture of gray imaginable, one of the subtleties that makes it the most beautiful city in the world to my mind. But such perceptions come slowly and it takes time to get dark-adapted or color-adapted or whatever. My present difficulty was due to being in a new land, a different country.

"Look," I said, "I've read probably a million words or more about the experimental districts, about ghetto schools, about you and Rhody McCoy and Ocean Hill–Brownsville and all that, about Albert Shanker and the teachers' union, and community control, and confrontation and so on. But the one word that never seems to appear at all is 'children.' "

"That's simple enough," was his instant response. "Children have no power base." Then he added: "They all write about it. But no one has been up here to see what we're trying to do. Once in awhile I get a phone call from downtown: 'Hey, Charlie baby, whatcha into up there? What's new?'"

"Do you really mean to say that nobody has been up here poking around the schools, trying to find out what's going on with the children in them?"

"No, they come for the press conferences. Like the television people came the other day on the street when we had something to say about the seven teachers thing. Then they go away."

I found that hard to take, yet I believed it. I could see no conceivable reason for him to deceive me.

"One thing puzzles me. I wrote you a couple of letters explaining that I wanted to visit you, and I made some phone calls, but mostly I drew a blank. And I had to wait over two hours the first time I came up. Usually, even in the school system, one gets handed over to someone who handles public relations and things like that. So you go from there."

"Well, that's what I'm telling you. I'm a virgin. There's been no public to relate to, outside Harlem. So we don't have a PR man. I suppose I'm him."

I described to Charles Wilson the Bronx principal I had visited in his inner sanctum and his feelings that questioning the certificates of teachers was something quite out of order. Wilson snorted:

"As Clemenceau once said: 'War is much too important to be left to the generals.'" Then he took off on the subject a bit: "That man makes about thirty thousand dollars a year. Anybody in industry makes a salary like that, he'd better deliver a product, right? Otherwise that cat's out of business. In this case, your man there is supposed to be delivering education, though from what you say I doubt he is delivering much of anything. Will he get fired? Probably not. If his whole school

comes apart, to the point where he's so obviously incompetent
he has to go, they'll take him in at the Board of Education and
find a job for him there. They take care of their own."

I said I would like to explore the schools of the Complex,
and Charles Wilson gave me a vote of confidence by turning me
over to a young black man on his staff named Joe Brown. Joe
had been athletic director at P.S. 24 the year before and was
now in charge of summer programs for all the Complex children. Joe would take me around and introduce me to the principals of the five schools in the district. After that I could visit
them as I saw fit. Our first stop was Joe's alma mater, so to
speak. P.S. 24 was a typical old school, built along lines I have
already described. Joe Brown and I entered the building and
started down a quiet hallway. Instantly children appeared from
all directions as though they had sprung out of the walls of
the old school. They came running from everywhere shouting:
"Joe Brown! Joe Brown!" Boys and girls of all sizes and descriptions swarmed over the young man like bees, clinging to
his legs, arms, and shoulders or just touching him for a moment,
to look back again as we passed on. Joe recognized almost
every one of the leaping, darting figures who rushed up with an
affectionate greeting. And he spoke to each in turn:

"Hey, Charles, you been behavin' yourself?"

"Yes, Mr. Brown."

"Louie, have you been staying out of mischief?"

"You bet, Joe."

"You better. Where's your brother Robert? Is he in trouble?"

"No, Mr. Brown, he sick today."

"Well, tell him to get better."

"Have you come back to our school, Mr. Brown?"

"No, just for today."

"Will you come back later, Mr. Brown?"

"Maybe. Maybe. I don't think so."

"Why not, Mr. Brown?"

"Well, we got a lot of things to do around here. But I'll see you."

"Good-bye, Mr. Brown."

"Good-bye,"

"Good-bye, Joe Brown."

On one hall after another the scene was repeated. I don't understand to this day how so many children knew that one man was in that school, but they did. We entered the classroom of a young white man. Whatever had been going on ended abruptly as quiet, whispered confidences spread through the class:

"Joe Brown."

"It's Mr. Brown!"

"Joe Brown!"

"It's Joe Brown!"

The teacher greeted us, or rather Joe Brown, and then me. We greeted the teacher and the children. At the teacher's urging a number of the children read us poems they had written. Some were quite good and Joe and I applauded spontaneously. I don't remember the poems anymore; I was too impressed by the scene to remember. The teacher drew Joe aside:

"Look, Joe, I was thinking of taking the children to Central Park on Saturday, just for an outing with some sandwiches and pop or something. Do you think you could come? I mean, it would be great if we could do it together. What do you think?"

"I'll try to, but I'll have to let you know. Okay?"

"Okay, Joe."

"Good-bye."

"Good-bye, Joe. Say 'good-bye' to Mr. Brown, children."

"Good-bye, Mr. Brown."

"Come back to see us, Mr. Brown."

"We'll have some new poems next week, Mr. Brown."

"I'd like to hear them."

"Come back next week and hear them, Mr. Brown."

"I'll try and do that. Good-bye."

"Good-bye, Mr. Brown."

As we walked out the door I could hear the children saying quietly to one another: "That's Joe Brown. Joe Brown."

Joe introduced me to the principal and then we left the school. On the street some kids were hanging from the grill-work over the school windows.

"Get off there!" Joe shouted. "Get off there right now!"

The children dropped from the meshed wire as though a jolt of electricity had suddenly surged through it. But instead of hightailing it down the street they rushed over to Joe.

"Look," said Joe, "you behave yourselves, you hear?"

"We try, Joe Brown. We try."

"Well now you just try a great big bit, and you succeed! Do you hear me?"

"We hear you, Mr. Brown."

"Well," I said as we walked down the street, "I know now who the big man around this place is. His name is Joe Brown."

Joe shrugged. "Yeah," he said. "Yeah."

From P.S. 24 Joe took me to P.S. 68 and, since the black principal, Mr. Nailor, was absent that day, he introduced me to one of the white assistant principals, a corpulent, tall, and open man with a clear sense of purpose and self-confidence named Mr. Goldstein. I explained that I was looking around the Complex schools to see what was going on and would like to return another day to talk with him and Mr. Nailor. He said he would pass the word to Mr. Nailor, and I would be welcome any time. At P.S. 133, another of the "feeder" schools, I was received by Mrs. Dellora Hercules, an attractive black woman who was also a member of the governing board of the Complex. Then we walked to the intermediate school which the other four fed, I.S. 201, the windowless building that had been the center of so much controversy in Harlem some years before. The principal of this school was Ronald Evans, a jet black man well over six feet tall. We caught up with him not in his office but on the prowl in the corridors of his school, a practice I later learned was an incessant part of his routine. In the course of this he adjudicated altercations among various children, admonishing boys and girls as he moved about. "See that candy wrapper on the floor there? Pick it up, please, girls." The cleanliness of the Complex schools was obviously on everyone's minds.

Joe Brown introduced me to Ronald Evans, and I asked if I might look about his school a bit. He stared at me coldly from his formidable height as though he had just been introduced to some new and undoubtedly poisonous species of white snake.

"No," he said firmly, "you can't look around here. You'll have to talk with Charlie Wilson about that. He handles those things." By which he clearly meant white people.

I felt I had no grounds for remonstrating with Mr. Evans. If he had decided that all whites were devils, as Malcolm X had at one point, I could not fault him on that. The polarity was that extreme, now. I also knew he had his hands full, for his children were older and this implacable attitude might win him greater respect from the youngsters. The evils of the ghetto beckoned more strongly now, as they grew wise to the ways of the streets, and some of his kids would be into that. Small hustles to get some sporty shoes perhaps, or worse, the dope scene. I recall seeing on the corner of 125th Street and 8th Avenue one day a violet-colored Continental which had pulled up in front of a dry-cleaning establishment. A big black man got out dressed in a violet sharkskin suit and violet-dyed alligator shoes and went into the store to pick up some clothes. When he emerged there were greetings on all sides. Everyone on the corner knew who that fat cat was; everyone but me. Afterward I walked along 125th Street looking into shoe-store windows. Genuine alligator shoes were prominently displayed in practically every store and they cost seventy-five to one hundred dollars or even more, depending on the style and the store. I could scarcely believe it, but that was what the price tags said. Sporting such shoes was obviously a status symbol in Harlem. Kids could hardly miss the point or fail to want some semblance of the same in their own poverty-mired lives. There could be but one way to acquire such icons, and it wouldn't be legal.

I had lunch downtown shortly afterward in an excellent French restaurant with a sardonic and civilized gentleman concerned with urban education in various ways. He was connected with a foundation that had helped to convert an unused supermarket into "Harlem Prep," a school for older dropouts with an astonishing track record of getting its graduates into college. I had visited Harlem Prep one day, reported my very favorable impressions of the school to the head of this foundation, and was greeted with the astonishing response: "Gee, maybe I should go see the place. How do you get there?" I started to say: "Well, you get on the 'A' train . . . ," but I quickly thought better of it and instead told him he could easily get there by taxi. I don't believe he ever went, though, possibly out of some unrecognized fear that he might "get involved," an unfortunate eventuality which could prejudice his position and his "extreme concern about things" as the head of a foundation. I told my luncheon companion that it seemed to me the presence of young, viable black males in ghetto schools was important. I mentioned briefly some impressions of Charles Wilson, Joe Brown, and Ronald Evans. I said I felt such individuals were particularly valuable for children whose images of "making out" were largely confined to hustlers of one sort or another. How many Joe Browns did these kids ever see? My companion's response was rather negative:

"You can't get young men like that into the school system. They get paid the same as women teachers under the U.F.T. contract. The only way they can make extra money is by extra work — teaching gym classes for instance. So how are you going to get your Joe Browns, or whatever his name is, to want to teach in a ghetto school? Do you think that through some sense of obligation black people should feel more dedicated to one another than anyone else? Or work in some substandard and overextended way more than anyone else?"

It was a reasonable enough argument. Why should a young man like Joe Brown work for low pay simply out of dedication to a racial cause? Yet that was not the definition of Joe Brown in the Complex community. Not as far as I could see anyway. He was a valued and respected person. I am sure Charles Wilson scrounged every penny he could find to make sure Joe Brown made as good a salary as the circumstances permitted. I am sure Joe Brown knew that, too. I thought about Joe Brown; what two or three or maybe even half a dozen Joe Browns could mean to the spirit and feeling and hope of a school if they were circulating about, talking to kids, teaching, as an everyday part of school life. So that kids who knew all too well the hustling side of the picture could look up and say to one another: "Look! There's Joe Brown! Hey! That was Joe Brown! Look! Watch me sink this basket like Joe Brown would, like he taught me!" So I left the restaurant feeling that what the man had said was simply not acceptable. It was not acceptable that New York's ghetto schools were not enlivened everywhere with little Joe Brown scenes like the one I had observed.

I paid another visit to Charles Wilson. I had been reflecting on the emphasis on cleanliness in the Complex schools, reinforced by my encounter with Ronald Evans urging girls to pick up candy wrappers on a corridor in I.S. 201. This had struck me at first as a simplistic and almost pathetic gesture: "Okay, people, let's clean up this dump and get to work!" But as I thought about it, I realized this simple directive could carry a considerable message to children accustomed to an environment of broken glass, graffiti, neglect, and indifference. If I were a child in one of the Complex schools I might possibly think to myself: "Gee! Someone cares about me! Someone close by! Maybe I'd better get to work!" Since the school custodian is the person responsible for the upkeep of the building, I asked Charles Wilson about that particular office, mindful of the drunken, absentee noncaretaker of P.S. 158 in East New

York. I learned that custodians have their own maintenance budgets, and consequently the principal has no real authority over the custodian or how well he performs his duties. Though the principal might know the caretaker's overall budget, he would have no way of telling if it were being used effectively other than in a flagrant case of neglect such as P.S. 158. Thus a custodian could order good-quality fixtures, paint, and other supplies and yet have a tacit arrangement with the supplier to deliver second-rate materials — leaving the two of them to pocket the difference.

Most custodians seem to follow their job definitions with some professional, if casual, sense of duty. But the helpless, hopeless, day in and day out pointlessness of the average ghetto school infects everyone, including the custodian. While in one such school, I noticed the cop on the beat saunter in, seeking out the custodian for his morning coffee break. Between them there was the easy rapport of city functionaries. They sat in the custodian's small office on the ground floor drinking coffee from plastic containers, the officer with his blue jacket hanging on a folding chair. The two chatted convivially and, when the custodian had to go out into the building briefly, the policeman picked up the ever-present copy of the New York *Daily News* and glanced leisurely through that chauvinistic rag. They were comfortable with one another, the cop and the custodian. They knew how it was in the school — just another mindless, pointless situation which was part of their lot. They did what was required of them, but it did not seem to occur to them to contribute anything to the situation, like patting a kid on the head for instance. They were just doing their job. But what did they offer when the wine bottles gathered and broke on the school steps and in the playground at night? Clean them up? Start a program with the kids to wipe out graffiti?

So the custodian locks up the school around three-thirty in the afternoon and goes home to his white enclave, having done little all day in the least way satisfying, though well paid none-

theless. There, in the friendly neighborhood tavern, far removed from the bean school and black children bouncing off
the walls, he belts a few Rheingolds with his peers — the off-
duty patrolman, a couple of construction workers, a parking lot
supervisor. And if it's Friday night and they stay long enough,
they will end up talking about how it is to have to work in a
place like that and how the goddamn niggers better stay out of
their part of town. Who is to fault a person because he has only
a weak grasp of his own identity to begin with, or condemn him
if job definition and big-city ambiance and the *Daily News* and
commercial television transform him into a self-accommodating,
self-congratulating parasite?

Charles Wilson, having a relatively free hand in the I.S. 201
Complex, had certain options. He could solicit special funds
for the district from foundations, businesses, and other sources.
He explained that he had raised $1500 and hired an architect to
explore the custodial problems of the schools. The architect,
knowing the costs of paint, windows, cleaning equipment, and
other supplies was able to come up with explicit recommendations as to what a school could realistically expect from a custodian's budget. In this way he executed an end run on the
prevailing custodial mystique of closed bookkeeping and the
Complex schools began to look a little better. As I left his office, Mr. Wilson handed me a bit of "homework" to study up on,
something he had begun to do from time to time to help me get
a better idea of what the Complex was all about. It was a 245-
page document the district had printed called *The I.S. 201
Complex COMMUNITY INFORMATION MANUAL.* I was becoming aware that one important aspect of the experiment was
the involvement of parents and other community people with
the schools. The manual contained a wealth of information
useful in the area covering such subjects as welfare and social
services available in central Harlem, the locations of clinics,
hospitals, and police stations, advice on employment, night

courses and equivalency courses offered by the schools, addresses of narcotics centers and day-care centers, family, health, and legal aid services which people could use. Aside from its pure usefulness, which must have been considerable in such a community, the simple fact that a cluster of Harlem schools had undertaken to do something for people in the area and elected to make itself a focus for information must have had quite an impact on people who have long felt that schools were administered from a headquarters quite remote from those who live "out here" in the distant provinces.

As I stood waiting for the elevator Charles Wilson unexpectedly caught up with me: "Say, I just thought of something that would interest you, since you're involved in films and things like that. Take a walk over to two-o-one with me." Inside the windowless school we encountered Ronald Evans, and I received the same frosty look as I had on my first meeting with the gentleman. He said nothing, however, since I was operating under the visiting rules he had laid down himself. Though I tried on several subsequent occasions to break the ice I never succeeded. And because I felt I could not presume on Charles Wilson to escort me around the district personally, this was my first and last tour of I.S. 201. What Charles Wilson wanted to show me was a multimedia center he was setting up which consisted of several large rooms cluttered with several million dollars' worth of sound, film, and videotape equipment, most of which he had acquired gratis from various electronics manufacturers. The center was designed to produce all sorts of educational materials which could then be piped to television sets in individual classrooms throughout the district. In this way, the best math teacher in the Complex could do a program for all the children in a particular grade; similarly for science, reading, or whatever. This led us to speculate whether or not such a cluster of schools might one day obtain a broadcast channel of its own to reach home television sets in the neighborhood, making possible a "live" Community Information Manual which would present all sorts of exciting prospects for cohesive school-community action.

I returned to P.S. 68, which was located in a rather tough section of Harlem, to talk with Mr. Nailor, whom Charles Wilson had managed to recruit from the meager black administrative personnel the city school system offers. Despite his training as a traditional "line officer," Mr. Nailor showed a considerable interest in seeing if something could be made to happen in what had been a typical reject school. He visited classes, talked with teachers and children, and made a dedicated effort to run a school open to new ideas rather than one run by the numbers. Yet I detected a touch of ambivalence in his attitude. Despite being black, he had worked his way up through a dominantly white school system. Achieving the status of a principal had been accompanied, I feel sure, by swallowing many a bitter pill along the way. To expect an all-out, gung-ho attitude from such a traditionalist, whatever his secret feelings might be, seemed unreasonable in light of the manifest ill will with which the educational establishment now regarded the experimental districts. Though Mr. Nailor was quite open to visitors, at least to those approved by Charles Wilson, I had a feeling he was covering his rear and was prepared for retreat, so that should the experiment abort, he would remain acceptable in the established order of things.

The corpulent Mr. Goldstein, whom I next visited, seemed to have no reservations whatever about the experiment and was quite frank in saying so. He explained that P.S. 68 had been a complete disaster before the new district was established, a school ridden with strife, conflict, rumor, confrontation, and a vacillating administration incapable of getting anything together. Now, under Complex direction, he clearly felt things were shaping up. These impressions came through in what I can only describe as fragmentary conversations during various visits to the school, for one child or another was continually ap-

pearing in Mr. Goldstein's office, or he was abruptly bolting out
to attend to some matter which had popped up in a distant part
of the building. A number of these interruptions involved an
unfolding drama which I began to piece together: a problem
with an older white male teacher. This gentleman, confronted
with the idea that the school should be turned around and that
maybe the children in P.S. 68 might actually achieve something, had gone into a sweating and nervous funk. He had
realized, much to his credit and yet to his distress, that he could
not relate to the children in his class at all, let alone teach them
anything. He wanted to be transferred out. To discover at his
age that a long tradition of custodial baby-sitting might not be
acceptable struck me as admirable and led me to think there
was life in the old man yet, though elsewhere. Mr. Goldstein
was not the least embarrassed at my observing this situation. In
fact, I felt he had come to be a bit of a radical in the district,
more so than Mr. Nailor could be himself. It is easier to be a
radical in the New York City school system if you happen to be
white and Jewish than it is if you're black, but this simple fact
did not diminish my faith in Mr. Goldstein's belief.

At Mr. Goldstein's suggestion I spent some time in the
classroom of a young man named Tom Drager, a graduate of Dr.
Martin Deutsch's Institute for Developmental Studies at New
York University. Deutsch and his associates had pioneered experimental programs in selected ghetto classrooms for some
years to determine what attitudes, approaches, materials, and
classroom arrangements might best come to grips with the educational problems of poverty children. These studies were the
first to reveal the now-classic pattern of failure as children drop
farther and farther behind between the first and third grades, a
sequence which all too frequently culminates in giving up and
dropping out in the later grades as a growing sense of inade-
quacy and pointlessness envelops a nonemerging young personality.

The revelations disclosed by Deutsch's research led di-

rectly to the whole concept of Head Start, programs for preschool poverty children which would provide a kind of intellec-
tual fork lift from which they could then be channeled off into
the established educational system.

I once had the opportunity of observing a very fine Head
Start program set up in a Cleveland school by a bright black
woman named Christine Branch, also a graduate of Deutsch's
Institute. The teachers involved understood what they were
doing, had experience and training in the program, and, perhaps most important of all, believed they could achieve results
with the children — a belief supported by the participation of
many community parents in the effort. A success-oriented atmosphere hung over the project which could scarcely escape notice by the "subjects." It was a pilot program, Christine Branch
explained to me, adding that almost no such efforts were really
off the ground in any big city she knew of. Later I remarked in
the presence of a New York City school official that there were
precious few working Head Start programs in ghetto schools.
He bristled:

"Why, we have Head Start programs in all of our city
schools!"

He walked agitatedly across the room and brought back a
large bound folio, which he opened up to point out that Head
Start was listed in school after school. I knew perfectly well
that just because a school was listed as having a program it
didn't mean that the teachers who were running it believed in it
or cared about it or understood it, it didn't mean that the children enjoyed it or benefited from it, and it surely did not mean
it worked. To his mind, however, it said on the books that the
city had Head Start and that was that. The bureaucrat appeared
satisfied because in his big ledger, for all to see, the requirements of social fact had been met. That there might be a
serious question of social truth as to whether the programs were
actually working was neither his department nor his concern.

Recently Head Start has come under attack because a lot of

people apparently thought that it alone would solve the ghetto education problem, people who read and believe in big ledger books, people who presumed that if you gave a child one bright year, he should make out okay thereafter on being returned to the same old cobweb-lined system. This they believed despite the fact that even in our affluent suburbs a dozen years of at least dimly lit schooling often don't do the trick. It was a cheap hope, another truckload of shoddy thinking which was dumped onto the ghetto, typical ghetto goods, dropped from the mile-high end of the bridge that does not touch down.

Tom Drager's second grade classroom, which he managed with a young female assistant, presented a fascinating picture of apparent disarray and chaos. It took me several days and many conversations to sort out the underlying meaning and purpose behind the surface confusion. Instead of the usual teacher's desk and rows of chairs for children the room was broken up into various work areas — one for reading, one for math, one for science (with a variety of live animals for the children to observe or play with), one for conferences, one for writing and reading stories. Each child had a small locker with his or her name on it to help start the day off with an established sense of individual identity. Depending on how the previous day (or night) had been for the child, or what was on his or her mind upon arriving at school, the child could select whatever area seemed desirable. Tom and his assistant worked with small groups of the children while most of the class was absorbed in the study areas in one way or another. When the children felt like it they wrote stories, often in small clusters and with Tom's help. A typical story then in progress was called: "How Momma Threw the Junkie out of the House LAST NIGHT!" The children at that time also had a class project going. They were keeping a chart of the lunches they had in school each day, recording who liked and did not like what lunch. It added up to an overall exercise in identity and opinion, with natural

mathematical tabulations built into a context of clear and direct
interest to the children themselves.

Mr. Drager was concerned that the children acquire verbal
and reading skills. He told me about one boy whose vocabulary was so limited at the beginning of the year he was quite unable to ask another child to play ball with him in any direct
way. Instead he could only mumble and gesture in an effort to
make this simple social contact. Tom Drager did not baby talk
such children. In fact, one of the things that surprised me
about this very articulate young man was that he used only his
own natural vocabulary, big adult words and all, despite the fact
that the children clearly understood only a fraction of what he
said. He did this, he explained, because he believed he should
always be himself. As far as I could tell the children appreciated his integrity, whether or not they always understood him.

One of the most interesting inhabitants of the classroom was a
character Tom introduced to me as the class psychologist. This
was a large, female white rabbit named Peter, naturally, who
had the run of the room and whom the children all cared for.
They fed Peter and also cleaned up her urine and feces. For
some reason, possibly overcrowded living conditions, poverty
children frequently have an aversion to feces. Peter and her
needs enabled the children to face this natural problem in an
open, routine, and casual way. Peter's role as psychologist was
quite different from her biological one. Tom told me of one afternoon when several children had been fighting. He held a
discussion with those involved and inquired about what had
happened. At one point he asked a rather aggressive boy if he
knew of anyone who didn't fight, who might be peaceably in-
clined instead. At that moment, quite fortuitously, Peter
hopped across the boy's foot. "Peter!" the boy exclaimed radi-
antly. "Peter doesn't fight!" Since everyone in the class
cherished Peter, this aspect of her rabbit behavior was noted
and remembered by the children.

I happened into Tom Drager's classroom one day at lunch-time, a period I had noted was the best for asking questions without interrupting his work with the children too much, and found him eating a sandwich with several other young white male teachers I had noticed in this wing of the school. Most were draft evaders and were frank to admit this was the reason they had become teachers, but there was more to the matter than that. Many draft evaders were socially motivated to begin with, and this group had elected to come to the Complex, knowing it was an educational experiment, to see if they could contribute something that was humanly worthwhile. They gravitated to Tom Drager's room because they knew that quite a bit of research lay behind the way he ran his class. The group met frequently and exchanged ideas and experiences in a mutual effort to improve their teaching. Because the school year was now nearly over, one of the things which concerned them was what the next year would be like, what teachers would be in line for groups of children each of the individuals had been working so hard with. There was a general feeling among these teachers that they would personally like to carry the classes they knew through the next grade rather than abandon them to someone else and, God forbid, plunge them back into "the system" again. In doing this they could begin to construct an educational ladder children could climb from one grade to the next, built upon a continuity of perception which might indeed lead to a real ghetto schoolhouse. The group resolved to confront Mr. Nailor with their plan at the school's weekend "retreat." As lunchtime ended I was chatting with one of the young men who remarked in passing that he and his wife lived in the community, a few blocks from the school. I asked why.

"I think it gives me a certain credibility with the children and with their parents as well. I mean, part of Tom Drager's whole thing is that the parents should come to the school and get to know us and what their kids are doing, be a part of the thing.

And I think he's right. I mean, like, look, out here most parents think a school's a pretty hostile place, a kind of put-down. And I think they have a lot of good reasons for feeling that way."

"What kind of building do you live in?"

"Oh, it's a small apartment building."

"How does it work out?"

"Well, like, you could say we integrated the building — a kind of reverse blockbusting. It took a while, I mean for people to believe I cared about what I was doing. After all, for years they've seen these teachers scramble out of here in their cars at three o'clock, going back to their white world. They know that scene, you know? So if you say you're making a different scene they wonder about that, because the old one's been going on so long now. Like, for instance, we got robbed once. People around here if they get robbed don't like to call the police. Why? Because it can always turn out that the TV set they bought from the cat up the block had been stolen from somewhere. Who knows? So people keep it to themselves. But the stuff we had that got taken, I know where it came from. So I called the police. Two cops came, a white cop and a black cop. They were nice enough, but they sure were surprised to find a white couple living in that building. I explained I was a teacher at P.S. 68 and that was all right with them. But as they left the black cop looked at me in a funny way:

"You're a teacher around here? Are you writing some kind of a book or something?"

During the rest of that brief Friday afternoon I wandered about the school, looking in on one class or another. Then I walked out on the street where all the teachers' cars were parked, as school closed for the weekend. It was a warm, sunny spring day that promised more of the same for Saturday and possibly Sunday as well. One by one the cars buzzed off as children made their own ways in small groups down the side streets of Harlem. Then a battered Volkswagen bus sputtered out of a lot alongside the school, driven by one of the young men I had met in Tom Drager's classroom. Half a dozen black faces peered out through the dirty windows, reflecting a sense of joy and anticipation at what lay ahead. I did not know what adventures this young man had arranged for the children. It was the scene that caught my eye, even through the dingy windows of the old bus, a scene of faces aglow with expectation.

P.S. 133, Dellora Hercules's school, was located at 130th Street and Fifth Avenue. Harlem's share of that particular elegant downtown boulevard, though a bit seedy, presents none of the shocking contrasts afforded by the two Park Avenues. Uptown it is still a broad street in a partly middle-class area with a number of pleasant, tree-lined side streets occupied by brownstone houses set back from the curb to make room for small, tidily kept front yards. Because of the better quality of the neighborhood, P.S. 133 was by no means a hard-core ghetto school in the usual sense and so presented a less disruptive challenge than P.S. 68. Mrs. Hercules was a handsome, light-skinned woman who, like Mr. Nailor, was a qualified principal in the city school system. Her husband was a writer and she told me the two of them were planning a vacation in Morocco when the school year ended. Though she was a member of the governing board of the Complex, I detected in her the same touch of ambivalence toward the experiment I had felt in Mr. Nailor. She had worked long and hard for her prerogatives within the system, such as her planned vacation with her husband, and though she was clearly in favor of the experimental district, she was not about to make a major issue out of it. One of the basic concepts of the Complex was that the four feeder schools would funnel their graduates into I.S. 201. But Mrs. Hercules told me quite frankly that many of the parents of her children were determined to avoid that if possible, because they were fearful of what might happen as a result of continual contact with the "harder" ghetto kids. Instead, if they could afford it, they hoped to send their children to intermediate schools elsewhere in the city, or even to private schools. In fact, the level of fear and distrust of Harlem schools was such that many poor people, stuck in the ghetto, were shipping their children back to the Southland to attend the frankly segregated "down home" schools there in preference to having them grow up on the streets of Harlem, "mean streets" as Piri Thomas so aptly called them.

One thing that could hardly escape the notice of any visitor to P.S. 133 was a portrait of John Kennedy on the wall, just inside the main entrance to the school. It was a profile in color, obviously done by one of the children from a photograph, and it was not very good. Yet the identity was unmistakable. I asked Mrs. Hercules about it.

"He was the closest thing to a white god that these children know," she said.

The school was preparing for graduation exercises that spring, and a major item on the agenda was a production of the musical version of *The Wizard of Oz*. Bulletin boards in the hallways displayed drawings, costume designs, and posters all concerned with the forthcoming show. Mrs. Hercules suggested I might like to meet the school's library teacher, Charles Click, who was involved with the production. I was escorted down the hall and introduced to this young black man. His appearance was wonderfully appropriate to his name, for he was a fastidiously mod dresser, though not flashy. He wore a natty jacket tailored trimly at the waist, modified bell-bottoms, a lavishly striped shirt with large, jeweled cufflinks and a broad, billowing necktie. He also sported a number of elegant rings on his fingers. The children who filed in and out of the library by classes had a quiet rapport with Charles Click and he with them. They did little exercises he invented or borrowed books. Sometimes he read stories to them. The whole library had a free and relaxed atmosphere, thanks to Mr. Click. All the books were on open shelves which meant the children could explore the room, take books which struck their fancy, and sit at little tables to read them, or sign them out at the end of the period and take them to their home rooms. Mr. Click had both a slide and a movie projector and put on frequent shows for his classes. Occupying a place of honor along one wall was a small book-shrine dedicated to Dr. Martin Luther King, Jr., with a lettered title: The Journey of the Black Man.

I sat in Charles Click's library for several days observing how he worked. He was an open, welcoming, and pleasant person, self-assured in his role at P.S. 133 and aware of how much it was appreciated by the children, Mrs. Hercules, and the teachers as well. I arrived at the school one day before the lunch period had ended and, knowing the library classes would not have resumed yet, wandered about the building a bit to kill time. By accident I entered the gymnasium just as children were coming in from the playground to be sorted out and sent off to their afternoon classes. There was a somewhat subdued version of the confusion and bedlam I had observed in other schools. But there were no bullhorns, police whistles, or broomsticks. Instead, Mr. Jackson, a dour, compact, and strong assistant black principal strode purposefully into the midst of the melee, raised his right hand with fingers spread in a Churchillian V, and shouted in a resonant and commanding voice: "Signals!" At this order a forest of small arms shot up to duplicate the gesture, a chorus of piping voices repeated the command, and the children sorted themselves out and filed quietly from the gym with their respective homeroom teachers. I filed off quietly to the library.

On this afternoon Mr. Click wheeled a spinet piano from a large storage closet off the library and conducted a singing class, rehearsing a chorus he had organized in the school. I asked him if he doubled as music teacher, and he explained that since the school had never been assigned a music teacher, he had elected to play that role himself, since he was among other things a musician. Extending himself this way meant that he had to give up his "preparation period," not a trivial sacrifice since prep periods are an important item in the U.F.T. contract with the city allowing teachers to prepare themselves for their classes. I imagine in many instances this is a euphemism for composing themselves. At 3 P.M., just as Mr. Click was closing the library along with the rest of the school's closing, four of the more unattractive black preteen girls I have ever seen entered the room. Two were scrawny and gangling; two were obese. The girls wished to stay after school to rehearse some of the songs from *The Wizard of Oz,* and Charles Click agreeably decided to work with them. Since the school was now growing rapidly empty, the general noise level was diminishing accordingly, adding a dimension of intimacy to the activities of the quintet of performers. Charles Click proved to be an excellent pianist with long, thin fingers accentuated by the rings he wore. All four of the girls had surprisingly beautiful voices. Mr. Click rehearsed the girls in a number of songs and then, in the dead silence of the library within the total silence of the empty school, the group took up "Over the Rainbow." I had become an ignored fixture in the scene by this point, both to the group and to myself, sitting immobile at the librarian's desk and watching. In such a relaxed and quiet setting I had no inkling at all of how vulnerable I was until a bit of the lyrics came over, well harmonized by the girlish voices:

> Somewhere, over the rainbow,
> Bluebirds fly.
> Birds fly over the rainbow,
> Why, oh why can't I?

I left the library quietly, walked along the empty hallway to the main entrance of the school and out onto Fifth Avenue. I felt in no hurry to leave the neighborhood, so I wandered around the building, down the side street and across the back where the playground was. There, on a blank wall otherwise undefaced by graffiti, was written in bold, red, spray-paint letters:

THIS IS YOUR DAY — MALCOLM X — 5/19/69

It was indeed May 19, and the man's birthday was well remembered, by how many young people I cannot imagine. In the mind's eye, fragments of a century-old promise of emancipation clashed with newer images of a pernicious disenfranchisement which incredibly still endured.

Charles Wilson invited me to the weekend "retreat" for the teachers and staff of P.S. 68 at Tarrytown House, the elegant estate he had mentioned the first day we met. I said I would like very much to come, if I could pay my own way. "We got forms for that," he replied jovially. In my files today is one of the few canceled checks I have come to regard as a memento of something worthwhile that money could buy. It is made out to *The I.S. 201 Complex*, for twelve dollars. On a Saturday morning in June, I drove over to Tarrytown in our old Falcon stationwagon and pulled into a parking lot on the estate. All around were recognizable faces — Mr. Nailor, Mr. Goldstein, Tom Drager and his assistant teacher, and the other young men who had gathered for lunchtime sessions in his classroom; also several women in charge of various programs in the school who had been involved with the problem of the older teacher who wanted out. The estate was absolutely beautiful; it must have been built by one of those classically wealthy families of bygone times, in the old days before the income tax. The house was a sprawling stone mansion with spacious rooms, high ceilings, and broad verandahs. There were vast expanses of lawns and gardens, some quite formal, others casually rustic. Here and there were cozy niches a well-planned estate always affords for delight and surprise — a marble statue and stone bench nestled in the corner of a hedgerow, a spouting fountain in a garden alcove, a small shelter enveloped in ivy and wisteria. Several tennis courts and a large swimming pool, complete with dressing rooms and bath houses, rounded out this scene of majestically careless opulence. What a marvelous conceit, I thought, to transplant the staff of a central Harlem school to a place like this! Particularly on a sunny and sparkling June day! How even more marvelous it would be if the whole place — with its flowers and trees and lawns and gardens and singing birds — could have been transplanted back to Harlem. Such a notion was hopelessly romantic and childish, spun out of young and budding images and memories of growing up in the South. But then the South was always a romantic place, despite all its manifest evils.

I knew immediately that this was no conceit at all, but an inspiration, an ingenious and tangible affirmation of the value of schools and teachers and administrators which had been conceived in Charles Wilson's mind. If it had once seemed a flamboyant idea to me, it did not seem so now. I knew the big-city school system was locked into a line and staff pattern of prerogatives and responsibilities and assumptions which, within any school, operated "by definition" to produce a frozen educational waxworks. Zombielike, day in and day out, this securely fixed carousel sprang into motion at the ringing of a bell. The staff carried out responsibilities as defined. The teachers filed into their boxes to confront several dozen children, taught or failed to teach, maintained order or failed to do so, to the best of their individual capabilities. All in an effort to maintain a tight ship. This rigidly defined system made any suggestions for improvement — any recommendations, any griping or bitching or, God forbid, any insurrection or outright mutiny — inconceivable within the schoolhouse. So everyone did his duty, and it never occurred to anyone that by making noise in his own pigeonhole he could send signals to a fellow-teacher next door, let alone to the captain's cabin. And no one asked the ever-puzzling question about who were the keepers and who the kept. The lawns of Tarrytown made just such interchanges possible. Teachers assembled in clusters on the sweeping expanses of grass or on the verandahs to discuss their mutual problems. Staff people — Charles Wilson, Mr. Nailor, Mr. Goldstein, and others — circled to monitor these working sessions. After this work-up there came encounters. I sat in on one in which Tom Drager and his young associates confronted Mr. Nailor with their proposals for carrying on with the children they had taught during the current year, and their idea of beginning to construct a ladder of continuity which children could climb, accumulating experience by which teachers new to P.S. 68 might profit. Mr. Nailor's traditionalist past proved a bit resistant to many of the propositions presented by these young men. He regarded them as youthful and transient enthusiasts who would be gone one day, leaving the system as it was before they either came or went. His attitude was: "When you've been in the school system as long as I have, son, you will come to realize that changing things in any significant way is simply impossible." He remarked on a number of previous proposals in a similar vein, saying they had been tried in the city before, but had simply not worked. The young men pressed him nevertheless, countering that just because something had failed traditionally was no reason for it to fail in *their* school, which was, for now, free to try things with Mr. Nailor's support. Mr. Nailor met these demands as best he could, taking refuge in past failures from time to time. But the seminar ended in a mutual understanding of what new ideas might be implemented in the fall and in a resolution to work out arrangements when the new school year began. Mr. Nailor's hesitancy was based on a long-term perception of what always happened to hopes for change within the city school system: they were inevitably snuffed out. On that count his reservations were well taken. Yet after listening to the discussion, which lasted for several hours, I knew that Tom Drager and his associates had the right idea — and for a very simple reason. They knew what they wanted to do. They knew how to do it. Their collective experience could build the educational ladder they were now urging Mr. Nailor to endorse. *They* knew this; Mr. Nailor certainly knew it, too. Yet this very fact presented a basic problem, one which was certainly on Mr. Nailor's mind though he did not say so explicitly. If such a ladder were to be built only these individuals could build it. They could not hand over the sawmill to a green platoon and expect the ladder to ever get constructed. Not now, anyway. Perhaps in the ensuing years they could bring new teachers in and train them and so gradually relinquish control. But that would take time. Drager & Company would have to be considered valuable enough to continue their operation and would have to be free to carry it out. This, in turn, would require judgment, an evaluation, and a decision. Where could that come from? Not from Mr. Nailor, who was only temporarily the principal of P.S. 68. Not from Charles Wilson, who was only temporarily the unit administrator of the Complex. From where, then? The educational establishment? The teachers' union? Never. Mr. Nailor's hesitation seemed understandable in these terms, but what it meant did not seem in the least bit acceptable to me.

The morning work sessions ended and lunch was served, a wonderfully classy buffet on the big verandah of Tarrytown House. It featured cold shrimp with a variety of dips, cold roast beef and ham and turkey, cheeses, cole slaw and relishes, potato salad and noodle salad, cakes, pies, and ice cream — "the works." Teachers whom I had come to know in various classroom settings chatted and joked and told stories and laughed just like any other complement of bright businessmen or women one might expect to find in such a setting. Aside from the confrontational interplay of the morning work sessions, it was a first-class social event, just the right kind of event for people — as Charles Wilson had suggested to begin with —

who did a quarter of a million dollars' worth of business a year with the city. There was a feeling of openness and worth that proclaimed P.S. 68, on a particularly rough piece of turf in Harlem, was a free, operating, and important institution in American society. Everybody came and dressed and talked and played in just that spirit. As opposed to the traditional school fiesta featuring sandwiches made of stale bread without much filling, lots of cookies and cupcakes, coffee in plastic cups with a little Preem if you want it, thanks, and much constricted small talk befitting the usual American treatment of teachers and clergymen, too.

I had some shrimp. Then I made myself a delicious over-stuffed sandwich crammed with goodies. Afterward I had a cup of coffee — perked, in a cup, with cream — with Charles Wilson and asked him how he had managed to spring the funds for such a munificent affair, held on separate weekends for each of his five schools. I had come to see that the man was not only a mandarin and an epigrammatist, but also a rather canny hustler as far as his district was concerned. He had obtained a grant for these outings from an institution downtown. Yet to this day I remain mystified as to how he found the funds for something which made such extravagantly good sense given the prevailing parsimonious attitudes toward education in America.

After lunch there were more encounter sessions and then playtime, which for most guests focused on the estate's huge swimming pool. The center of attraction was Mr. Goldstein, whose galloping and galumphing dives were a source of great amusement because of the resounding splashes they generated. Since this was the first time I had a chance to see the school staff in one place, I wandered about to check on who had actually come. Most of the young teachers were present and so were the supervisors, but there was a gap. Very few of the middle-aged teachers who had been in the school system for years were on hand.

After Mr. Goldstein had knocked himself out in the pool he

settled down on a nearby bench, and I got the chance to question him a bit, as a viable male who had nonetheless elected to teach in the city school system. It was clear that a person of his intelligence and strength of character could have done well in any number of occupations in the "outside world." Aside from the younger, dedicated types like Joe Brown and Tom Drager and his group, most males I had come across were mousy, fussy, insecure types who had taken refuge in the school system and would have been failures in a more aggressive, competitive arena beyond the bounds of Academe. Mr. Goldstein had elected teaching deliberately, with no sense of emasculation whatever, and this was obvious to everyone in P.S. 68. Children and staff alike looked up to him and respected him as a man, a big man in several ways. I asked him about the salary problem which had come up during lunch with my sardonic foundation friend downtown.

"That's all over the hump, now, for a man," he said, "and you have to hand Al Shanker a lot of credit for that. Because the United Federation of Teachers has brought things to the point where if you're a man and want to teach you can do it without feeling like some kind of second-class reject. Not that I wouldn't be doing this anyway. But I make about eleven thousand dollars a year. That doesn't seem like much on the face of it, but if you add in medical insurance and an annuity plan and quite a few other fringe benefits I don't pay a lot for, if you add it all together, I make an adequate salary for something I really like."

So my sardonic friend was wrong. Perhaps he was simply behind the times, out of touch and desensitized at a time when it was just becoming apparent to me that there were all kinds of prospects out here. The importance of two simple words had been building in my mind: power and freedom. Charles Wilson in Harlem and — I felt rather sure by now — Rhody McCoy in Ocean Hill–Brownsville, were free to ask "the forbidden question": "Why can't the teachers teach?" and were indeed obliged to ask it, because they possessed the power to do so. Far from turning teachers off, the challenge had actually turned them on and made all sorts of things possible that would otherwise not have happened or been thought of or undertaken at all. For instance, Mr. Jackson discarding the traditional bullhorn put-down to invent such a simple, positive notion as "Signals!"; frosty Ronald Evans deciding he did not want any white snakes crawling around I.S. 201; Charles Click volunteering to give up his prep period to double as a music man since his school needed one; Tom Drager and company perceiving the need to build a whole schoolhouse, or to live in Harlem, or to take a class off for a weekend somewhere; or the presence of men like Joe Brown. Power and freedom were clearly crucial to the administration of the little district as well. It permitted Charles Wilson to execute an end run on his custodians and to scrounge funds for a marvelously uplifting retreat and to solicit the electronic equipment for a new multimedia center. It meant that parents and the community were involved with the schools and the children instead of being put off by them. I knew all of this was extremely difficult to get going. Yet the growing result was there to perceive. A gentle breeze of social truth was beginning to blow in what had until this time been a petrified forest of social fact.

Monday morning after the Tarrytown weekend I paid another visit to Charles Wilson. A new collection of questions had germinated in my mind. One persistent puzzle was whether there was some significant difference between black children and white children which might suggest something about how to approach the problem of teaching ghetto kids. The prospect of cultural differences seemed reasonable enough. What would happen, what adjustments would be in order to introduce Chinese children, or Cuban children, or Slavic children, into a school system in a strange place known as America? I recalled one experience of discovering a small hand in mine and how I had responded to it.

"That's characteristic of lower-class children. They have a low vocabulary, because they don't hear too many words, except the very simple ones. Yet they have a lot of things they would like to express. So they do it physically to make up for a lack of words."

"It strikes me there's a lot of natural warmth there that too heavy an overlay of formal learning would mask or somehow inhibit."

"Yes, it would be nice if you could have the whole thing; the heart and the head together and free. Then you'd have a whole man."

"You know," I said, "there are two completely contradictory propositions building up in my mind. One, which I see up here, goes:

" 'If something is necessary, it can't really be impossible.'

"But the other, which I am getting downtown, reads:

" 'If something is impossible, it can't be really necessary.' "

I had become accustomed to prompt, bright responses from Charles Wilson to my verbal probes. I was completely unprepared for his instant response to this one:

"That's like saying: 'Let them eat cake!' Isn't it?" He snapped it off.

For the first time I detected a tinge of anger and bitterness in this otherwise outgoing, open, and hopeful man. Charles handed me a digest of the Marchi Law, the new legislation which had just emerged for supposedly decentralizing the city schools at the end of the following school year. Though I had been aware that this was in the works and that technically the experimental districts had a three-year franchise which would end with the new redistricting, I had completely forgotten about it because I had become so absorbed in discovering what was going on here in Harlem. The document had been prepared by a community group called the United Bronx Parents and bore the title: *Summary and Analysis of School Decentralization Bill.* While Charles made a few phone calls and attended to other matters, I sat in a corner of his office and read the summary. It did not take long to come upon several strange provisions. One of them read as follows:

No [new] district may have less than 20,000 pupils in Average Daily Attendance.

I looked over at Charles Wilson, who had just put down the telephone:
"How many children are there in your district?"
"About four thousand."
"And in Ocean Hill?"
"About eight thousand, I believe."
The other provision that jumped from the paper went this way:

With respect to special, federal, state and private funds, each community board may contract for such funds to be transmitted to the city board and disbursed through the Chancellor.

That one, I could tell, was aimed at the Ford Foundation, which had provided small funds directly to the experimental districts to help them get started. From now on any such monies would have to go to "headquarters," and it was obvious what that meant. So there it was, a neat and simple legislative wipe-out of the districts. I asked Charles Wilson if this was indeed true.
"As of the first of the year, officially at least. Of course, the district will run until its lease is up next spring."
"But how did this happen?"
"Well, you could call the new law Albert Shanker's contract

with the state of New York. He carried a lot of political muscle with him to Albany when it was being written."

Once again I left Harlem in a bewildered state of mind. Wiping out these schools, even though new plans were being drafted for the system as a whole, seemed mindless, insane, or even worse. I did not understand how or why such a thing could happen. At this time the dear old Metropolitan Museum of Art was featuring an exhibition called "Harlem on My Mind" which was proving to be one of the most popular shows in the museum's history. I went to see it and found it splendid indeed. There were big pictures of Marcus Garvey, the black revolutionist of the 1920s who had inspired Malcolm X's father. The pictures indicated that Garvey had ultimately gone to jail for his crusade in behalf of the black man (with implications that he had been involved in some kind of swindle), but the captions said nothing about his ultimate fate. I later looked up Marcus Garvey in the biography section of the big second edition of *Webster's* dictionary and also in the collegiate edition with the hope of finding out. He was not listed in either place. There were famous photographs of Malcolm X at the Met, too. But the basic motif of the exhibition was what Harlem had been historically and how it had developed from a farming suburb north of the city into, finally, a teeming ghetto. Jazz music played in the background — Duke Ellington, Fats Waller, Chick Webb, Jimmy Lunceford, people like that. As a long-gone jazz lover I wondered why there wasn't something deeper, like the real blues:

> Trouble in mind, I'm blue.
> But I won't be blue always.
> 'Cause the sun gonna shine
> in my back door someday.

But that's "down home" music, not the swinging uptown beat this exhibition was all about. As I wandered about the darkened rooms, listening to this other music I also knew and loved,

a feeling gradually came over me that something was awfully wrong, a feeling connected with memories of a Father
Brown story in which that spry, sly priest felt that a knife was
"the wrong shape." A word came to mind: accommodation.
What this exhibit was really about was "accommodatin' Harlem."

> Fascinatin' babies hangin' 'round,
> dancin' to the meanest band in town . . .

or

> Hey! Let's take the A train!

or

> Old Bojangles of Harlem . . .

Accommodatin' Harlem. Images from the 1930s. Shirley
Temple getting tap dancing lessons from Bill Robinson (tap off,
now, Bojangles, this is a white man's flick). Accommodatin'
Harlem. Innocent fun and games uptown, back when we were
all broke together and poverty was a great equalizer during a
great depression, as indeed was wealth if you were some
"swell" from downtown. Fun and games. And a whole lot of
"mixin'." Mixin' to the point of getting black people with a
little bit of an Irish look, a little bit of a Jewish look, a bit of an
Italian look, a German look — in other words, fuck the nigger.
In those old-timey times no one thought of or cared about the
wasted lives or the destroyed children it took to bring a Bill
Robinson or a Paul Robeson or a Sugar Ray or an Ellington to
the surface.

I had come to see Harlem as a monument to death, imprison-
ment, misery, and despair — a nightmare perversion of the
American dream of life, liberty, and the pursuit of happiness.
But downtown a great museum was celebrating accommodatin'

Harlem as a place which had given something to the city and so should be honored and remembered. But does it make sense to extol a ghetto while it still exists? The mind count of children lobotomized and destroyed in such a place is far greater than any body count in Vietnam, gooks included. It seemed to me that Harlem should be eliminated rather than commemorated. Or is American society so precariously founded that it requires skulls imbedded in the bottom mud to support it? Are we a society of rednecks that needs someone to stomp on to build up our own egos?

Wandering about this elegant exhibit I could not help feeling finally that only an end to Harlem would be something to celebrate, perhaps with a New Orleans style funeral and big brass bands bouncing along. That would be a day to remember! If something could be done to bury Harlem rather than to praise it, then indeed would there be a reason to rejoice. The only way to do that would be to spring the kids through the schools into an outside world that was now beginning to open up. Consequently this commemoration of Harlem just did not take. It was, I have to say it, a white man's show. I later learned that some black groups protested the whole thing, much to the dismay of the well-intentioned aesthetes who had labored so hard to make a grand exhibit. I was not surprised. The fact that well-meant white maneuvers frequently only outrage desperate black people is part of the chasm.

As a person who was becoming something of a building observer, I felt I should take the pulse of other places. So I headed for the City Hall area of lower Manhattan to explore parts of the bureaucracy involved in education apart from the central board in Brooklyn: bureaus concerned with finding sites for schools, producing lunches (little old ladies making hundreds of thousands of peanut butter and jelly sandwiches and thousands of gallons of soup and kettles of beans for delivery to the schools); bureaus that purchased desks and chairs and all sorts of other hardware; bureaus for books and materials, pencils and paper and, elsewhere, audio-visual materials. Included, of course, were bookkeeping, accounting, payroll, and specified interrelationships with a dozen other city agencies like the Fire Department, the Police Department, the Health Department, the Department of Water Supply, Gas and Electricity, the Parks Department and, for reasons I could not understand at all given the almost uniformly dull and dreary look of the schools themselves, the city's Art Commission, whatever that was.

The two impressions which dominated all these places were grayness and entrenched monumentality. The grayness was apparent enough in the cheap paint that had been universally, if grudgingly, applied to corridors and rooms, suggesting ground-down budgets and a corresponding low evaluation of all that occurred here. But the real grayness was in the people who inhabited these spiritless caves and corridors. Their complexions were literally gray to begin with, and they were just as indifferent physiologically. Little old ladies with gimpy gaits or a somewhat hunchbacked cast moved slowly along the corridors, as did occcasionally a man with a clubfoot or with one leg a bit shorter than the other. I do not mention this out of cruelty; it's only that it was so completely evident. Handicapped or not, people moved about with an almost unbearable slowness, as though a movie projector had unaccountably slowed down, with the vacant look of mechanical dolls, acting out a ritual devoid of all meaning. They carried papers here, filed them there, entered numbers in big ledger books and then transferred them out again, stared at mountains of papers or shuffled through them with an air of long-resigned lethargy.

The city bureaucracy was originally established to protect the public from predators like the old Boss Tweed machine which had controlled and systematically fleeced the city in a bygone era. The basic idea was to insure that government operated without the possibility of individual corruption. Each office, each niche, each function was defined and prescribed so that it could be carried out no matter who occupied the slot. But I had become acquainted with what could be called "the problem of problems." In any bureaucracy new problems crop up continually. When they appear, particularly in the pyramid of interlocking bureaucracies with which New York is saddled, the inevitable response is to define new functions for new clusters of pigeonholes and thus create the need for additional functionaries to roost therein. So the bureaucracy expands geometrically while its ability to deliver actual goods and services by some inevitable law of inertia declines proportionately. Ultimately these structures become cancers devouring our society. As far as I know there is no recorded instance in history of such a beast going on a voluntary diet; on the contrary, it simply gets fatter and fatter and consequently becomes increasingly lethargic and inoperative. When Jonas Salk developed the polio vaccine did the March of Dimes close up shop? No. When talk began about winding down the war in Vietnam did the Department of Defense propose cutting its budget? No. Instead it discovered a bunch of new and urgent military problems which somehow had never been identified before. I suspect the Pentagon has a whole task force devoted to identifying and preparing for just such contingencies. In fact, long ago I invented a riddle about that unique place. Question: "Why does the Pentagon have five sides?" Answer: "So that every angle encountered in it would be obtuse." New York City has, among its many woes, an astronomical garbage bill thanks to the sanitation workers' union. It was recently discovered that private carters could do the job at half the cost or less and at good private wages. But little has been heard from the union about rolling up sleeves and going to work for the city with more determination, instead of milking it. How many of these sugar tits can our multititted society underwrite?

As far as the city schools went it seemed that the bureaucracies involved were simply producing more functionaries to

identify more problems which then required still more bureau-
crats to deal with them, yielding an expanding population of
gray, emasculated people which could only increase the yawning chasm between the nonpeople downtown and the little non-
children uptown who were not making it in the city's non-
schools. The end result was nothing short of a huffing, puffing,
mindless and undirected juggernaut which was slowly creeping
over and snuffing out the minds of countless children. One
conversation more or less crystallized this situation in my mind.
I had telephoned a man named Mr. Cohen and made a date to
visit him at a specified time one afternoon. I appeared and told
the receptionist I had an appointment.

"Oh!" she said. "But I'm not sure Mr. Cohen is in! I'll
have to go check. Did you write him for an appointment?"

"No, I called him on the phone twenty minutes ago. He's
in."

The receptionist disappeared in a hostile huff. Five minutes
passed, I don't know why. She did not have to go to another
floor, or another building, or another part of town. Or to the ladies' room, either, as far as I could tell. Finally she returned to
her desk.

"Mr. Cohen *is* in," she said with ill-concealed surprise which
bordered on amazement. "He'll see you now."

It turned out that Mr. Cohen's office was only about eight
doorways down the hall from her reception desk. But the lady
who was so obviously programmed and conditioned for difficulties, obstructions, and problems, was unprepared for my telephone call; her function had been shorted out. This baffled
her, in fact irritated her. Quite possibly it even infuriated
her, though I doubt it. I couldn't help wondering what might
happen if someone suddenly shouted down all these reverberating corridors of nonfunction:

"Hey, everybody! Let's go *do* something! Something real!
Something useful!"

What a marvelous army of cripples, misfits, and nonentities

would emerge! Like Jean Valjean shouting into the ancient echoing sewers of Paris: "Hey, you scum! Let's go sack the city! Let's build a *new* city. *Aux armes, citoyens!* On to the Bastille!"

Wow!

Slowly, gradually, painfully and to my consternation and horror I was finally beginning to perceive a diabolical paradox which I otherwise would have had no inkling of whatever. Since I had now observed so many felicitous things going on in the district, I naturally thought, given the nationwide hue and cry about the disaster of ghetto education, that the school establishment would have been watching these developments closely, formulating plans to incorporate the results throughout the city-wide system and perhaps even proclaiming proudly to other cities that little old New York had finally found a way to turn the corner. That's what I *thought*. Yet no such thing had occurred. Quite the contrary, the edbiz power brokers downtown had not bothered to look at all or even to send in observers. In fact, they simply considered the whole experiment irrelevant — completely irrelevant. Why? The experimental districts were obligated to ask "the forbidden question" in order to succeed. But such an assumption of independence, power, and freedom to hold teachers accountable for what they delivered to children — the essential ingredients of schools that work, in other words — could not but challenge and ultimately threaten to erode the central authority of the educational establishment. So "the system" developed a self-protective reflex response to save itself at any cost, the cost in this instance being the destruction of the experimental districts and the instant denial that anything at all had been accomplished. And who could gainsay such a denial since no one in authority had even looked? To those dedicated to preserving "the system" there was no real alternative; consequently there could be no curiosity about or interest in what the experiment might in fact be demonstrating. Put in simplest terms, then, the paradox was that if the experiment succeeded, it would have to be destroyed and denied, cast off like some illegitimate child of the city. One begins to see a certain rationality in what is commonly called black paranoia. It is intrinsic to the very nature of the system that minority needs and rights and aspirations should be "systematically" destroyed. From this perspective, a word like genocide no longer seems inappropriate.

I have never been one for protests, overtly anyway, though I have had thoughts from time to time. For instance, a strange emotional response occurs these days when I hear the White House mentioned. I experienced another such reaction when a huge George Wallace for President sign suddenly appeared on a neighbor's lawn across the road from us. I considered putting on our lawn, in appropriate gothic lettering, a sign which read: *Wallace über alles*. I never did it, though. But now a rather severe sense of defiance was building up. About this time a vogue developed for displaying American flag decals on car windows and fenders. A major purveyor of these emblems was the Gulf Oil Company, so I picked up one at our local service station and read the copy which accompanied it:

Your Flag . . .

has been unfurled by brave men in countless places around the world. It has been seen by stars and planets far beyond the earth. And now it stands on the moon!

But is it seen . . . is it honored . . . enough right here where it all began? Originally it was a symbol only of a dream — the American dream of building a country unique on the face of the earth. It has flown as a proud sign of a proud people for nearly two centuries. Today, it characterizes America's unquestioned greatness . . . and all the privileges we enjoy through being Americans.

By flying our flag regularly we can strengthen our personal belief and pride in America. And thus does America grow stronger.

As a person who, until this point, had considered himself a
bona fide inheritor of and subscriber to the American dream,
but who happened to be standing on the other side of a newly
discovered chasm at the moment, I was infuriated by this piece
of cloying, chauvinistic copy. It was not the astrophysical inan-
ity that stars and planets could "see" our flag that bothered me.
Rather, it was the strident sense of power and smugness and
posturing around the world, something I had never regarded as
the essence of the dream at all and which I surely believe Jef-
ferson, Emerson, Thoreau, and other early keepers of the ideal
would have disowned and regarded as completely contradictory
to the whole American enterprise. They had championed independence in order to make something else possible — life,
liberty, and the pursuit of happiness. When those goals have
been achieved for everyone in this land then, I think, we can
justifiably talk about "America's unquestioned greatness." But
to one standing "out here," corporate drivel about "all the privileges we enjoy through being Americans" just did not cut the
mustard. I peeled off my decal and pasted it on one of the rear
windows of our old Falcon wagon upside down, in the traditional Navy signal for a ship in distress. I learned later that
others had done the same thing to protest the abominable Vietnam war and that this dishonorable and unpatriotic act had
come to the attention of the police, whereupon some of the per-
petrators had been arrested.

I telephoned Charles Wilson and invited him to have lunch
with me — our first purely social meeting. I returned to Harlem with something on my mind on a Friday morning a week
before school would close for the year. I arrived a bit early and,
since Charles was involved in a meeting, I dropped by to see
Joe Brown in his small office in the Complex. We had not met
for some time so I explained that I was beginning to see a few
things. One was why it had taken me so long to get there in the
first place. I had received no inkling from any of the official

sources downtown that anything significant was going on in the Complex schools. Even Ken Marshall and Vera Paster, two people who might have been expected to understand the district, had suggested visiting it more as a hunch than anything else. Though millions of words had appeared in print about the strike, the seven teachers incident (though not as I have described it), confrontation and so on, almost nothing had come out about the schools themselves — either in Harlem or in Ocean Hill–Brownsville. Reporters had taken the normally accommodating route: the Board of Education, the U.F.T., and the districts whenever trouble erupted. I explained that in retrospect I felt lucky to have turned up at all. Now, knowing how far away the I.S. 201 Complex was from the education establishment, I felt negative and hopeless. There was clearly a conspiracy afoot to destroy the Complex, to liquidate the hopes and the programs and the attitudes and the freedom and the optimism I could see surfacing in old buildings and on the faces of teachers and most importantly on the faces of children. I did not feel the conspiracy was deliberate. It was just that the mills of the establishment, like the mills of the gods, ground along on an inexorable course, and in *their* course, they would grind into oblivion this small and happy cluster of schools which was just beginning to flower.

In this "down" frame of mind I wondered aloud to Joe Brown how it was possible to defend or to declare the value of such an intangible achievement. Not by a piece of real estate known as a school with a number engraved in stone over the portico. Yet the people at 110 Livingston Street seemed capable only of handling such mute numbers — lists of teachers, supervisors, materials, programs, hardware and software, buses, lunches, and so on. In fact, somewhere along the line I once heard a story of how, through some clerical error, a whole school had once been lost. It simply disappeared from the list. No one could find it. Consequently, no one opened it, no one staffed it, and naturally no children came to it. Somehow, later in the

school year, the existence of this Flying Dutchman came to
light — with what felicitous results, besides balancing the
ledger, I cannot imagine.

Since we live in a supposedly accommodating society, the
word "compromise" is frequently heard. Yet given the paradox
I had come to perceive, and the two propositions which had finally become formulated in my mind to express it, an analogy
had occurred to me which I tried out on Joe Brown:

"Suppose I'm an athlete and I develop a sore leg. And I go to
the doctor and say: 'Say, Doc, I got a real sore leg.' So the doctor looks me over carefully and says: 'You got a real sore leg all
right, son. In fact, I'm going to have to saw it off to save your
life.' To which proposal I naturally respond: 'But gee, Doc, I'm
an athlete and I need that leg.' So then the doctor naturally
nods his head sympathetically and thinks about that dilemma
for a moment, whereupon a look of revelation comes to his face:
'I think I have it. We'll compromise. I'll only cut off your
foot!' "

Joe Brown leaned back in his chair, stretched out his legs,
and relaxed his lean, athletic frame. He looked me straight in
the eye with a directness I knew meant that one human being
had encountered another human being. We speculated about
whether our mutual country could somehow shape up as far as
the rights and expectations of people went so that there might
indeed be freedom and justice abroad in the land, short of a revolution. I asked Joe about himself. He told me that some years
back he had been a SNCC (Student Nonviolent Coordinating
Committee) worker in the South, had later become a Muslim
and a follower of Malcolm X, and was now a Panther. But he
was distressed about the leadership problem:

"We get a leader and then they all get shot down — Martin
Luther King, Malcolm X, and now this last week Brother 37X [a
charismatic young Muslim who had been murdered in his small
Harlem storefront headquarters]. The leaders rise and get
killed. So where does that leave you? The leadership cult

doesn't work. Not for black people, and I suppose not for any people. If we had in this country only Jack Kennedys, Joe Browns, and Bob Campbells we'd be all right. But we don't. So then what?"

"Maybe," I suggested, "this kind of back and forth talking and sensing is growing in the land. I think it is. I think more and more people are coming to know what other people are all about, despite what you see on the boob tube. Don't you?"

"Yes. With some of the young people, yes. But time's long ago run out. You know?"

"Yes, I know. So how are we going to catch time? The lag between some people knowing something and enough people knowing something to get something going, that's a ten-, maybe a twenty-year lag. And if you throw in that a lot of people hearing about something don't want to hear that news at all and hope it will just go away, then that's got to make it even worse. We can talk about a revolution that has to happen, maybe even a violent revolution, but those folks who don't want to hear anything also don't want to learn anything about other people. Besides, they got all the guns."

"I know that," said Joe Brown flatly.

"So how do we get caught up to where we should be?"

Joe Brown shook his head: "I don't know, man."

Charles Wilson popped his head into Joe Brown's office. "I'm ready," he said. We walked across town to Seventh Avenue and 137th Street to the Red Rooster, a favorite Harlem restaurant and bar, very different from accommodatin' Frank's on 125th Street. Since I had perceived the real nature of the wipeout in progress, I had also acquired unwittingly a moral obligation to try to prevent it if possible. I felt that a magazine story might be done, or that I might find funds to film activities in the schools during the final year and so get some information back across the chasm which might help to stay the execution and at the same time encourage other cities by showing how ghetto schools could, in truth, come alive. How wonderful the Joe

Brown scene I had witnessed at P.S. 24 would be on film, if that could be done! Or Mr. Click's music class! Or the poor but inescapable portrait of President Kennedy! Or Tarrytown! So much was there, and still would be, if it could only be recorded. I expressed these thoughts to Charles during lunch. "Good!" he exclaimed. "Good! It would be important to have a real record of what was attempted here and almost accomplished! Then they could not just walk away as though it had never happened and forget about us, the way so many things get forgotten." He chuckled at the thought: "If you could do that then we would have something alive to haunt them with!"

Charles Wilson and I were gradually becoming friends, and one natural consequence was that we now spoke to one another on a first-name basis. I have always regarded addressing another person by his first name as an act of some social significance, suggesting that a perception of the other individual has been gained, some identification has been made as to who he or she actually is. This is, of course, a two-way street, since two quite distinct sets of antennae are involved, and occasionally one gets dissonant vibrations. In principle I feel one should persevere in formality under such circumstances, despite the perception. Yet in the easy and casual world of business I have occasionally violated this principle and addressed by his first name a person I had come to detest, because that was the easy way out and everyone involved accepted it; if I had resisted, the performance would have seemed strange and almost perverse to the point of possibly blowing the matter at hand out of the water. I hate myself for so dissembling, and I continue to believe that addressing another person by his first name is an act of mutual respect. I detest seeing this violated.

Among his other activities Charles Wilson taught a class at New York University, downtown at Washington Square. One day he invited me to attend, because he had shown the class the film I have mentioned and the students would be discussing it.

This was the first time I had seen the man in the role of teacher and he was simply terrific. A big-city university is generally a credits-and-degree factory with students attending classes or not, according to their private evaluation of what will satisfy the teacher, cramming in the clutch, and otherwise getting by with not much enthusiasm. There are exceptions, of course, and somewhere within these exceptions one generally finds an exceptional teacher, distinguished from the "big name" personality who is usually absorbed in the "publish or perish" racket at the expense of his students. So when the bell rang at the end of the hour I expected the class to get up and file out of the room. Nothing of the sort happened, however. Nobody moved. One person or another remained intent on asking one last question, because the kinds of Wilsonian responses I have already suggested kept coming. After a while Charles walked over and opened the classroom door and most of the students took the cue. Some still lingered, however, and continued to ply him with questions, not so much out of interest in the answers as out of interest in the man. It wasn't until about fifteen minutes after the hour that the spellbound young people finally left the room. In this respect a big university is not far removed from a ghetto school. If you hit one good teacher, you're damn lucky.

After the last student had gone Charles said to me: "Hey, let's go have a cup of coffee in my private lounge!" He knew, of course, that still another collection of questions was on my mind. His "private lounge" turned out to be a coffee shop across the street, naturally. There he was intercepted by a lanky, elderly, gray-faced white N.Y.U. teacher who pulled him aside: "Hi, Charlie, how about you and me having a rap session sometime soon?" Aside from his use of the word "rap," which I regarded as the property of young people, but which the old geezer had blithely appropriated for his own vocabulary to suggest to Charles he was really "with it," "hip," or something of the sort, this instant and convivial familiarity with a man I simply knew *he* did not know at all was infuriating. Such a self-styled Yankee liberalism, which I had begun seriously to suspect, was based on the completely false assumption that a terrible racial problem had long ago been solved, that everything was now hunky-dory, and that we could proceed on a course of heavenly equality on a "Hi, Charlie" basis ("Hey, Charlie baby, whatcha into uptown there?"). Superficial familiarity is as endemic in America as spray-can antiperspirants (caution: Keep out of reach of children). To some degree Charles brought this on himself, or made it possible, by his open and convivial style; yet to presume on that style was something else again. I knew that a great and hopeful experiment was about to be destroyed by this kind of glib accommodation, or as a consequence of it. Given this, I have never referred to Charles Wilson as other than Charles, a man I respect. It has always been his prerogative to break the pattern if he chose to do it. He did one day in a memo to me:

> Hi! Bob Campbell.
> Here is the material I promised.
> Keep up the good work.
>   Mr. Charlie

He said it, not I. And I have never presumed upon that.

We had a pleasant and leisurely lunch at the Red Rooster. Afterward we strolled back toward the Complex office. I asked him how he personally felt his cluster of schools was doing at this point.

"It's happening," he said. "It's just beginning to happen. I don't know all the answers yet, but we've turned the corner here."

I knew enough to know what that meant. Two years of trying had gotten something going with children. Then, casually and almost as an aside, Charles said:

"I have handed in my resignation to the governing board as unit administrator."

I asked why.

"Well, a kind of madness has taken over the governing board. We should be building an institution up here that can carry on into the future. But some people are so upset about the problems we have right now with the establishment that they think the Complex should be marching on the street and protesting."

I knew what that meant, too. Charles believed the 201 Complex should be a purely educational experiment and that if it were used for political purposes, it would make it just that much easier for the education power brokers to point an accusing finger and say: "See, we told you so." Now Charles Wilson was out of Harlem and so was I. This pretty well washed up a lot of things including my own hopes of doing something about the district while it was still alive. There remained one option, however: to try to do something similar — a story or film or whatever — in the Ocean Hill–Brownsville district the following year where, I anticipated, I would find many of the same elements of success I had observed in Harlem. Charles agreed and said he would introduce me to the "sinister" Rhody McCoy.

III

A Schoolhouse
in
the Ghetto

EARLY ONE MORNING in the spring of 1970 I took the A train again, this time in the opposite direction from Harlem, south and then east beneath the East River and on toward central Brooklyn. Charles had said: "Get in the last car." It was a fairly long trip, forty minutes or so compared to the very few minutes it took to get from midtown Manhattan to 125th Street. But finally the train reached Rockaway Avenue, the Ocean Hill–Brownsville stop. The subway platform was typically long like others in New York, built to accommodate a train of eight, ten, even a dozen subway cars. Emerging from the last car, I had a full view of its length, and I was startled because the end was enveloped in darkness. In my travels I was becoming increasingly aware of a simple geographical fact about the city: the farther one ventured from Manhattan's showcase hotels and office buildings, fancy restaurants and elegant theaters, well-manicured and brightly illuminated boulevards, and tastefully appointed shops and department stores, the more everything deteriorated in a simple geometric progression. Even Park Avenue, which abruptly becomes pure ghetto at 97th Street, indicates it is on its way if one drives north on it, for above 72nd Street the road becomes lumpy and patched, with unfilled potholes in increasing numbers. So it was on any radius that led away from the center of power, affluence, and security. I was beginning to perceive that "my city," a city I had loved for a

quarter century now, had become not too different from a Western cow town with its typical Long Horn saloon whose inviting
facade on the street only served to conceal the actual offering: a
sleazy one-room gin mill lying just behind. New York was putting up a good front downtown while many of the surrounding
provinces were dying.

Nowhere was this fact more apparent than in the subways,
unique in New York, because they are the main arteries of
transport in the city. Downtown the platforms are reasonably
clean and well illuminated (by U.S. standards). During working hours they swarm with people and the police are clearly in
evidence to protect the crowds, even at 125th Street. But then
Harlem has always been regarded as the city's "elegant" ghetto,
whatever that perverse play on words means, which is why the
Metropolitan Museum elected to celebrate it. But any subter-
ranean voyager who ventures far from the bright lights of Broad-
way finds himself moving into an ever-deepening gloom the farther he goes, a gloom that hides from the casual visitor the
essential shame of the city. Into the luminous midtown termi-
nals come subway cars from the distant provinces. Increasingly
in recent years they have been used to transmit messages, like
the pneumatic tubes in old-time department stores that carried
orders and receipts to and from distant parts of the decaying
emporium. The messages take the form of colorful and wonderfully inventive spray-paint graffiti — initials, street addresses,
names, slogans, obscenities — and cover nearly every subway
car in the city today. One can usually tell by the subway line
which of the provinces the trains come from. And the harder
and more despairing the area, the south Bronx or central Brooklyn for instance, the brighter the message and the more flamboyant the display, to the point of being virtually psychedelic.
New York's talented ghetto dwellers have invented an authen-
tic new art form. But no one downtown seems to have been
able to decipher the symbols or understand the message.

The Rockaway Avenue station clearly lay along one of these

communications channels that transmits signals downtown. It was enveloped in a murky gloom that completely blacked out the far end. The platform was strangely deserted. Though it was now mid-morning, only a handful of shadowy figures boarded or left the train. It was a lonely, abandoned, and frightening place, and I hastened to get above ground and out into the daylight. I emerged from the rear subway exit and turned right on Hopkinson Avenue as Charles Wilson had directed. Abruptly I encountered half a dozen young black men in their twenties congregated at the doorway of a small and delapidated apartment house who were sharing a bottle of wine wrapped in a crumpled paper bag. I proceeded on down the block and approached Atlantic Avenue, one of the main thoroughfares of the borough. To the west, in the direction of the Brooklyn Bridge, the avenue supports a second and elevated subway line. But as the tracks extend eastward and approach Ocean Hill, they vanish underground and Atlantic becomes a broad boulevard, covering the subway beneath and providing an open view of this particular ghetto.

Though I had been driven through the area before during my brief exploration of Brooklyn courtesy of the Board of Education, it was now as if I had never seen Ocean Hill at all. Cruising a ghetto in the comparative safety of an automobile is one thing; being alone and on foot is quite another as all my senses promptly notified me by tuning up into a silent jangle of apprehension. Harlem is an intense ghetto with tenement buildings five or six stories tall packed one against the other, shops and stores and churches at street level, life swarming on all sides — old and young, children and cats and dogs, activity everywhere, a sense of life which at least gives the illusion, in daytime anyway, that one may possibly pass by safe and unnoticed. But the streets out here gave quite the opposite impression. The reason one could see so far was not only Atlantic Avenue, but also the low profile of the whole area, which consisted largely of decaying brownstones left over from bygone middle-class residential days, a vista made even broader by the fact that complete blocks and even groups of blocks had been leveled into rubble to make way for urban renewal projects which never materialized. ("Urban removal" was the local term for this phenomenon, I learned later on.) Alongside these were other blocks whose burned-out or boarded-up buildings also awaited the wrecking ball. Still other streets appeared near death yet were not altogether deceased, streets that had obviously once been part of a living community with the typical corner drugstore, cigar store, apparel shop, delicatessen, grocery, bar, hardware store and liquor store, the ubiquitous funeral parlor set aside with its own special architecture. But now the signs which had proclaimed these amenities of urban civilization were fading, the once-welcoming doorways were grilled over and heavily padlocked, windows which had displayed enticements of one sort or another were now blinded by heavy sheets of galvanized tin nailed securely over them to protect some absentee landlord's decaying property. Here and there, amid the overall sense of resignation and collapse, an establishment still endured — an automobile salesroom, a dingy luncheonette, a gas station and wrecking service. But mostly Ocean Hill was a wasteland where the hopes of small entrepreneurs had simply died.

Now, at the height of the morning, people were missing as well, though one could see a figure and occasionally even groups of them moving about amid the ruins. Ocean Hill seemed much worse than Harlem, a place devoid of the means for supporting life and yet still inhabited in some underground fashion by people who went where if they needed medicine? Where, if they wished to die? Where if they simply wanted a Coke? Walking these streets I felt as if I were entering the ruins of Berlin after the Russians had shelled the city. The sound of ground glass crunching underfoot persisted whether I was walking on the sidewalk or in the street, as I did at times to avoid the carcasses of abandoned cars docked on the sidewalk by the police, their windows knocked out by neighborhood children.

In the midst of this wasteland, across Atlantic Avenue, was a modest, high-rise housing development which I knew from Charles's description contained the Ocean Hill–Brownsville district offices. A tall, black, privately employed policeman controlled the main entrance and directed me down a ground-floor corridor to the right, off which was the district's small reception room. With impressions of desolate, deserted streets still on my mind, I entered and found I had plunged into a beehive of human activity. A stream of people flowed into and out of this particular human hive, moving with a sense of urgency as though something important was happening, something paradoxically related to the wasteland I had just seen. There was no protocol of the "sign in, purpose of visit" nature. Rather, it appeared as though the individuals who came and went had already "signed on" for something crucial to all of them. Most were young, and there was a fairly even mixture of blacks and whites. About half were young men, a novelty itself in a school system dominated, for the most part, by older white ladies.

The reception room contained two desks manned by two young ladies and, for visitors, several chairs and a long, black couch. One of the women proved to be Sylvia Betty, whom I had telephoned for an appointment with Mr. McCoy. She introduced me to her associate Henriette Hunter, whose first name she pronounced as " 'enriette," giving it a French flavor which I observed everyone else did as well, myself included later on. I never learned the rationale for this, because every time it crossed my mind something more urgent cropped up to divert me from my simple sociological curiosity. Sylvia asked me to take a seat and I settled into the unexpectedly soft black couch to await my appointment, glad for an opportunity to observe the office in more detail. Virtually all the people who came and went seemed to know one another quite well and to understand what each was involved with. This led to passing exchanges and queries as well as occasional impromptu conferences as one person drew another aside. These people seemed to have long ago transcended basic issues like color and were onto something else together. One striking thing about them was that aside from being mostly young, they were also attractive, purposeful, and self-confident, men and women alike. Some dressed casually in jeans and other informal clothing, some were mod in currently fashionable bell-bottoms. Many of the young men wore their hair long, but not scruffily so. There were miniskirts, Afro hairdos and wigs, Muslim turbans and togas, amulets and tunics and ordinary suits and dresses as well. In other words, real live people, the kind one observed downtown making their way in the big, legitimate outside world as opposed to the sociological refugees who frequently seek asylum in a big-city school system.

Off to the left of the reception room there were other offices. At the back was a conference room, with a long table and quite a few chairs, that could be closed for privacy by an accordion partition. Occasionally individuals or small groups entered the conference room only to disappear through a doorway to the right and into an inner sanctum which I could not see from my vantage point on the black couch. One such visitor emerged escorted with an affectionate arm-on-the-shoulder gesture by a slightly stocky, light-skinned gentleman with a large head, closely cropped hair, and a pot-bellied pipe in his mouth whom I instantly recognized as the head man himself. Then he retreated to his office once more. On several other occasions in the minutes that followed Rhody McCoy emerged to escort one visitor or another out or to have a brief word in the reception room with someone who had popped in with an urgent problem. I sensed he knew I was waiting to see him, because Charles had laid the groundwork for our meeting. But it had also become evident to me that running his district was a strenuous and a time-consuming job. So I sat on the

couch patiently and watched and waited. After a while, saying
good-bye to still another caller, McCoy looked at me:
"Mr. Campbell?"
"Yes."
"I'm sorry to have kept you waiting. Come on in." His voice
was soft and mellow, with a quality of human affection in it that
seemed to have been wrung almost dry. I could tell that he did
indeed regret the delay, but there was a quizzical quality, too,
as though I were some belated visitor to death row in the big
house, with what in mind at this late hour?

It was now early in March. By the end of June the district
would close for good as far as its experimental status was concerned. Yet there was still time left during which a stay of execution might be won. Back during the winter I had set some
wheels in motion with that in mind so I did not come empty-
handed to my meeting with Rhody McCoy. My immediate
problem, after spending so much time in the I.S. 201 Complex,
had been to do some work to shore up family finances, which I
had allowed to drift to the brink of disaster. Then I surfaced
and began to consider what might be done. My first thought
was my journalistic alma mater *Life*. I still occasionally did assignments for the magazine with generally felicitous results and
I knew I would get a good hearing from the editors. I felt a
large picture essay in *Life* with a fair amount of text could stir
up quite a row. I felt also that to really lay this one on the line I
needed a strong ally in confronting the editors. I telephoned
Gordon Parks, that gifted black photographer, writer, composer,
and filmmaker whose feature, from his book *The Learning Tree*,
had just opened. Gordon and I had never gone on an assignment together, and we did not know one another very well in
the usual sense. But we had conversed briefly along the corridors of Time, Inc., and at various social functions and had, I
knew, an instinctive rapport. There had been a time when Gordon had played the role of the white editor's black photog-

rapher in the ghetto. He played the role still to a degree,
doing stories on the Panthers, or as the only acceptable photographer in Muhammad Ali's dressing room after the fight with
Joe Frazier — a scene of defeat he was simply unable to photograph. I knew Gordon was onto things more important to him
now as a talented human being, like the elegant new black magazine *Essence,* other films, and so on. I phoned him nevertheless, feeling his endorsement and, with luck, his participation
could be critical under the circumstances.

"Gordon? Do you think you might be up to one last good
street fight?" I went on to explain briefly what the fight was
about.

"Come on over," said Gordon, perceiving that since I had
never presumed to call him before, I must now have something
on my mind worth calling about. I went to Gordon's city hide-
away on Beekman Place, one of the more fashionable residential
areas on the East Side. It soon became evident that the man
was split six ways to Sunday. Our conversation at one point
was interrupted by a phone call from London; then, a bit later,
by one from the West Coast. Gordon explained that he had half
a dozen scenarios going and was really in a bind. Still, with occasional interruptions, we talked for well over an hour. Gordon
had been living in Paris during the big teachers' strike and had
missed all the flak, which had presumably been reported in the
papers. Yet his intuition told him that I was onto something important, that my picture of the wipe-out I was describing was
accurate, that something critical to the fate of countless ghetto
kids was at stake; it was a subject he knew about and still
clearly cared about.

"Look," said Gordon very seriously, "I don't know what I can
do. I'm really committed all over the place, as you can see.
But I do have an agreement with *Life* to do a certain amount of
work each year. They just offered me twelve color pages if I'd
do another fashion story. I turned it down. That kind of thing I
just don't care about anymore. To me it's a waste of time. Now

what you're telling me is something else again, something I do care about. But only Ralph Graves [the managing editor] can decide on my commitments to the magazine. So you'll have to talk to him. I think I understand what you're saying and I'll do anything I can. But the word will have to come from Ralph." That was certainly fair enough. I phoned Ralph and for openers set up a screening of A *Child Went Forth*, which he and Gordon and the two assistant managing editors, Phil Kunhardt and Bob Ajamian, attended. A considerable amount of personal commitment had gone into putting that film together; on my part, of course, but perhaps more importantly on the part of young Larry K. Madison who directed it and who is to my mind one of the most gifted, intelligent, and human people in the motion picture business. For more than a year our respective Abou Ben Adhem complexes had been dedicated to producing something we felt would have social significance. The film reflected this, at least in the way it presented the ghetto education "problem," though it didn't really come to grips with any solution — a matter in which I had now become involved on my own. A *Child Went Forth* had the impact I anticipated it would on four old journalistic colleagues, and after the screening we all retired to a pleasant private dining room on a top floor of the Time & Life building so I could talk about the story I wished to do. It proved to be a rather long lunch for several reasons. One was journalistic embarrassment on the part of a collection of top editors who naturally felt they were on top of things and who had either read or at least skimmed the same lengthy litany of words, pictures, and images that had emerged from the provinces as I had, early on.

Phil asked: "Are you saying that all the stuff we've read about the experimental districts is just plain wrong?"

"No, the problem is that it's mostly irrelevant. How many times did you see the word 'children' appear in print, for instance?"

"I guess not very often, as I think about it."

"Right. Everybody covered the strike, confrontations, and all that flak. But nobody, it seems, went to look at the schools to see what was going on there with children and teachers. It may seem incredible, but it's true."

Ralph remarked: "As I recall we did get a suggestion from someone in the *Time* education department that maybe we should do a story from Rhody McCoy's point of view. But we turned it down."

"Of course! Rhody McCoy's point of view just confuses the issue. The real issue is what's happening or not happening to the children. And that's what I'm talking about."

Initially a cloud of suspicion if not downright disbelief hung over the luncheon as I described what I had observed in the Complex schools in Harlem, why they were to be wiped out, why something vital to ghetto education should not be blindly destroyed, and the story I felt could certainly still be done in McCoy's district, though I had not yet explored it. The skeptical reception of the editors led me to feel like someone newly returned from discovering a lost continent, some latter-day Trader Horn come back down the Niger River with a long yarn about miraculous things no white man had ever witnessed before. Glances were cast at Gordon from time to time to determine if what the madman was saying might possibly be true. Gordon's quiet, attentive interest answered such queries as far as he was concerned.

"You know," Bob Ajamian exclaimed, "if anyone else had come in here with this tale, we'd have thrown him right out the window!"

Phil said: "Well, I guess we have to realize we never had very many great reporters around, you know."

"The trouble is," Bob said, "what you have is a New York story. Why is it that the only good story suggestions we get are either from here or the West Coast?"

"It may be a New York story by accident, but it's really a story about ghetto education. And if I'm not mistaken, there are quite a few ghettos in cities all over this land. To my mind that makes it a general story across the board and so much more important than New York."

Ajamian had planted the seeds of possible equivocation, seeds that could bear fruit by defusing the absolute moral imperative I had tried to confront them with. I knew they really believed me finally, but I could not see that there followed from this a sense of caring and possible responsibility in the matter. Now they could walk away, consult about what they regarded as the real and immediate interests of their magazine, and let me know. I sensed the prospects of getting Gordon assigned to the story were slim, given his many obligations, and I knew the magazine well enough to know that without such a commitment the whole project could sputter along indefinitely and possibly fizzle out. Time was too critical for that, so, for a change, I gave Ralph a deadline. When time ran out I turned to Plan B.

I phoned Gordon again, told him of my misgivings about *Life* and that I was considering *Look* instead, a move Gordon felt, with some reluctance, was probably best under the circumstances. This left me with the problem of finding another Gordon Parks, a duplication I doubted was possible.

"So where do I find your alter ego, Gordon?"

"John Vachon at *Look*," he responded instantly.

"Is he black or white?"

"He's the whitest man I know," said Gordon in a wonderfully ambivalent recommendation. "He took me under his wing when I was just breaking in, back in the old Farm Administration days. There is no one finer."

"Okay, I'll try John. By the way, remember back in the old days at *Life* when you were more or less the 'in-house' black photographer?"

"Yes."

"Well, now that you've got your new elegant black magazine going, maybe what you need there is a good 'in-house' white writer."

The suggestion elicited a long, mellow laugh from Mr. Parks.

I phoned another old friend, Joe Roddy, a senior editor at *Look*, told him what I was onto and of Gordon's recommendation and asked about Vachon. It turned out that Joe had worked on many stories with John and regarded him as both one of the rare photographers and rare people of the world. He suggested John and I get together first and that if John were for the story, a meeting could be set up with the top *Look* triumvirate. I called John and we agreed to meet several days later for lunch at the Oyster Bar in Grand Central Station, which was convenient both to the *Look* building and the Madisons' office where I would be that morning. Though we must have exchanged a few words about how to identify ourselves, we ended up standing on opposite sides of the same doorway for ten or fifteen minutes looking for each other. Finally I became aware of another individual who seemed to be glancing about vaguely, just as I was, so I asked if *he* were John Vachon. He was. John turned out to be from Minnesota, of French-Canadian ancestry, a remarkable-looking man with a great, craggy face, bushy eyebrows, iron gray hair and a hesitant, rasping voice. We quickly found we had quite a few things in common, including a love of early jazz — Jelly Roll Morton, George Mitchell, King Oliver, and the other New Orleans greats, as well as a few white musicians like Bix and a piano player named Paul Lingle. John was astonished when I mentioned Lingle, an obscure but extremely gifted San Francisco pianist who had worked out his own very sensitive renditions of the classic Morton compositions; as far as he could recollect I was the only other person he had met who had heard of the man. During lunch I discovered Gordon's recommendation had not been made casually, that John was indeed a perceptive soul whose pictures — I had no doubt — would show it. I explained the Ocean Hill story as I saw it, or rather anticipated it, and John said he was available, eager to do it, and hoped we could get the assignment.

We reported our agreement to Joe, who set up a meeting for the following afternoon with Bill Arthur, the publisher, Pat Carbide, the executive editor, and Martin Goldman, the managing editor. At the last minute Pat Carbide got preempted and could not attend, but the others did. As with the *Life* group I began by showing the film. Impressed, the *Look* editors began a quiz session not surprisingly parallel to the one at *Life*. Joe, acting as host, asked:

"In that section on the Head Start program in the film I was struck by how clean and well-dressed the children looked, particularly the little girls. Are those really poverty kids and did they just get spruced up for the camera?"

"No, the families of all those children are welfare families."

"Then how come they look so clean and dressed up, not bedraggled or ragtag at all?"

"I'm glad you asked that question, because there's a funny thing that happens. Those little girls, most of them anyway, have only one or two halfway decent dresses to wear to school. Consequently momma washes and irons nearly every night so her child can show up the next morning looking neat and clean. Why? Because she hopes her gesture will deliver a message to the school system that possibly the child is worthwhile."

From comments and questions about the film the conversation turned to the matter at hand and whether the magazine would assign John and me to the story. Martin said, expressing a final consensus:

"From everything we know about what we are doing this is *not* the kind of story that sells *Look*. On the other hand it *is* the kind of story to which we feel a journalistic obligation. Accordingly we can't pay you much, but you and John have the assignment. Go to it."

I didn't care a whole lot about the pay provided the story got published. In any event, this would buy time to explore Ocean Hill at some length and to observe the programs there in detail, by way of preliminary research, before John was called in.

Rhody McCoy's office in the Ocean Hill–Brownsville district was small and cluttered, and its walls decorated with photographs of his wife and many children as well as honors and awards he had received as an educator. On his desk was a small plaque which read: Do Everything With Love.

Like the cleanliness of the I.S. 201 Complex, this new admonition did not communicate much on first encounter. I explained to McCoy some of my perceptions about the importance of the experimental districts and my belief that they had been badly reported at best, that even now in the last hour I had an assignment I felt could produce some useful result.

"I've been trying to find a rabbit, and I think I have a piece of one now anyway. Maybe, if things work out, we can make a rabbit stew."

"Fine," said McCoy. Then, after a short pause: "You can keep the fur."

The first thing I wanted to know, as we sat in his office with the typical stream of interruptions, was how the district had been organized initially. I learned that at first people had been dispatched to explore programs, materials, teaching methods, and a variety of innovative approaches which appeared to have worked in bits and pieces with poverty children in other schools and in other cities. If a program seemed promising, one or several teachers might train in it and then import it for implementation in the district. In a reverse arrangement, educators from the outside who wished to try out approaches of their own were invited to do so in selected classrooms. In this way a whole spectrum of methods was launched ranging all the way from highly permissive classroom procedures at one end to hard-nosed drill instruction at the other. Teachers who had learned about the experiment and had personal feelings about the possibilities of change applied for work in the district. Since I felt I should explore all these classrooms, as well as activities involving parents, which I also knew were a critical part of the overall effort, I requested McCoy's permission to do so. He introduced me to several of his staff members and asked them to arrange for me to observe whatever I wished. So I began my rounds.

The Ocean Hill district consisted of six elementary and two intermediate schools. But by a logistical accident my first stop was not a school at all but rather a small, comparatively modern two-story brick building about a dozen blocks from district headquarters and close by P.S. 137, one of the feeder schools of the project. It happened to be next door to the Westminster-Bethany United Presbyterian Church on McDonough Street, a byway quite at odds with the overall devastation of the area in that it still supported living trees at intervals along the sidewalk and, back from the trees, relatively unmolested and still-occupied two-family houses. Like the distant district offices McDonough Street was, amidst this vast wasteland, an unexpected oasis that seemed to have been overlooked both by urban decay and urban removal, its trees providing pleasant shadows on a sunny spring day. I would like to think it was the solidly built church with its facade of arched windows and its sturdy square bell tower nestled alongside that had cast its shadow over the neighborhood and so concealed it from the view of the urban "developers" who otherwise seemed to have mapped this whole area of Brooklyn for destruction. I would also like to think that the current pastor of the church, the Reverend C. Herbert Oliver, an ally of Dr. Martin Luther King, Jr., in his Southern Christian Leadership Conference and now head of the governing board of the experimental district, possessed some kind of spiritual "wolfbane" that had magically immobilized the approaching wrecking ball. But, of course, that is only fantasy. A more likely explanation was that this warm and sunny block had simply become lost in the overall scheme of things like the Flying Dutchman of a school I have mentioned, and so had continued to survive by accident.

The little brick building, an annex to the church designed for various community activities, had been leased by the district as an adjunct to P.S. 137 nearby, and so was naturally known as the "Annex." There were shops on the first floor and, on the second, half a dozen classrooms, office space, and one large conference room with movable partitions so it could be opened up fully for special assemblies or closed to provide enclaves for small classes. The Annex housed a kindergarten program known as Bereiter-Engelmann, named for the people who had developed it at the University of Illinois. I met Miss Jackie Rogers, a young black woman who had trained in the program and its special materials at the university and was now in charge of it in the district. She explained it was a strict drill approach designed to overcome a number of obvious disadvantages of poor children at a preschool age, among them a lack of identity and confidence, a low vocabulary, and a consequent tendency to mumble answers, which is a natural defensive response for any child a bit lost within himself and hesitant to project a germinating inner world, being unsure of what it means or how it might be accepted.

In the Annex children gathered in clusters of about six with a teacher and competed aggressively with each other to be the first and the loudest with the correct answers in the reading and math drills. They were encouraged to speak up and their answers were frequently rewarded in tangible fashion by a Frito or a pretzel stick, proffered then and there by the drill teacher. The children worked with materials they could master, step by step, and in so doing gradually developed their own potential. An example will indicate how the procedure went:

Mrs. Holloway, a black teacher, shows her children a simple line drawing of a lamp — with shade, light bulb, switch, cord, and plug connecting it to a socket in the wall. She points to parts of the picture and the children shout loudly and in unison the anatomy of the lamp, under her guidance:

> The lamp has a *stand!*
> The lamp has a *shade!*
> The lamp has a *light bulb!*
> The lamp has a *switch!*
> The lamp has a *cord!*
> The lamp has a *plug!*

Mrs. Holloway pauses before the critical words whose symbols she is pointing to with a pencil — stand, shade, and so on — and urges the group to shout out the identification of these objects in the picture. Like a Marine Corps drill instructor she encourages the cadence of the children: "All right! Get it going!" And as the children swing into the routine:

"That's good talk! Good talk! Get smart! I hear Charlene talking now. Here!" She proffers Charlene a Frito.

The same kind of drill applied in the math sessions. The children got with it, shouted out the answers, and competed vigorously with each other to have the loudest and surest response and be rewarded. At times this aggressive behavior threatened to erupt into open fistfights. But the well-trained leaders of these small combat platoons seemed quite sensitive to volatile points and prevented such explosions from occurring. It struck me that having words and numbers as outlets for aggressive childhood behavior made a lot more sense than having windows and possibly each other as the objects of pent-up steam. I asked Miss Rogers how well the children were doing, and she replied their reading and math levels were comparable to late second grade, quite an achievement for one year of kindergarten.

The classes ended at noon and one of the young white members of the district staff, Fred Schulman, happened by and I scrounged a ride back to headquarters with him in his small, battered car. Fred asked me what I was doing, and I explained I was working on a story for *Look* about what was, to my mind, the real Ocean Hill, an idea of which he heartily approved. He had been a teacher in the district before McCoy had singled him out for staff work.

"Do you know any people in the publishing business?" he asked as we drove off.

"A few. Why?"

"Because I'm writing a book."

"About the schools?"

"Yeah, and what was really going on around here before the district took over."

"Meaning what?"

"Genocide, that's what. Pure and simple genocide."

I had met Fred briefly in McCoy's office, where we had exchanged a few words at most, but an intuitive liking had developed between us. I could tell he was a bright and dedicated young man. Now I discovered he was very angry as well. I made such suggestions as I was able to about his book, offered to help, and then asked him what he thought of the Annex program.

"Terrific!" was his instant response. "These kids don't have time to play educational games, that Montessori permissive 'What's on our minds today, children?' kind of thing. They don't have the time, man! The streets and the drugs and the whole ghetto scene gets to them too fast. So I think that program's great. Lock them in right away to achievement in kindergarten or even before that maybe, because time runs out fast on these kids. You got to lock them in and get them going early, and I mean really early. And no nonsense about it!"

Fred's logic was inescapable. Yet it conflicted completely with my recollections of Tom Drager's classroom in Harlem. Perhaps the conflict was more imaginary than real.

I dropped by the Annex several weeks later because some

questions had come to mind and, since I had already spent some time there, I could walk in without any formality attached — which proved to be a good thing under the circumstances. I greeted Mrs. Holloway and several other teachers and quickly realized I had unwittingly plunged into the midst of what was more a social than an educational affair, and a somewhat hectic one at that. It happened on a Thursday preceeding Good Friday, Maundy Thursday by the Christian calendar, and everyone in the Annex was busily preparing for an Easter program and luncheon for parents and other interested people in the community. Children and teachers bustled about putting last minute touches on costumes and arranging tables in the large room of the Annex. Miss Rogers managed to break away for a bit, and we talked in the office down the corridor from the main room. Then she invited me to stay and watch the children's program.

Parents began to arrive. Most if not all of them were well known to the Annex staff, which permitted an easy informality and led to many offerings of help with one or another work detail — a novelty for any "day" in a big-city school. The guest of honor was the Reverend Oliver himself and Miss Rogers introduced us. He was a trim, nice-looking light-skinned gentleman in his mid forties I guessed, well but modestly dressed. I told him briefly what I was up to. "Fine," he said. His voice was mellifluous and resonant without being in the least pontifical, a desirable attribute for a preacher. All too often one gets the feeling that this sense of audible spirituality terminates in the voice box alone, so that the medium is the whole message. I had no such impression of Reverend Oliver. On the contrary it seemed to me his voice reflected the resources of a deep humanity that had long ago determined who he was, who he might be, what he might do or not do. Consequently one had no need of trivial banter in speaking with him, a good thing because the show was about to begin. Reverend Oliver took his seat among

the parents at the "head table" and the children put on their
Easter show, the highlight of which naturally was Peter Cottontail in full regalia accompanied by a chorus of children's voices:

> Here comes Peter Cotton tail,
> Hoppin' down the bunny trail,
> Hippity hoppity, Happy Easter day.

In the midst of the act Peter Cottontail quite predictably lost
his large white tail. The accident produced a brief flash in my
mind about this same little black boy getting his ass shot off at
some later time if he didn't make it down Rhody McCoy's
bunny trail. I was reminded that Easter, the festival of resurrection, was being celebrated just as these resurrecting schools
seemed about to go out of business. "A crucifixion? Yes." But
a resurrection? Where? When? How?

P.S. 178, an elementary school diagonally across the street
from the district offices, was a huge traditional building which
contained a number of surprises. One, on the fourth floor, was
a second grade classroom with the following motto inscribed in
handwritten letters over the entrance:

> I hear and I forget. I see and I learn.
> I do and I understand.

The proprietor of this class (he gave more the impression of
being a host than a teacher, both to the children in the room and
to visitors) was a young white man named Gene Aptekar. Long
ringlets of black hair dangled onto his shoulders. He wore san-
dals and an embroidered tunic, and strings of beads hung from
his neck. He was the classic hippie incarnation of a Christ figure that infuriates most American adults and turns them off like
a light switch. My initial impression of his classroom, as with
Tom Drager's, was one of complete disorganization, but it did
not take long, with Gene's help, to discern order amidst the ap-

parent chaos. The visual chaos at least was a consequence of the arrangement of the room itself. It had been divided into all sorts of crazy Lilliputian areas by fiberboard partitions which were chin-high to the children but only waist-high to an adult. They were painted in a splattered and haphazard way with various forms and colors and squiggles of no apparent significance. The most interesting structure of all was a makeshift igloo in the middle of the room into which two or perhaps three children might squeeze, with an opening in the top should they wish to peer out. The other areas, as Gene explained them, had quite sensible purposes.

One, enclosing a small table and three or four childrens' chairs, was his own "homeroom" where he worked with several children at a time on some reading or math project. The sight of Mr. Aptekar, a full-sized adult, sitting on a child's chair in this small corral with two or three kids, half of him projecting above the waist-high walls, was funny indeed. Another of the enclosures was the class "library" that contained books and various other materials which could be taken out by the children and was staffed by girls who managed it in a rather bossy fashion. Next to the long, sunlit wall by the windows was a science and nature "bench" with plants and animals — mice and a couple of hamsters and I'm not sure what else. Still another area was the shop. There, on one particular day, I watched a small boy drive a nail into a block of wood. Having succeeded in this, he proceeded to pound on the head of the nail for at least three minutes, wielding the hammer ferociously as though hammering out and posting up some inner rage and retribution. While he was doing this two little girls danced nearby, oblivious to the scene of anger because they wore earphones connecting them to a phonograph only they could hear.

As for the igloo, Gene explained that was a place to hide in and be alone. Like if you'd had a bad night, or your folks had had a fight, or any number of things that could make a child want to be alone on a particular day, or a part of the day, or just

for a moment or two. Or just to go and pretend something if
you wanted to.

Gene Aptekar's faith in the way he conducted his class had
been only gradually arrived at:

"I had one boy that for three months did nothing but work in
the shop, hammering away on nothing at all. I would try to get
him into reading and a little math. No luck. It, like, bothered
me, you know? Because it was on my mind where he'd be at
the end of the year. What he could do. I let him alone for
three months, three whole months, and that worried me. But
then he began to look from the shop to the animals. And he
began to think. And so he thought up a whole kind of science
exhibit that he could make in the shop — name the animals or
what they were doing or what they were like and things like
that. So he began to come over to the reading group to get the
spelling he needed for his project. And finally — how excited,
relieved I felt, you know? — finally he made the connection to
reading. Made it out of himself. From that point on he understood, and he took off."

Gene told me most of the story over his shoulder for he was
continually circulating about the classroom in a completely informal manner. All the children called him Gene. It was part
of his idea of what their relationship should be. He was a love
person and his whole style with the class was in that vein. He
touched and patted and related to his charges with a physical
directness and innocence that could not possibly have been
feigned. I recalled discovering a child's hand in mine and
Charles Wilson's comment on the event, and it seemed Gene
Aptekar had put that and his own sense of love together and
come up with something that worked for him and his children.
One simple indication of how well it worked was the fact that
his classroom door was always open. Though I visited that
room on many occasions I never saw a child run out except to
go to the bathroom. Free as the situation appeared, Gene Aptekar obviously had it well under control.

As Gene circulated about the room children would reach up and tug at his arms with one question or another:

"Gene! Gene! Jimmy and I were playing a card game and he's cheatin' again!"

"I keep telling you if he cheats don't play with him."

He responded to all such queries about games, words, animals, books, numbers in his own quiet way, bending down each time to listen. His sense of patience, love, and quietude infected the children, and they behaved accordingly. This made possible a curious conversation on two levels: one when he tipped over to talk with a child and, in so doing, lost contact with me; the other when he surfaced three feet or so higher to continue where we had left off. In this way, strangely enough, neither stream of attention was broken.

"You got to dig kids, man," Gene said as he bobbed up on one occasion. "I hope to get each kid to know himself. After that he'll be okay. I want these kids to have faith enough in themselves to be creative. They're growing emotionally now and that's invaluable. To get that going you got to dig kids, man. You got to."

He went on to talk about parents:

"Like these kids come to school? All right. But they come to school from somewhere, right? They have parents and their parents are pretty well put off by school, from what they usually see. So I go see them and we talk. So they know who I am and what I think and they understand that I like their kid. No, that's not quite it, but part of it. They see that I know their kid, who he or she is. If you don't know a kid you can't talk about him. But if you do you can. Parents see that right away, so they dig, too, and get involved. They can come here, too, any time they want, just tell them in the office: 'I'm going up to room four-o-three to see Gene and Betsy.' "

During one afternoon visit to Gene's room the class became a bit restless, a typical school phenomenon particularly in spring when the weather is nice outside, and it's almost three o'clock

anyway. Gene naturally detected this before I did and interrupted our conversation to turn his attention to the situation,
but not before remarking:

"Sometimes the class gets restless, like now. When that happens maybe we just walk out of the school. Sometimes we
explore the neighborhood and make up games along the way,
like how many houses we see, how many are boarded up, say,
or how many still have people living in them. Or what the
stores are — like there are two grocery stores, one liquor store,
and six stores that don't have any business anymore and are
closed up. Maybe we come back and talk about that. This time
of year we take trips, too, like to the beach to go swimming, or
to Prospect Park, or the zoo. We travel a lot."

In the present instance, however, it was too close to 3 P.M. to
invent much of anything. Instead Gene went to a locker, produced a guitar, sat down on a child's chair, and strummed a few
chords. The children gravitated to him and Gene sang, with considerable accomplishment, a Pete Seeger song:

> Way down south in yankety yank,
> a bullfrog jumped from bank to bank
> just because he'd nothing better for to do.

The song developed into a whole musical story about all
kinds of animals and people congregating to enjoy a social gathering. Gene interpolated shouting lines:

> Everybody's drinking their free Coca-Cola!
> And eatin' their free soda crackers!
> And munchin' and chompin' and havin' a grand time!

So he got a whole "down home" festivity going, thanks to Mr.
Seeger, with the children joining in on the choruses. The children participated in other ways as well — touching or holding
his arms and clothes, putting hands and fingers on the guitar,

relating physically and emotionally to Gene's scene. The end effect was a glorious musical tableau celebrating joy and life and fun and marvelous goodies, a living classroom that dissolved as I looked beyond the cluster of happy singers toward the spacious windows of the room where the hamsters and plants bathed in the warm sunlight of the science shelf, then on to the view from the battlements of the old fortress, of the silent desolation of Ocean Hill.

Another of P.S. 178's hidden surprises was Everard Barrett, a nice-looking light-skinned young man with a slight accent, suggesting he came from the West Indies. Mr. Barrett was the mathematics coordinator for the district and circulated among all the schools though P.S. 178 was his headquarters. He drove a maroon Citroën and thereafter I was able to tell whether he was in one school or another by the presence of his very visible car in the neighborhood. He was a graduate of a Manhattan institution called Schools for the Future, established by Dr. Caleb Gattegno, a pioneer in the use of Cuisenaire rods in teaching mathematics to children. I had heard vaguely of this approach to math and was more or less prepared to take Mr. Barrett's word for the effectiveness of the technique. But being a rather methodical person, Mr. Barrett sat me down and insisted I understand what the rods were all about. He took out a set of them, explaining that the principle was based on the innate strengths any child possesses — he simply "says what he sees." The rods were small sticks of wood, square in cross section and of various lengths and colors representing the numbers from one to ten. The rod for one was a white cube. That for two was a red rod twice as long. The light green three rod was three times the length of one and so on up to the ten rod, which was yellow. Mr. Barrett then illustrated how any child could do a math problem using the rods:

"Suppose I say to a child: 'What is three fifths of ten — three fifths of the ten rod.' The child takes a ten rod, but the problem has to be broken down. So I say: 'Find five equal rods, and make a train out of them end to end on your table that is equivalent in length to the ten rod.' The child can do this because he sees the problem right in front of him. He may try a blue rod, or some dark green six rods, but he quickly sees that if he makes a train of five of them it will be longer than his ten rod. Ultimately he has to see that it is a train of five red two rods, end to end, that equals his ten rod. So you see he is working with his own perceptual strengths. He is playing a game he can see, and with a bit of encouragement he can't lose. At this point he has analyzed the problem, but not solved it.

"So far he has found one fifth of ten, a red rod. But the problem was to find three fifths of ten. What is three fifths of ten? What is that equivalent to? Now the child makes a new train of three red rods, which represents three fifths of ten. And what is this new train equal in length to? Having made the new train, the child then looks at his other rods and quickly perceives which one of them is the same length as the train he has assembled from the red rods. The only one that matches is the dark green six rod. And so, eureka, he has the answer: three fifths of ten is six!'

Mr. Barrett sat back and looked at me with arched eyebrows, crossing his arms over his chest and tilting back slightly in the child's chair he had been sitting on. In effect, he inspected me and he could perceive I had followed his demonstration exactly. The tableau carried me back to prep school days and to memories of an austere and exceptional mathematics teacher named John Campbell (no relation) and to my demonstrating the solution of a problem at the blackboard and, having done so, writing Q.E.D. after the final answer. Q.E.D. stands for *quod erat demonstrandum* in Latin, meaning "which was to be proved." In those days, confronted with such a canny old gentleman, one did not do the exercise or presume to attach the Q.E.D. lightly unless one was damn sure the solution was not only correct, but had been rigorously arrived at. So it was in these terms that I understood Mr. Barrett's demonstration.

But it was the psychology behind the rods that was the grand thing, for it was virtually fail-proof — a particularly valuable asset in a ghetto school where the prospect of failing hangs heavy in the atmosphere like a sulphurous inversion and is not all that dissipated in suburban schools either. Mr. Barrett informed me that Gattegno himself was a psychologist with a highly professional perception of the learning process and that he posed the problem this way:

"Look, any child who has learned to speak has already mastered the most subtle and complex human act there is. If a child can learn that surely he can learn simpler things, like math and reading."

Thus with the rods if a child simply listened to the problem, used his eyes, and then "said what he saw" as Barrett put it, he could not fail. He had to find the right answer. The whole system was predicated on the basic perceptual strengths any child has, no matter what his family or environmental situation. There was more to the matter than innate strengths, however, which came out as the conversation progressed. In school children are usually taught the elements of mathematics separately — addition, subtraction, multiplication, division, then improper fractions and algebra — all at different grade levels, a process which involves a considerable amount of rote learning meaningless to any kid, because meaning is missing from the procedure. But with the rods a child was working in all these elements simultaneously and so was, in fact, "doing mathematics." As this facility developed, the rods became increasingly unnecessary, for the child could then do a problem conceptually. I could see Mr. Barrett was dedicated to this method of teaching math, because it was simple, conceptual, and elegant. Sensing the elegance of mathematics is the key, I believe, to making a subject which is all too often dull, dry, and rote into an exciting adventure.

Mr. Barrett told me it had taken him two years as mathematics coordinator to get traditional teachers to abandon more formal approaches and take up the rods seriously. It is difficult for any teacher to go out on an experimental limb. But now, in the third year, several had come to understand as well as apply the program. That it had indeed gotten off the ground became evident in my own explorations of the district. Just as surely as the streets of Ocean Hill were paved with broken glass they were also paved with Cuisenaire rods. They were everywhere; in classrooms, of course, but also under desks, in stairwells, here and there on corridors, and sprinkled brightly along the sidewalks as well. I described this phenomenon later to a sister-in-law who had been a long-time student teacher in one of the "best" schools of the city on the upper West Side of Manhattan, a school that had a good racial mix in an area that ranged from lower- to upper-middle class, with a dedicated parents' association able to exert a good bit of concerted muscle on the education establishment and so command a good principal and well-qualified teachers for staffing the school. She was astonished by my description of the value of the rods and reported that though there were quite a few sets of them in the classrooms of her school, they were largely used for play, like building blocks. 'No one, as far as she knew, understood their real worth.

One day on leaving P.S. 178 I came upon a green six rod on the sidewalk which I picked up and idly put in my pocket. Thereafter it became a good luck charm in my mind, and I carried it all the time I was in the district. Along with my wallet, pen, and keys, it was deposited on our dresser each evening when I came home. Somehow, after my time in Ocean Hill was over, my six rod disappeared. Since I am not a superstitious person, at first I attributed the loss to our children, who lose or demolish almost everything. Yet this simple object would not have caught their fancy. I looked for it fitfully under the dresser, in the drawers, and ultimately all over the house, but I could not find it anywhere. It simply disappeared when Ocean Hill died. The charm was gone.

One of Everard Barrett's activities as math coordinator involved training paraprofessional school aides in the rods so they could assist in classrooms and, if they became competent enough, actually conduct classes. The concept of utilizing the talents of community people in the schools was, I came to discover, a critical part of the Ocean Hill experiment. Their presence was evident everywhere. Some acted as teachers' aides, thus permitting the regular teacher to work with small groups of children or even individual youngsters while the paraprofessionals handled more routine classroom instruction. Some assisted in the library; some supervised and scored testing. In some classrooms pairs of paras conducted classes largely on their own, under the visiting supervision of the subject teacher.

The reason behind this intense involvement of parents and community people in the schools was clear enough. Under circumstances prevailing elsewhere in the city, mothers went off to work as a maid or baby sitter if they could. The junior high school principal I have mentioned, with his quiet and secluded inner sanctum, rarely spoke to a parent. Had he deigned to receive one, the embarrassment would have no doubt been monumental for he would not have known, to borrow a line from Stephen Crane, "that there was a soul before him that needed saving." The parent, in turn, suffering from the helplessness and lack of confidence that result from poverty and ignorance, would have scarcely been able to formulate a question under the circumstances, let alone ask it. But in Ocean Hill funds had been found to pay many parents to serve in schools, thus reducing the traditional exodus to work elsewhere. It was not a question of altruism, though the financial assistance was helpful. The fact is that no school can work unless parents have some understanding of what it is about and are involved in the process to a degree, at least. If the only focus of the Ocean Hill experiment had been a massive effort to plug parents into the schools that would have been half the battle, right then and there.

Mr. Barrett invited me to a training session for paraprofessionals. One morning the following week I met him in one of the top-floor rooms with eight women. He gave each of them a box of rods and started in, beginning with the simple numbering system, explaining one somewhat novel word in his rod vocabulary. The word, which sounded like "tooth," was actually "twoth." It had been introduced to provide a consistency in language. We normally take a "third" of something, or a "fourth" of something, but when we get to a half of something the word "half" doesn't fit the pattern of the other words. So the coined word "twoth" had been substituted, as in "one twoth of six is three."

From this simple introduction Mr. Barrett led the group through increasingly complex problems until by the end of an hour and a half he had them doing rather difficult improper fractions and algebra that children would normally get only in the ninth grade. With one exception, everyone followed him extremely well. The exception was an older woman who struck me as being either below average in intelligence or perhaps so locked into traditional ways of figuring that a new approach was no longer possible for her. It was clear that with some practice the rest would be able to work with children in a very short time.

After the session Mr. Barrett invited me to sit in on a prep period with two of his fully trained paras who would be conducting a class of their own afterward, two young black men dressed in Afro style, Jonathan Clark and Robert Saunders. I had seen the pair before a number of times — in and out of the district offices, on the street, sometimes with groups of children. Their presence, activity, and visibility reminded me of Joe Brown in an earlier spring. Together they taught a third grade math class. I came to think of them as the Gemini of the district. Mr. Barrett and the Gemini discussed where the class stood and what problems might be presented to the children. Since Jonathan was to be the principal teacher after the bell rang, Mr. Barrett suggested they engage in some role-playing by way of rehearsal with him and Robert pretending to be students. Jonathan presented his opening problems. The presentation was rudely interrupted by Robert and Everard raising their hands in the roles of students:

"Say, teacher, did you say two threeths of the three rods or three twoths of the two rod?"

"What did you say?"

"Jimmy has my three rods."

"Teach, what did you say for us to do? I didn't hear what you said, teach."

"Can I go to the bathroom?"

Jonathan handled these fungoes adroitly. Then the bell rang. The third graders straggled in and took their places at small desks. Jonathan started the lesson off as planned, and it became quickly evident that the children possessed a thorough grasp of the rods and how to use them in solving the problems Jonathan and Robert presented. The two worked well as a team with Jonathan laying out the problems at the blackboard while Robert circulated quietly among the children to help with any hang-ups that developed. I did not know what these two young men earned as paraprofessionals, but I doubted it was very much, certainly well below what an accredited teacher could command. However they did have a class that was clearly going somewhere under their expert direction, and it struck me that in doing this they were making it, too, in another way, a better way than pushing carts of dresses or bolts of cloth downtown in the garment district, or pumping gas somewhere, which certainly would have paid more immediately but which just as surely would lead to a dead end. On this turf of education Jonathan and Robert were somebody, two young men looking out instead of falling in a darkening hole that has no bottom. The Gemini later went on to become students at the University of Massachusetts with McCoy's help.

Half a dozen rubble-ridden blocks from 178 stood another district elementary school, P.S. 144, which housed in several

large corner rooms on the top floor one of the most remarkable
math labs in the whole city. The space was brightly illuminated by the natural sunlight which streamed in warm and un-
obstructed through the big classroom windows, as it did in most
of the upper-floor classrooms in the Ocean Hill schools, because
what was a low-profile neighborhood to begin with had become
even more so thanks to urban removal. The lab was run by five
cluster teachers, and its presiding genius was a white teacher
who could scarcely have been more than five feet tall named
Steve Rothstein. In a school system run almost entirely on
specifications, I naturally wondered how such a diminutive individual could have qualified. This inventive young man had
filled the lab with a variety of inventions of which he was the
principal designer, inventions which the other teachers had
helped to construct and which children could explore, manipu-
late, and learn from. One area contained a makeshift "grocery
store" with an adding machine and a small counter behind
which stood whatever child happened to be the store's "proprietor" for a particular class. Inside the store were shelves lined
with dummy produce — milk cartons, cans of soups and vegeta-
bles, simulated loaves of bread, cans of coffee, boxes of cereals,
each item marked with its own price. Children, individually or
sometimes in small groups, visited the store with play money
and gave orders to the clerk, who added them up, took the
money, and made change — a practical lesson in arithmetic.
Across the room stood a clock pendulum and a darkroom timer
for clocking the swings of the pendulum depending on where
its weight was fixed, as with a metronome. A third part of the
lab featured vials of different sizes and sand to fill them so that
a child could make his own set of metric weights and, on a
makeshift balance, weigh various objects.

But the pièce de résistance of the laboratory was a genuine
electronic computer that Steve had constructed from cardboard,
wires, and tiny light bulbs. It was a digital machine with 10
rows of lights, each row containing 10 bulbs. The "input" was

handled with an ordinary telephone dial. If one dialed o (representing the number 10) the lights would flash on in sequence from the bottom of the first column to the top, which remained lit. If o were dialed again, the bottom light in the second column would be illuminated, indicating 10 times 10, or 100. So one could dial on up to 1000, 10,000, 100,000, 1,000,000, et cetera. Which left still quite a few columns to go and some really mind-bending numbers to think about.

Early in my explorations of the district the question of where one might find a noontime snack had come up and I had asked Sylvia Betty, McCoy's senior stenographer, what the sandwich prospects in the neighborhood were. She replied that the answer to that was singular and consisted of a luncheonette down on Rockaway Avenue at the far end of the housing development, about three blocks away. I left the district offices as directed and turned left. On my right was P.S. 178 with its large playground, about half of which was occupied by a dozen "portables," the temporary huts used by the city to provide extra classroom space for overcrowded schools. Given the city's penchant for securing its property in the provinces, the name was something of a euphemism. For these huts — prefabricated structures large enough to contain two full-sized classrooms — were also firmly anchored to the asphalt playground on cinder blocks. As one Board of Education man remarked to me one day: "If we ever have to pick up one of those damn pillboxes and try and cart it down the city streets, God help us!" The whole playground area, secured by a cyclone fence ten or a dozen feet high, had a street entrance complete with a small wooden guard house. Visitors came and went through a large gate as did selected automobiles, since there was ample room behind the huts to serve as a parking lot for people with business there. From time to time I was to see Mr. Barrett's Citroën on the playground. And in the weeks ahead, as my visits became more frequent and my need for a car rather than the subway more urgent, it became my parking lot as well.

Since P.S. 178 was no longer an overcrowded school, the portables had been taken over by the district for more urgent needs and now formed the headquarters for what was known as the Community Education Center. Here was housed a variety of activities related to home reading, classroom adjustment, family service, adult education, day care, preschool programs, career guidance, Spanish and Afro studies, and a newspaper and photography unit. The center extended its services into the community via a number of storefront operations concerned with drug addiction, counseling, and the like so that all kinds of services, abilities, and skills in the district were delivered at street level and by the same token the needs and requirements of the community fed back into the C.E.C. On my left in the next block loomed the big brick windowless school which I had thought looked something like the old Bastille, I.S. 55, the school my Board of Education guide of a few years back had said people in the area hated. Despite its formidable appearance I still liked it. I turned left past the school and could see the luncheonette two blocks away. With the now-familiar crunch of glass heralding my approach, I entered the place slowly and warily, not knowing quite what to expect or how to behave.

Along the left-hand wall were typical stainless steel delicatessen refrigeration compartments with sliding glass doors which displayed and provided access to the contents arrayed on shelves within — a variety of sodas, colas, milk, and beer. The small floor area in the middle of the luncheonette accommodated half a dozen tables. The right-hand wall was occupied by a small cigarette-and-candy stall which also held the check-out cash register and from there to the back of the store stretched a serving counter with stools which included a steam table, grille, and carving board for slicing hot meats, like boiled ham and pastrami. Later on, after I became better acquainted with the establishment, I discovered there was a toilet near the back end of the counter, a pay phone with an Out of Order sign on it, and a small shelf holding half a dozen assorted padlocks at least three times as large and probably many more times as tough as any I have ever seen for locking up the place in the evening. The pay phone, one learned on becoming a regular customer, actually worked. The sign was there to discourage strangers who might pretend to be using it while jimmying the coin box when no one was looking.

I sat down at the counter. Across the wall behind it was a long yellow panel with black lettering common to most New York delicatessens listing all the sandwiches, platters, and beverages the establishment offered along with the prices. The menu was about as varied as one might have expected downtown. As a stranger in Ocean Hill I felt far removed from such amenities and so did not quite know how to respond to the offerings, whether to assume what was listed could actually be provided or whether this was merely appearance, a facade to suggest options in a province where options had largely vanished. I decided to take the place at face value so I ordered a hot pastrami sandwich on rye bread. Then I went over to the cooler to find a bottle of beer, not anticipating too many choices. The labels immediately indicated that virtually all the goodies were there — Heineken's, Lowenbraü, Michelob, Beck's. I took a bottle of Heineken's back to the counter, found waiting there as nicely stuffed a pastrami sandwich as one could hope for anywhere, put some mustard on it, began to eat, relax a bit, and look around.

The proprietor was a tough old Italian who worked behind the counter with two young assistants. One was his son; the other a young black man. The parade of neighborhood kids that usually streams in and out of such a place was very much in evidence, in this instance mostly black and Puerto Rican with an occasional white youngster mixed in. They exited clutching soda, Devil Dogs, peanuts, Oreos, potato chips, french fries, and assorted other stuff that kids like or are permitted to buy. Over the parade the stern old proprietor cast a no-nonsense, no-stealing glance of vigilance which the youngsters clearly respected. Some of the lunchtime customers were obviously teachers from I.S. 55 or P.S. 178. A few had one or several pupils with them, a special social event which I later observed occurred most frequently on Friday as the school week drew to a close. These groups usually ordered sandwiches or whatever from the counter and carried them to one of the tables, a more sociable situation than lining up on the counter stools. Other adults came and went, but on a first visit I could not tell how the clientele broke down.

I became a steady customer at the luncheonette, having breakfast there as well when I came into the city to attend some particularly early classes in the schools. People felt free to join others at any table that happened to offer an unoccupied chair in this necessarily informal setting, so the luncheonette provided an opportunity for casual conversations with persons one might not have otherwise met and served as a kind of "off-campus" social club. One day I found myself at the same table with a tall, thin, and striking-looking young black man in his twenties. We began to talk a bit, since we'd seen one another around, and I learned his name was Paul Chandler.

"What do you do in the district?" I asked.

"Well, I'm one of the local militants. What are you doing here? I've seen you around for some time now."

"I'm trying to do a story for *Look* on what these schools are all about."

"I guess I heard about that." (As I thought about it, I realized probably almost everybody had, after a time. The word was "on the wire," so to speak). "What do you think of the schools here?"

"I think that's it. The pieces of it anyway. And I hope the story will get over what this is really all about for a change. What do you do, when you're not being a militant, that is?"

I had to ask the question because it was completely evident that this young man was *not* a militant, at least by the television definition of the word. He spoke in a soft and modulated voice. He was civilized, cultivated, and clearly intelligent and well educated. Obviously he was not rabid.

"I worked on Wall Street in a brokerage firm for some time and was doing very well there, but now I've slipped into a part-time job that pays my way but gives me time to work out here. This community needs all the help it can get. So I do whatever I can. If I have to stomp and shout and do my Mau Mau act when those television cats get here I'll do that. It's a kind of reverse Uncle Tomming, but they seem to dig that and I figure maybe if I can get a word in edgewise for the community on TV it beats just mumbling around."

On another occasion I met John O'Neill, a person I had heard about who had been Albert Shanker's right-hand man in the teachers' union before the showdown with the demonstration districts. He was tall, thin, and pink-complexioned with black hair that had begun to gray at the temples, as Irish-looking as his name. He had broken with Shanker over the school squabble, taking the position that the union should support Ocean Hill rather than wipe it out. He lost and was banished to the district, or perhaps McCoy had taken him in. I don't know which. In any case, he was now an assistant principal at I.S. 55. I asked him what had happened.

"Well, I felt it was not right, not morally right, to stamp out the districts because of this conflict over who really controlled teachers, whom they owed their allegiance to. I felt the district had a right to raise questions, to judge teachers in fact, as to whether they were delivering something to kids out here. In fact, I felt that taking that into account would be good for the union in the long run, that the union should open itself up and become concerned with the kinds of real teaching problems we have out here. I felt that maybe it would be smarter for the union to face questions about the qualifications of its members for teaching in schools like these. Maybe get with McCoy and try to develop something like that. But Al felt threatened, I guess. He felt that if all of a sudden he let other people ask questions about the qualifications of the membership, then that would blow the union."

"It seems to me it would make more sense," I said, "if the union itself recognized a serious question was on the agenda about delivering the goods. Wouldn't it be all the smarter to let the cat out of the bag and go after the question yourself, rather than let someone else chase it around?"

"I thought so, but Al felt that if you bring something like that up, you're raising the question of other people judging your whole operation. Then maybe you end up negotiating teacher contracts all over the city with different school districts instead of with the Board of Education down there, where you get a uniform contract for everybody."

"Sure. But maybe there should be some outside judgment, outside pressure."

"Okay, but it's an awful lot easier to negotiate a blanket contract with headquarters than with thirty or forty school boards, as to what the qualifications are and so on."

"Well, but what about the delivery question? Who's teaching kids in a place like this? What? How? Why? It strikes me that's a problem a blanket contract can't possibly cover. Or maybe you could still have the contract and yet raise qualification questions under it."

"The problem is there's power in a blanket contract. Big power in a city as big as this, and Al Shanker opted for power. That's why he's downtown at headquarters, and I'm back in my old role as an assistant principal in the New York City school system."

There was no bitterness in John O'Neill's voice, only the faint trace of a deep and apparently hopeless moral sadness.

I left the luncheonette and started up the street toward I.S. 55, bumping into Father John Powis along the way. He was pastor of the Roman Catholic Presentation Church nearby, had been in Ocean Hill a long time, and was a member of the governing board of the district. He was, or so I judged from several brief conversations we had had in McCoy's office, a rather severely radicalized young white priest, though this was not apparent in his quiet, almost diffident manner. He was a small man with a slightly owlish but otherwise unremarkable face, short sandy hair, and a very white, almost sallow complexion, as though he had been held prisoner in a tenement basement for years. I had heard he was almost never to be found at the church, though I assumed he conducted religious services on appropriate occasions. I had the impression he had come to regard the saving of souls as something of an indulgence in this ground-down ghetto where simply surviving in the present life was a tenuous, day-by-day affair. He circulated about the streets and in and out of the district office wearing faded slacks and an old sport jacket, cradling a large and well-stuffed manila packet under one arm. The packet contained papers, forms, blanks, and petitions of all sorts relating to his Christian duties as he perceived them under the circumstances — trying to prevent evictions, getting slumlords to make repairs to buildings so families could survive in them, relocating people and finding housing for new arrivals, explaining how to get services from the city bureaucracy, where jobs might be found and of what kind. Father Powis was, in effect, a walking Community Information Manual. If for any reason one wished to find him, standing on any corner in the area for a few hours would have been the most efficient way of doing so.

We chatted briefly. I expressed some feelings that had been building up with consequent hopes for a good story in *Look*.

"They'll never publish it," the priest said in a completely flat voice.

"What do you mean?" The thought fairly spooked me since there had never been the slightest question as to the validity of the assignment.

"Look at that." Father Powis pointed to a large truck parked beside I.S. 55 with a cargo of teaching materials to be delivered there.

"This is a billion-dollar business you're trying to buck. Many billions. Try if you want to, but you'll never make it. There's too much money on the line. They will get to them."

By "they" he obviously meant the people involved in the education business. By "them" he just as obviously meant the magazine, so he was suggesting that the powerful "they" could somehow put the quietus on "them," the journalists. I shook my head. I could not believe the man. I was convinced that journalism was alive and well in the U.S.A. I felt that perhaps Father Powis, who certainly had a far deeper perception of life in this desolate Brooklyn wasteland than I, who walked its streets day after day in a dehumanizing and suffocating atmosphere of broken dreams, abandoned hopes, and crushed aspirations, had himself become infected in the depths of his soul with the despair that hung listlessly in the air.

I walked up the block and entered, at last, the bastille school to meet its principal, Percy Jenkins. If I ever had the job of casting a black man for the lead role in I Am a Fugitive from a Chain Gang I would immediately select Percy. He was a big, hulking man with broad shoulders, fierce features, a glistening and close-cropped skull which, when outdoors, was topped with a mashed-down porkpie hat. From him emanated a resonant and commandeering voice. If the casting required a person of simple animalistic energy only, however, there would have been a problem of concealing Percy's other qualities. This strapping black man's physical appearance did not mask his great sense of soul, or his intelligence. Instead of issuing directives from the sanctuary of his office, he ranged and raged continually throughout the school like a bull in a china shop. Yet he never broke or even bruised the contents, namely the children and teachers. New York City has about 1000 schools, give or take a few, and so has about that many principals.

Among that number are what? A dozen, maybe two dozen, great ones? Whatever that limited number might be, Percy Jenkins has to come close to the top of the list — for a variety of simple but fundamental reasons. There were nearly 2000 children in I.S. 55. I followed Percy in his rounds for quite a few days as he visited classrooms, checked on programs, and confronted one child or another. Gradually I came to realize that he knew every child, or just about every child, in the school by name. Not only that, he also knew quite a bit about how each youngster was doing, what problems had come up, what was being done or not being done about them. More often than not he knew something about the kid's family as well — a far cry from what one young black man had told me about the principal of his ghetto school: "You're lucky if you see those cats two times a year, once when school opens and the second time at graduation exercises. If you see them more than that, it means some teacher has sent you to the office to get your ass chewed out."

I noticed that Percy, in the course of his day, chewed out quite a few black asses, but he knew exactly whom he was chewing on and why and he never drew blood. It was always in the interest of some positive encouragement rather than the typical put-down, "You're a bad kid and you better shape up." I asked Percy how many really disturbed and troublesome youngsters he had in the school.

"I have about ninety-seven," he said, "and with a little extra help and attention I think they, most of them, can make it. But I'm not sure we can get them all through."

With a school population of nearly 2000 that expectation was so far above normal as to be dumbfounding. Yet I believed it to be a hardheaded assessment, because Percy Jenkins struck me as a very hardheaded man.

In trying to locate Percy on any particular day I naturally dropped by the office first to inquire after him, usually to hear an uncertain "He's somewhere in the building, I think." After spending some time there I observed that one or another youngster was indeed "sent down" to be reprimanded from time to time. One day I personally ran aground on one such obstreperous boy, a real smart ass. He was in the office though I didn't notice at first, as I reached over one of the little gates to release the latch and let myself in. The boy, a Puerto Rican, appeared from nowhere and pushed the gate shut. Then he looked up at me with an expression that clearly said: "Oh, golly gee, I didn't know you wanted in." It was an obvious put-on. I removed his hand from the gate, opened it, and walked in, at the same time affecting a cringing body movement suggesting I had barely escaped the clutches of a terrifying monster who acted as the gatekeeper. Not finding Percy, I turned to leave. The boy saw the move and I saw the boy. I opened the gate and made a sweeping "after you, Alfonse" gesture. At this his character changed immediately. He drew back, assumed the self-contained air of a small but emerging personality, and said in a quiet and dignified voice: "No, please, you go first." I clasped him on the shoulder in a parting gesture of recognition.

Percy Jenkins simply did not accept having children sent down for disruptive behavior. On this particular day the teacher of the Puerto Rican boy was himself called down for sending the boy down. The teacher was a tall, lanky, and very Nordic young man named Jeff Nilson. Percy read Jeff the riot act:

"You lost your cool, sending that kid down here."

"I know that," Jeff said, "but he's a complete put-on. If I had him on a one-to-one basis he'd be the greatest." (A fact I could have attested to myself.) "But he comes on so strong he throws the whole class out. So what do you want me to do, forget the rest of the class?"

"Just try and do better, that's all."

"Okay, I'll try."

"Okay, that's all I'm asking."

Percy, when I could catch up with him, became my philosophical guide to I.S. 55 in terms of explaining programs, educational ideas, the running of the school, and so forth. Though he was continually on the prowl — something he considered an absolute necessity and his duty — he made time available for us to talk, sometimes remaining long after school for the purpose. This was a real gesture on his part since considering the way he managed the school he must have been exhausted by three o'clock. Still, he was a big man with a strong constitution, and he was proud of his school, his children, his teachers, and his programs. Once he perceived I really wanted to understand what was going on, he found time for discussion. Judging from the nuances of our various conferences, he had come to regard me as a rare visitor, and I certainly got the impression that almost no one else had taken the time to explore the school fully. Yet a school with 2000 students, 100 teachers, and a whole assortment of programs is a complex organism to say the least. One has to come to know people, both students and teachers, to get a feeling of it. I required patience and even indulgence from Percy and everyone else if I were to acquire some reasonable understanding of the school, and Percy sensed this.

In the course of our conversations I asked the man about a piece that had appeared in *The New York Times Magazine* by one of the most reputable figures on the New York education scene, an article devoted mostly to behind-the-scenes operations that developed in setting up the Ocean Hill experiment. In it Rhody McCoy appeared as a rather devious and almost Machiavellian character, the Reverend Oliver came across as inscrutable and even perverse, and Father Powis seemed to hover over the whole experiment like a white Rasputin who concealed under his spreading clerical habit the seeds of some mysterious conspiracy, though his church had been identified as about the only legitimate local institution qualifying as an acceptable conduit for money from the Ford Foundation. One put down the article feeling "a plague upon both your houses," and I asked Percy why nothing much had been said about the schools:

"That son of a bitch!" he snorted. "He spent one day here, asked what kinds of programs we had going, and then went off and wrote that crappy thing about the district. You can't just make some kind of a list of programs and evaluate a school that way, even if you've been in the system a long time. Look, man, suppose I got six 'programs,' right? And suppose five of the six teachers I got running them are schmucks. Then have I got six programs, whatever the hell that means, or haven't I? These cats just move words around, man, like here we got this and there we got that, and never know what they really got. I *know* what I've got. I've had three years to do it. I've got a good staff. That cat Jeff Nilson, the one I chewed his ass out the other day, he's beautiful. He cares about his kids. He works hard with them. And that little bastard that bugged him so [Percy laughed], that kid is one of the smartest kids in this school. Jeff knows that. I know that. I know that kid can drive you right up the walls. But that kid can go somewhere, too, if he'll just cool it a little. So Jeff gets mad at the kid, and I get mad at Jeff. Forget it. It's the kid that counts — and we both know that."

Percy escorted me along a corridor to the opposite side of the building to show me a facility he was justifiably proud of — the school library. It was a large, well-illuminated, and spacious area the size of about three classrooms, with open shelves along the walls containing a large assortment of the hardcover books one might expect in a good intermediate school, suitably organized according to subject. There were reading tables and one area of the big room was set aside as an audio-visual center where youngsters could view film strips or listen to recordings with ear phones so as not to disturb anyone else. Several tables contained assorted magazines which were presumably appropriate reading material for intermediate students in New York

City. I could not help noticing one cover in particular: *Better Homes and Gardens*. One could easily interpret such an incongruity as a deliberate put-down of the natives in this bleak province, to remind them of where they were at. Rather, as I learned later, the standardized librarians of the city's middle-class oriented school system selected their own periodicals, which frequently included magazines they felt would be of interest to middle-class teachers. Either way the end result was the same. Aside from open shelves and some incongruous offerings there was a novel aspect to the library which, I could see, was the source of Percy's pride in this large warm-hearted room. The shelves contained literally thousands of paperback books. I asked how they came to be there.

"Well, we have some freedom under Rhody, you know. I've got a budget for library books. Normally I'd have to buy what the Board of Ed is selling, hardcover and expensive, like *Dick and Jane* books. You know? Crap like that." He laughed. "Well, I do buy a lot of reference books I figure the kids can use, but I also invested a big chunk of the budget in all kinds of paperbacks, several copies of each in some cases, so we have everything the curriculum needs but other stuff as well. Like six copies of *Soul on Ice*, for instance, though they've probably all disappeared by now." Percy chuckled.

"What do you mean, 'disappeared?' Do kids steal books from the library?"

"That's the whole point of the paperbacks. They're cheap. Kids steal them. So what? Do you know what it means when a kid steals a book? It probably means he's reading it. And when he's through with it somebody else out there will be reading it. So what does that mean? It means reading's back in style. How did Malcolm X learn to read?"

"He got fascinated with a dictionary in prison," I said. "Ruined his eyesight doing it."

"Right. So if you learn by reading *Soul* or whatever, it doesn't matter. You're reading. I don't mind losing paperbacks, because I figure some cat's out there with that dog-eared book learning something. The more he learns, the more good he may be to my school one day. What the hell's a school for, anyway?"

We had left the library and crossed back to Percy's office. A moment later the 3 P.M. bell rang. Percy ambled over to a coat rack in the corner and put on his coat, clamped a porkpie hat on his head, and anchored a large pipe in his mouth.

"Time to hit the street," he said.

I followed him out of the office and down the broad corridor to the main entrance of I.S. 55 which, like the nearby housing development, was guarded by a privately employed black policeman. He never questioned me on my many visits to the school or other adults, either, and as far as I could tell, his main duties were to maintain order among the flocks of kids who piled exuberantly in and out of the building and to make sure those who entered belonged there. Out on the sidewalk Percy patrolled his turf — a daily ritual of his at opening and closing time. He made his rounds vigorously, breaking up scuffles, settling disputes, and quashing an occasional spontaneous crap game. But his main concern was controlling marauding bands of high school students who sporadically invaded the district with an eye to conning younger children out of something, some loose change perhaps, either through a fast-shuffling card game or a quick but menacing confrontation, or who hoped to inveigle them into dope, or recruit them for one nefarious scheme or another. Percy considered himself responsible for his charges even after they were out of school and on the street. He watched over them as they disappeared in groups down the side streets of the area. After that there was little more he could do. Often, of course, something in the neighborhood waylaid one group or another, like one of the numerous abandoned houses — more than enough to go around — which could become an instant club to play in for a while and explore, providing a setting for any number of games which children can dream up on the spot. There are advantages to be found in a disadvantaged neighborhood like Ocean Hill, but this was one of the few I ever saw or heard about.

After the street scene faded out, I returned with Percy to his office, and he took the time to explain one of the less tangible aspects of his school. He had actually divided I.S. 55 into four subschools to get at more individualized instruction. He was working toward a completely nongraded system so youngsters could progress at their own speed, advancing quickly in areas where they were strong, moving more slowly and comfortably where they needed extra support. The usual practice was to sort children out so that the so-called "bright kids" attended advanced classes whereas the slower ones were confined to other tracks. That system was, as Percy observed, the perfect put-down:

"What does that say to a kid? The kid knows what it says. It says: 'You're a dummy. Everybody in the school knows that. That's why we've put you in this class — dummy.' Oh, nobody comes out and says it overtly, you know. But that's the effect, and the kid gets the message. More often than not it simply helps confirm an attitude he has secretly held for a long time anyway. Only now it's out in the open. He knows it. But what's much worse than that, his classmates now know it, too. Though it may not really be true at all, and likely isn't, the kid will believe it's true. That may be the first and the last positive thing he learns all the time he's in school. 'Cause from there on it's nothing but straight down and out."

With Percy's blessing I set out to explore a number of individual classrooms and situations in the school. One of my first encounters was with a young white man whose style was completely in contrast to Gene Aptekar's. Jay Schoenfeld conducted a lively sixth grade social studies class, mostly boys. When I say "conducted" I mean this in the orchestral sense. He presided over the youngsters like an authoritative, baton-waving maestro, and the decibel level in his classroom was

high. But so was the interest level. Mr. Schoenfeld's style was
to encourage his youngsters to get interested in what they were
studying, get involved, get with it, and talk it out — and so begin
to open up and learn something. We had a brief talk after one
such session, and I asked him how he had managed to get the
whole band playing together so well:

"It took me two years. Like a lot of young men who came
here new, new teachers, wanting to try something, it took me
two years to learn how I as an individual could work with these
kids. I've learned that now, I think, though there are always
new things to learn. Now I know how to get my kids to respond, to go on. And you know something? Something I'm trying to get over to them? Let me back off a minute. There are a
lot of nowhere teachers in the school system, right? Well I
want my kids, when they leave here, not to settle for that. I
think I'm a pretty good teacher now, though I could be a lot better. But we're moving. When my kids leave me I want them to
know what a teacher is and not to settle for some ordinary deadbeat. So when they hit a deadbeat they'll know it's *his* fault,
not *their* fault. So they'll know enough within themselves not
to get brainwashed into that failure scene. I want them to bug
that bummer if they draw him — or her or whatever it is. If
they leave this class knowing that, they'll have some feeling of
how to get on, play little games with teachers if they have to,
but believe in themselves and so get through. I want my kids
to get through."

Months later I heard stories second-hand which supposedly
emanated from several high schools in the city about Ocean
Hill graduates — that they were contentious, disruptive, un-
ruly, and poor students. Some of the stories were patently absurd since one high school mentioned was in such a far corner
of the city as to be virtually inaccessible from central Brooklyn.
But others were not. I imagined that the expectations which
Jay Schoenfeld and other kindred teachers had aroused in their
pupils had simply boiled over when they encountered one or

another "bummer" later on down the line, someone quite satisfied with nonteaching the way it was and always had been. Infecting young people with the idea that there might be such a thing as students' rights, the right to a good teacher in this instance, can start an epidemic which is very difficult to bring under control. Of course, these rumors were circulated to suggest that the Ocean Hill graduates were academically unprepared, that they had been coddled and cottoned to and so didn't quite cut the mustard when it came to the rigorous requirements of Academe. And when the elementary schools of Ocean Hill were tested, a year after the experiment, it was discovered much to the system's amazement (and satisfaction) that the children had scored worse than would have been expected if the experiment had never occurred at all. Well, if a kid starts out with nothing, and then you give him something, something quite exciting for a time, and then you take it away, what response should you expect? To me, these results seemed more like proof of accomplishment than the opposite. The pious and absurd misinterpretations, springing from a belief in the God-given grace of the system, sounded like the self-congratulatory pleasantries exchanged by vigilantes on breaking up after a hanging:

"Well, guess that's that."

"Sure is. Right enough, too."

"Right enough if you ask me."

"He was a mean one all right."

"Had it coming. Saw it coming all along."

"Yeah. Saw that."

"Well, he's dead as a doornail now."

"That's for damn sure."

"Real dead."

"Guilty as sin, he was."

"Must of been."

"Whaddaya mean, 'must of been'?"

"Well, otherwise we wouldn't of hung him, would we?"

One large classroom in I.S. 55 was devoted to the teaching of typing and contained several dozen practice typewriters. It also contained, across the back wall, the beginnings of a mural which, once completed, would be nearly twenty feet long and about eight feet high. The centerpiece was already painted. It was a black panther, big and grand, with piercing, glowing eyes that almost impaled the viewer, contrasting strongly with the dark yet carefully and accurately modeled face. Around the panther, covering the rest of the panel, were sketches of other cat motifs which had yet to take on form and color. From the scale alone it was clear that the creator of this spectacle was a budding artist who was really beginning to open up. He was a student named George Pender and his latent talent had been discovered by the typing teacher, which explained the presence of his spectacular offering in that unlikely setting. And why not? Why shouldn't the typing teacher discover a kid with artistic gifts, if the whole temper of a school is to find out what kids have instead of posting on a bulletin board or storing in school records the accomplishments they lack?

Around the school George Pender was known as "Tiger Boy," because he loved to draw and paint tigers, panthers, and the other big cats. I met him in the hall one day carrying a portfolio of his sketches and paintings and, in a small room, he showed them to me, shyly at first. As one who has lived with cats for some years and observed their remarkable qualities, I could readily see how accurate his own perceptions of cats were, especially in the details not easily discerned if you don't dig cats. The paws were correct. The tails were right, so were the expressions and the whole feline feeling. George was good all right. He told me he made frequent trips to the zoo just to watch and sketch the big cats there. One painting showed a leopard lying on a platform, looking out from its cage with one paw draped languidly over the edge of the shelf. At the bottom was the caption:

Do you think the cat is happy in the zoo?

I complimented George on his work, not to flatter or encourage him, which I think is a silly way to behave with children, but because it was so clearly evident how well he saw the cats. George was pleased, because I saw what he'd seen, too. On that basis we were essentially equals, the supposed child and the alleged man. A bit of George's reticence left him, and he presumed to ask me a question:

"What do you think about their putting big cats like these in zoos?"

"Well, I don't think they should be there."

"Why?"

"Well, what do you think?"

"I think they should be free to run in the wild."

"How come you paint cats?" I asked.

"I like to go to the zoo. I just sit there and watch them. I like them. And when they move or just lay there I make sketches and bring them back to the house and work on them."

"Well, if all of them were free and none of them were in zoos to look at, what would you think about that?"

"I would rather go watch them where they live, see what they really do." The boy hesitated. "But I guess I can't do that."

"Well, maybe that's why they have some cats in zoos."

"Yes, maybe. But I don't like to look at cats in zoos."

Afterward I asked Percy Jenkins about George.

"That kid has talent. You can see it. You saw it, you said. He has problems, too. His family is poor, terribly poor. You know, some kids don't feel poverty. It just runs off their backs like water off a duck. They accept it. That's the way it is. But George sees it. He knows his family is poor. Hopeless. Stuck. And he's smart enough to see the contrast. Like stuff on TV about making out, flying off somewhere, stuff like that. George sees that. So poverty, being poor, hurts him, and every day that kid comes to school with a big ball of hurt inside."

Percy shook his head, thinking about it.

"That kid digs cats, right? You know what that kid would

like to do? He'd like to go down to the Amazon and really see
those cats in the wild, right? See them. That's what he'd like.
But he knows in his soul he's just poor George Pender, poor boy
in Brooklyn, who can never do that. And it tears that kid apart,
because he wonders why he can't."

One of the mainstays of the I.S. 55 teaching staff was a highly
qualified reading teacher in the form of a young, blond, and
willowy lady named Becky Taylor who had been attracted to
Ocean Hill from the outside because of the experiment in progress. Aside from professional qualifications, she came to
Brooklyn with a unique personal one as well — an unmistakable North Carolina accent. If Percy Jenkins, the ship's captain, was ideal for the role of a chain gang fugitive, Becky Taylor could just as easily have played the lead part of the
wide-eyed, fearful yet strong flower of white Southern woman-
hood in my imaginary melodrama of agonizing conflict and sus-
pense. Except that this was not a remake of D. W. Griffith's
Birth of a Nation. Here there was no conflict whatever.
Among the many fine and decent human relationships which
flowered as a consequence of the experiment, that between
Becky and Percy stood out because of the quality of apprecia-
tion, confidence, and trust that was so immediately apparent.

The kids dug Becky Taylor's "down home" accent immediately. Most of their parents and relatives were refugees from
the South, displaced persons uprooted by an agricultural revolution. She did not trade on this asset, but it was astonishing to
watch this slim, soft-spoken young woman working with young
people who, I knew, could tear a classroom apart if a teacher
turned them off. Not even the most mellifluous and homelike
voice in the world could have prevented that. Becky Taylor's
quiet and seemingly casual relationship with her students was
made possible by the fact that she knew what she was doing
and was a master at it. It was apparent to the students that her
whole effort and attention was focused on them, that the class

was a mutual enterprise devoted to success. The room was quiet as all individuals worked together. As I sat in a corner and watched the scene I got the point, almost as if a voice from the wall beside me had suddenly whispered: "They are all going to make it together or else they aren't. That includes the teacher as much as any of the children. And that is what they all know together."

Becky Taylor's pupils were girls, half a full class that was divided while someone else took the boys. She worked with a paraprofessional, Miss Tucker, and had the room arranged so that a number of activities could proceed simultaneously. While Miss Tucker worked with a group of girls in various ways, like playing Scrabble at a big table as a spelling exercise, individual students did other things. These included arranging books in the class "library" — a section of a small supply closet off the main room that had been converted for this function — reading or writing stories at the smaller tables in the classroom, or using a typewriter set up in one corner. Becky herself worked with one or another subgroup and periodically had sessions with individual students at her small desk in another corner of the room where she kept a progress chart on each child. During that period pupils would come to her desk, and she would have each girl read a story aloud to her. Then she would quiz her about the story, going into it rather thoroughly as she gauged word recognition, comprehension, and other skills.

On one of the last days of school she gathered the girls together at the big table and they had a seminar, discussing what had been good or bad about the school year, what they had accomplished or failed to accomplish, how things might be improved. There was not the slightest intimation of what "you have failed to achieve." Rather it was what "we" have managed or not, all together. They reviewed their working methods as a group and made plans for improvement next fall.

Becky Taylor anticipated following through with her class in the coming year to maintain continuity, presuming that "next year" would actually come.

I was curious as to how Percy Jenkins had become a principal at all since I knew he was the only fully accredited one in the Ocean Hill school district. The others were assistant principals whom McCoy had selected for the top positions in their respective schools. With one exception they were either black or Puerto Rican, which McCoy felt was important for the experiment. The exception was David Lee, a Chinese gentleman, who ran P.S. 178. This move of McCoy's had originally incensed the Council of Supervisors and Administrators, the city's union of principals, because of the long waiting list of accredited candidates, virtually all of them white. McCoy had been adamant in his demand because practically all the children in his district were black or Puerto Rican. His argument was too reasonable to be denied, and Dr. Bernard Donovan, superintendent of schools at the time, agreed the waiting list could be suspended in this instance. The council went along "for the time being." Considering that only seven out of a thousand principalities were involved, it was no great concession.

"I had to prepare myself for those exams, you know," Percy said when I asked about his status. "Shoo man! They were something else! For weeks I drove to the school I was in then and back home again with a couple of dozen cards stuck on the dashboard with questions I knew I had to memorize the answers to. Like: 'Who wrote the *Decameron?*' or, 'Who painted the *Rape of the Sabines?*' or, 'What was Ockham's razor?' Imagine asking that one in this school. 'Who? Wha? I didn't steal it!' Well, I passed. Then I threw all those damn cards away. And I bet you I couldn't answer a single one of those questions today." Percy hesitated. "Well, I'm not so sure that's so. I might remember a couple of them. The point is, does knowing answers to questions like that mean a goddamn thing when it comes to being a good principal in a school like this? Or any school in the whole city for that matter? Does answering questions like that indicate one solitary thing about whether I can handle kids or not? Or understand them, or care about where they are and how they're making out?"

Percy shook his head in disbelief. "You know, there are a lot of fine things in this world that kids should get with — music, art, reading — things we're trying to build up that turn kids on, like Eddie Bonnemere who runs the band and has a lot of kids into music. He wrote a whole musical mass, you know. And like Becky Taylor and the way she handles reading. She's something else. And the whole Gattegno thing I'm building in the school, not only the rods but his 'Words in Color' system that does for reading what the rods do for math, you know? (I didn't know though I found out about it later on.) Gattegno has that set-up over in the next room there. So all this stuff they lay on you and you have to memorize, does that make you a good principal?"

"Well," I said, "that's the kind of thing that would get you a good job in a fancy Anglo-Saxon prep school. Except," I looked the man up and down and then shook my head dubiously, "I don't think you'd ever qualify."

Percy leaned back and laughed heartily: "You're my man!"

In my explorations of the district I gradually became aware of the periodic testing of children throughout the grades in an effort to measure how well they were doing, a major component of an ongoing evaluation of the experiment. I went to see Liz Gebiner, a young woman on McCoy's staff in charge of this activity, to find out what it was about. I had chatted with her casually on several occasions for she was a fixture around headquarters. Liz was thin and stylish, and I had assumed she was a light-skinned black woman, part Indian perhaps because of her finely chiseled features. She had been a teacher in Ocean Hill for about twelve years and was on the scene when the experiment began. She told me she had been a darned good one and I certainly believed her; she was too open and frank a person to have volunteered such information otherwise. Rhody McCoy had made a similar estimation when he took over the schools, and now Liz was a valued member of his staff. Though I had thought she was black she told me later on she was actually of Russian extraction, but did not particularly go out of her way to correct any misperceptions other white people had of her. I suspected Liz had come to feel, after long experience in a ghetto, somewhat black at heart from rooting for the children who passed through her classroom and trying to get them to succeed in spite of a suffocating system she understood all too well. Quite a few white people seemed to develop black heart conditions in Ocean Hill.

Liz explained that McCoy felt the standard achievement tests normally used in the schools were deficient on several counts. For one thing the process took forever, and when the results finally came in all a teacher got back were averages; a third grade child, for example, might score 2.4 in reading and 2.7 in vocabulary, which would be below grade level, but show 3.2 in comprehension, or above grade a bit. Such numbers tell a teacher nothing about why a child is behind here or ahead there. They do not identify any particular difficulties or hangups so that the teacher has no way of knowing what help a specific child needs. McCoy believed testing should benefit the teacher and should make children more accountable to the teacher by providing immediate specific feedback on what a child knew or didn't know, and what the difficulties were. Several university testing experts were brought into the district to design tests which would make this kind of instant replay possible. Paraprofessionals in each school gave the tests to children individually, graded them, and got the results to the teachers the same day. Under Liz's guidance they became sophisticated enough to detect small difficulties individual children were having which would not have been noticed at all otherwise.

At P.S. 73, about ten blocks from McCoy's headquarters and not far from Reverend Oliver's church and the Annex nestled beside it, I sat in on a testing session with second grade children. The tests were administered by a group of paraprofessional ladies who worked in the school in a variety of capacities besides this one and were such an established part of the staff they had their own equivalent of a "teachers' lounge," complete with a coffee urn, comfortable chairs, and other simple amenities. The chief of the group was a woman named Barbara Covington, a neighborhood mother of some experience and skill who was also in charge of the school's testing program. The other women were neighborhood mothers as well. Two of them caught my attention for reasons quite irrelevant to what they were doing. One was Emma Kelly, a slim young lady who was very bright and very black. The other was Glendora Pender (no relation to the artist, George), a large, warm-hearted, and outgoing person who wore dresses so billowy they could have sheltered a small child or two and whose proportionately large head supported an incredible Afro wig that towered nearly a foot in the air like a curly black pagoda. Glendora was, as they say, a sight to behold.

At testing time the paraprofessionals gathered in a vacant room high up and to the rear of this particularly ancient school building and arranged themselves at small tables. Children were brought in by class and each took a seat beside one of the ladies. The paraprofessionals, well trained in the testing materials, then took over. The tests included identifying pie-shaped wedges in terms of what part of a whole pie they represented — a third, a half, a quarter. There were various other math problems. There were language problems, such as deciding whether certain pairs of words that looked alike also sounded alike or different: "cake" and "make" or "cake" and "Coke." The children also identified and pronounced some

rather large words for second graders. One which struck me
like a zap in the head was "stormtrooper." I could
hardly restrain myself from lifting a fist and exclaiming:
"Right on!"

From Liz I also learned a number of things about the test
results. At the beginning of the experiment, programs had been
implemented in the district, as I have mentioned, ranging from
very permissive situations at one end to hard-nosed drill at the
other. Today the laissez faire "Let's see; what's on my mind
today?" approach is in vogue among most of the large, well-established corporations and research institutions which generate
programs and teaching materials for sale to the nation's school
system — the educational-industrial complex, to borrow a
thought from Father Powis, which is a multibillion dollar operation. Like the country's major laundry soap manufacturers the
educational-industrial complex swings in slow, product-
oriented cycles and what is fashionable one year may be un-
mentionable the next — at least if one is to play it safe and
maintain the appropriate edbiz stance and an acceptable status
within the vast matrix. I once confronted a highly respected
member of this pedagogical elite with a description of strict
drill as practiced in the Annex. He threw up his hands in horror at such a fascistic approach to children. I have had similar
reactions from other educators when discussing various hard-
nosed teachers and approaches. Advocating a "fascistic"
schoolhouse would probably lead to ostracism if not actual un-
employment.

The most surprising thing testing revealed was that among all
the factors which appeared significant in contributing to a
child's success in school, by far the least important to the point
of being virtually negligible was what program the child was in.
After I thought the matter over I knew it had to be true and for
the simplest of reasons. If I were a child at P.S. 178 learning
math with the rods and I had Mr. Barrett or Jonathan Clark or
Robert Saunders as my teacher, I could hardly help succeed-

ing. But if I were in my sister-in-law's school with a teacher who was trying to work with the rods but didn't really understand their value, I would simply goof around childishly and get nowhere. Similarly if I were a kindergartner drilling with Engelmann materials, but did not have the likes of Mrs. Holloway for a drillmistress, I would fail. Clearly it would be the teacher who made the difference, not the program. In fact, Liz told me about one typical middle-aged black woman who was a stern traditionalist and wanted nothing to do with any experiment whatever, yet whose class scored quite high in achievement. Though she was severe with her children, she was impartially insistent about one thing: that they master the work and get on with it. Some of them rebelled and asked to be transferred to other classes, knowing there were other options in the wind. Most had second thoughts, however, and fearful that they might draw a new teacher of less caustic merit, returned to the old austerity regimen which Carol Gibson offered relentlessly. They knew Miss Gibson would demand that they not fail, be nagging, and sometimes abrasive about it. She would insist that they succeed, and the children appreciated that.

So, in the end, it all boiled down to the teachers. It also boiled up with unfortunate consequences, for the tests showed that some classes did better than others in comparable situations and with comparable materials. This led to the inescapable conclusion that some teachers were able to deliver whereas others were incapable of doing so, at least at the time. This revelation naturally put quite a bit of pressure on the teaching staff. The more open-minded made a determined effort at self-improvement, exchanging ideas and experiences and discoveries, much as had been the case with Tom Drager and his group at P.S. 68 in Harlem. Others went into a funky huff and fell back on union status.

The great majority of Ocean Hill teachers tried very seriously to do their best. They cared very much that the experiment succeed, and they came to see that success was very much up to them, a matter of individual personality and style in the final analysis. Some, like Gene Aptekar, normally took a completely permissive approach and made it work. Others, like the sterner Jay Schoenfeld, developed a style of controlled orchestration. For others, the role of a demanding martinet was most in character. Whatever the style, the teacher who opened up and developed a consistent idea of his or her own personality in relation to the class came to be a good teacher and a good actor as well. It is inescapable that a fine teacher is also a fine actor. Yet the role had to be played well, from genuine inner conviction, for one of the great gifts of childhood is the ability to detect hypocrisy. Whatever style emerged was not important to the children as long as it was genuine. Whether their teacher were a fascist or a total permissive didn't matter much at all; how "teach" worked out his approach was his own bag. What counted was whether *they* counted or not to the teacher. The intention and the insistence and the dedication was all that mattered to the children. An occasional outraged slap in the face is one of the things which offends children the least. It is aloof indifference, or the cool lack of response or interest, that destroys them.

So there it was. Half anyway of what the experiment was all about. It all simmered down to a question of children and teachers. To "the forbidden question," the only question that made any real sense, the only way for the experiment to get off the ground and demonstrate that it was possible for ghetto kids to succeed in school.

Rhody McCoy blew himself to a new automobile toward the end of the school year, a sleek, green, pulsating, bucket-seated fastback complete with racing stripes. After that I could easily tell whether he was in the district office or not by glancing at the parking lot in front of the housing development to see if the Green Hornet was in evidence. Though new questions popped into my mind every day, I was only able to corner him occasionally and briefly. His time was completely consumed with the moment-to-moment management of the district, and I felt I could not impose on the man too frequently. From early morning until late afternoon there was an endless procession of people in and out of his tiny office — Reverend Oliver, Father Powis and other members of the governing board, children with and without parents, individuals involved with various community projects, members of his staff, teachers and principals. In the midst of all this he also seemed to be constantly on one or another of several telephones in his office talking with all sorts of people including individuals at the Board of Education, to which he paid frequent visits.

One afternoon I noticed a teenager sitting quietly on the long black couch in the reception room. He had been waiting for some time, as had I. As McCoy escorted a visitor from his office the kid popped up off the couch:

"Mr. McCoy!"

"How you been, Jerry?" McCoy asked quietly, as though he had seen the young man only a few days earlier and now had all the time in the world for him.

"Fine."

"It's been a while." Some years earlier, I knew, McCoy had been principal of one of the city's "special" schools for highly disturbed and disruptive kids who simply could not be accommodated in the regular system. He had made quite a name for himself there, because of his record of shoring up many such youngsters and getting them back on the track again. This was one of the reasons the Ocean Hill–Brownsville Governing Board had picked him to administer the district. Jerry had obviously been one of his students back then, very likely a severely disturbed one. Now, although he seemed to have good control of himself, he was still quietly disoriented.

"I know it's been a while," Jerry said, "but I like to drop by here now and then and sit a bit. I'm checking up on you, Mr. McCoy."

"Do that any time you want to, Jerry." McCoy put his arm around the young man affectionately.

"You don't mind?"

"Not at all. How you making out?"

"I'm doing okay, Mr. McCoy. How about you?"

"Okay, I suppose." There was a note of deep weariness in the man's voice. I could tell that now, as the year ground down, he was not only involved with his schools, but also innumerable other activities concerned with whether anything at all could be saved the following year, including himself. That afternoon he happened to be driving into Manhattan, and since I was on my way there as well, he offered me a lift. I was concerned with an overall evaluation of the schools now that I had a fairly thorough impression of what the district was achieving and how. I asked McCoy how he would describe the three years.

"Well, the first year we cleared the rubble out. In the second year we put in the foundation. This year we've built a schoolhouse, though we don't have all the plantings and trimmings yet."

I nodded, confirming my own perception of the achievement. Rhody McCoy, his staff and principals, the teachers, children and the childrens' parents had put together the first full-scale ghetto schoolhouse in the land. I knew what he meant about plantings and trimmings. That positive educational ladder extending up through all the grades, a ladder a kid could climb successfully and so reach the bridge that does not touch down, was still a bit rickety in the individual schools. Even rungs were missing here and there. One could hardly expect that every second grade class in, say, P.S. 178 had a good teacher and was up to its expected level. Undoubtedly many children and possibly whole classes had moved up from the first grade with insufficient preparation, and so throughout the schools. It would take another three years, possibly even more, to acquire the "plantings and trimmings." But the hardest work had been done.   Clues to success had sprouted all over the district and were now waiting to be compared, evaluated, and disseminated throughout the schools, the essential one being the need for teachers free to try different approaches, compare notes with one another, and so develop their own individual teaching styles with a large degree of self-confidence. I told McCoy I certainly anticipated that the *Look* story would reflect these elements and that shortly I would be bringing John Vachon out to photograph the situations I have observed.   First, though, I had to explore the other side of the coin — parental involvement — aside from the paraprofessional roles I had seen. He suggested I drop by the office next day, and he would introduce me to Eva Kerr, a lady in charge of some of those activities.

I had made a number of rather simple observations about how to build a schoolhouse in the ghetto.   One of which I had been aware for some time was the need for real power and freedom at the local level — to ask "the forbidden question," to involve parents, to disseminate this freedom down the line to the point of providing options for the whole staff, like Percy Jenkins's paperback purchases or Gene Aptekar's neighborhood explorations with his class.   This led to the question of how many schools should be in such a district if it were to be managed in this fashion.   "Ten, at the most," was McCoy's response.   Considering that he already had his hands full with eight schools I realized he was projecting a bit from an extremely complex and time-consuming three-year shakedown cruise to a point beyond where everything no longer had to be done "yesterday."   Since there are about 1000 schools in the city this conclusion suggested they should be broken up into 100 local districts, which naturally brought a financial question into the picture.   McCoy told me that the Ford Foundation had contributed $100,000 a year for setting up and planning his district. For 100 such districts this would mean an increment in the city's school budget of $10 million or thereabouts.   The Board of Education already spends over $1.6 billion annually so this additional financing would hardly amount to a drop in the bucket. However, about half that vast sum goes for the support of a largely irrelevant headquarters, so one might even consider such a novel move as substantially reducing the budget. Of course, there would be howls of outrage at this suggestion, including: "How can we maintain educational standards in the city if we cut back our staff and delegate most of our central authority to one hundred little local districts?" Since "the system" is delivering precious little product, one would think it would be happy to pass the buck — except that one gets a feeling they are afraid the folks in the provinces might up and deposit the loot in a bank somewhere, even, God forbid, in a school safe. It would be comparatively easy for the central board to sample systematically the "product" delivered by its subcontractors in order to insure it measures up to standards, standards the system itself fails to fulfill. But a strange hesitancy in delegating authority to the provincials emanates continually from headquarters, with overtones that they will somehow goof up or water down "our" long-standing educational criteria. What gets forgotten is how much these potential subcontractors care about the product to begin with, and how much better able they are to whup asses to make sure it is produced. By the same token the teachers' union could maintain its blanket contract with the city while permitting the schools to be controlled at the local level, because, from my observations, the vast majority of its membership cares deeply about achievement when it is expected of them or permitted. Whatever the surface appearances or the political posturings, no man or woman at heart willfully assumes the role of a drone in human society.

Aside from the *Look* story, another question was on my mind as we headed toward Manhattan.

"Since you've gotten the district off the ground, I would think you'd be having visitors in here from other cities to see what's going on."

"We've got more than we can handle now. Coming in from all over the world in fact, looking for a piece of the carcass."

"Well, bits and pieces are all right, but it seems to me what it comes down to, what you have in Ocean Hill, is the first actual working model of a ghetto schoolhouse. Now that's something that's needed and ought to be replicated in every damn ghetto in the country — South Chicago, Watts, Detroit, name it. But it takes a lot of time and looking around to perceive what it's all about and how and why it works. Scrounging around for bits and pieces won't do it. So why not turn the thing around and take Ocean Hill to them? What I'm thinking about is film. It's a terrific medium for showing and telling. There's nothing like it, really. Why, if you had Becky Taylor on film or Percy Jenkins's day, Gene Aptekar's crazy classroom, Jonathan and Robert teaching, the Annex, all these things it would almost be like being able to spend a couple of months out here personally. There's just no substitute for actually seeing how someone else who's good handles it. That's the great thing about film. And along with other kinds of materials you'd really have the means of replication. On top of that I think it would add up to a terrific documentary, a network special perhaps."

"One film would be all right," said McCoy, "if you want to do something on us cats out here for NET or something like that. But if you're talking about replicating teaching situations you should be talking about twelve or fifteen or maybe even twenty-five specific films. Maybe mostly short films on specific things. That would make more sense as far as documenting the district is concerned."

The thought had not crossed my mind, but it obviously made good sense. I could see half a dozen short films just on different roles paraprofessionals can play. I could see a whole film on Percy's day, or Becky Taylor's class, on almost any of the other situations I had observed. I agreed this was the proper approach and that if I could somehow find the money, I could put together a special out of the same footage as well. I added that I wasn't at all sure I could manage this, but that I would certainly like to try.

"Good," said McCoy.

The next morning McCoy told me he had spoken to Eva Kerr, and she would be by very shortly. I sat down on the comfortable black couch and relaxed a bit. One thing seemed obvious to me about getting parents involved with the schools, aside from actually working there in one capacity or another. This was the need for them to understand the school work in order to support the efforts of their children and the children's teachers. My wife and I live in a rural township in New Jersey that supposedly has a fairly good school system which our two young sons attend. We understand the system and what it's aimed at more or less and can help the kids with their homework, she largely in the reading areas and I in math. (I managed to fathom the new math this way.) Without support I seriously doubt our kids could make it, particularly the older boy who is very bright and rather hyperactive. Much of school and homework is meaningless to him, and I can see why. So a bit of quiet pressure is necessary. Fortunately his teachers understand this, too, and know though the boy is exasperating a large part of the time, he can make the grade. Yet without support and insistence all along the line I seriously doubt he ever would. If I were a poor person from the rural South, without any real knowledge of the whole formalistic and future-oriented construction that is known as school, I *know* he would not make it, despite whatever natural perception and wisdom I might possess which could have more human value to him than anything he would ever learn in school. Transplanted to central Brooklyn and confronted with the failure-prone fortresses of education to be found in a big city, I think I would come to feel as intimidated, put down, ineffectual, frustrated, and despairing of any control over the fate of my children as any parents in Ocean

Hill. I was anxious to see how the district was dealing with this critical problem.

Eva Kerr appeared shortly and Rhody McCoy introduced us. She was a white woman with jet black hair that was cut short, and like Liz Gebiner, she had been involved in the city schools for some years. She was in charge of a group of about twenty neighborhood parents who had been trained as paraprofessionals in the district's home reading program — explaining to parents what was being taught in the schools and working with them so that they, in turn, could help children with their homework. Her headquarters was Portable #10 in the P.S. 178 playground and, seeing it was now late morning and that she had some things to attend to, she suggested I drop by in the early afternoon. I walked down to the luncheonette on Rockaway Avenue for a sandwich and a bowl of homemade soup which, I had discovered, the stern old Italian proprietor made with very favorable results. Then I returned to the playground and up a couple of steps to the door of #10.

Eva's assistant, Judy Frazer, a young Muslim lady to judge by her dress, met me at the door. As I entered she greeted me with a frostiness that let me know exactly where I was at, glancing meaningfully toward a number of women within Eva's hut. She might as well have said it: "Ladies, here's another white bastard come to look in on the zoo." As to whether I might enter and be "cleared," let alone do anything, she deferred that to Eva. For good reason as I would learn later on.

The portable was divided into two large rooms, the home reading program occupying one of them. There were filing cabinets along the side wall and two desks and a blackboard at the far end, but most of the space was taken up with a huge rectangle formed from about eight library-type tables put together to provide a very large conference spread. Here were seated about a dozen women and, since the table could have accommodated twice as many, I guessed that perhaps a dozen other members of Eva Kerr's group were out visiting parents in their homes or engaged in other community business. The ladies were both black and Puerto Rican. Most were young, but a few were older. Some drank coffee and chatted, some were going over school materials. I walked to the back of the room to one of the small desks and Eva asked me to sit down.

I explained the *Look* story, which was what I had come to see her about. I said quite simply that despite all the things that had been written about Ocean Hill, from what I had seen no one had done even a halfway decent piece on the district. I recalled my puzzlement as to why the word "children" had never popped up in all the flak and Charles Wilson's marvelous response: "Children have no power base." Eva knew and respected Charles, had attended his N.Y.U. class several times, and had also seen *A Child Went Forth*, because I had lent Charles my print of the film. So, aside from McCoy's introduction, she knew I was at least vaguely headed in the right direction from her own perspective. I explained that taking pictures of some of her ladies working with parents in the community was an important part of the story.

"Look," Eva said, "I think that's okay. I would love to see even a halfway decent story on Ocean Hill before . . ." She didn't finish the sentence. "But you have to understand that these people have had it up to here from the media for almost three years now. They are really turned off, tuned out. They've had it."

"I guess I got here a little late."

"Too late, maybe, as far as attitudes go. These people have been hoping for too long now."

"Didn't McCoy, earlier on, explain to reporters who came out what he was trying to do? Didn't he sit them down and try to explain the experiment and work with them?"

"McCoy gave them all the time in the world. He tried to explain. He was very patient, remarkably patient. And what came of it? What was 'news,' that's what came of it. And what was 'news'? Excitement. Confrontation. Hassles in the street.

About the Reverend Oliver, Father Powis, the governing board, McCoy himself. All that baloney, that was the news. The schools weren't 'news.' "

"I understand that. I think — no, I take that back. I was about to say I think I understand how angry people must feel. But that's silly. No one can put himself in someone else's shoes. I do think I see the shoes, though."

"Okay, but let me talk it over with the ladies. Let me see what they say. I'll let you know."

Several days later I bumped into Eva in McCoy's office. "I've talked to the ladies," she said. "They will listen to you. Why don't you drop by the hut this afternoon sometime? There are some things going on you would like to see anyway."

Mr. Barrett had given Eva's paras a number of sessions in the use of the rods so that they could acquaint parents with them. Other people active in other aspects of the curriculum had done the same thing so that the ladies could work with their materials as well. On this particular afternoon some of the ladies were engaged in role-playing, one pretending to be a mother as the other introduced the rods to her. The exchange which resulted was fascinating, as they acted it out with feeling and perception:

"Mrs. Jones, I'm here to introduce you to the rods which your child Jimmy is using in his math class."

"Rods? Them don't look like no rods."

"Well, blocks maybe. But look at them. See, this is the one rod. That means one. And then the two rod for two, twice as long. I'll spread them all out of the box and you'll see we have the numbers from one to ten in different colors. That's how Jimmy is learning arithmetic."

"Games. I told that child if he's just gonna go off to school and play games I'm gonna whup his ass!"

"Well, see, it's not really games. Like suppose Jimmy has a math problem in school, a good problem, like . . ."

So it went in the group, trying to discover how best to explain the rods so that parents could understand and work with them, too. It was a good session. As it wound down Eva interrupted the ladies to introduce me, said a few words about what she thought I wanted, and asked me to explain this personally to them. There was an instant silence in the big room which, I suppose, surprised me more than anyone else. I got up from my corner and started off by saying I was quite unaccustomed to addressing groups, which was certainly true. I said more or less what I had said to Eva to begin with about the story I hoped to do. In the course of my doing so one young lady caught my eye, because I had noticed how bright and articulate she was during the earlier role-playing session. She was a thin, light-skinned woman in her twenties with finely chiseled features, a flaring Afro hairdo, and large, slightly tinted mod glasses. She looked at me intently as I was talking, never taking her eyes off me, and about the time I finished what I had to say I realized something quite startling. She had never even blinked. I concluded my nonspeech and sat down, a bit unnerved.

"Any questions?" Eva asked in good classroom fashion.

The young lady's hand shot up immediately.

"Yes, Linda?"

"Mr. Campbell, you have told us what you want to do. Could you now tell us also what your real motive is?"

The question, out of the blue, might have stupefied me a year or so earlier. Now it did not, except momentarily. All my own sensitizing, plus what Eva had said when we first talked, indicated how badly burned, frustrated, and suspicious the Ocean Hill community had become, particularly of anyone connected with the public media. After a brief pause I replied:

"I don't see any way of separating my real motives from what I am trying to do. It seems to me that they're the same thing." That was true enough, certainly, but I felt it was a hopelessly inadequate answer.

"And what do you think this will do for the parents and the community?" she persisted.

Several obvious answers which someone else might have given crossed my mind instantly: it would be "good publicity"; perhaps *Look* could pay the parents involved "a little something." I rejected them as quickly as they occurred to me as being fatuous and even insulting.

"I don't know," I answered hesitantly. "Maybe nothing, but I'd still like to do the story."

There were no further questions. I think Eva Kerr said a little something in my behalf, like that McCoy thought what I was trying to do was worth it or something of the sort, but I'm not sure. Obviously the ladies trusted Eva. I felt inadequate and somewhat confused by my first confrontation with what I knew were the real feelings of this oppressed and put-upon community. In the schools I had fared better, probably because I sensed or understood the situation better. But here "on the street," so to speak, with community adults who knew exactly where they were at from long experience, I was very much a stranger. I had not crossed that part of the chasm yet. Not by any means. I left the hut and headed for home in something of a daze, thinking about Linda King's questions (that was her full name, I had learned in passing).

The next day I returned to Portable #10 and by luck Linda King was there, working on some tests at the big table. Judy Frazer said "Hello" when I came in this time, indicating a partial switch in attitude. I sat down beside Linda.

"Look, I've been thinking about your questions. I'm not very fast on my feet, as I said I guess. I'm used to thinking while staring at the typewriter or at the wall or out the window. Now I want to say something more. A fellow I used to know slightly, John Hersey, wrote a book called *The Algiers Motel Incident.* There must have been a dozen or so reporters who covered those shootings, but only John stuck around to find out what had really happened. Well, his book did nothing for the black kids who were shot by the police. It did nothing to change the mind of the idiot or bigot or whatever you want to call the De-

troit judge who acquitted the police. But I don't think, after
that book, that things will ever be quite the same in this country
again. So when you ask about my motives I think something
like that is what I feel, what I would like to try."

Linda King smiled. It was a genuine smile. "Okay, try," she
said.

"Thanks. I'm going to."

In my continuing rounds of the district I was gradually becoming aware of something which had begun only as a vague
feeling. There was an atmosphere of openness and mutual trust
in these schools and these people just as there had been in the
I.S. 201 Complex, a sense of purpose and dedication that over-
rode any formal position or prerogative, a unity that had long
ago passed beyond superficial perceptions about black or white.
Behind it lay a growing confidence in the enterprise itself, the
only thing that makes openness possible. A feeling of camara-
derie infected the district so that once a person was accepted as
having a legitimate purpose there, welcome followed without
question. Now, finally, I was one of them and the only question remaining was how one or another individual might help.
The acceptance, I knew, had come initially from McCoy. And
now in my occasional brief visits to his small and cluttered office my attention was increasingly drawn to the plaque on his
desk that said: Do Everything With Love. I had begun to understand what it really meant. That was the essence and the
anchor of the dedication and confidence I had come to perceive,
made possible by the independence of the district itself. Who
can love somebody or something if he's not free to do it? I also
felt with a growing intensity how badly the district had been
mauled by the media, which had portrayed it as contentious,
hostile, suspicious, devious, deceitful, highhanded and downright sloppy and inept in its procedures. Then why had this reporter been accepted as having legitimate business there, particularly in its third and terminal spring — "let in," so to speak?
Even as the question crossed my mind so did the answer. Had

the experiment actually been an educational abortion, the people involved might very well have developed a group psychosis, growing increasingly suspicious, alienated, and withdrawn. Quite the opposite was the case, however. Everyone felt the experiment was alive and well in central Brooklyn and was hoping it would continue to survive. Anyone who joined the embattled company, if he came unarmed or not booby-trapped in some way, was identified as a friend.

When people are forcibly isolated from the rest of society, either because of their own convictions or by the hostility and antagonism of know-nothing minds or merely by the inertia of indifference, bonds of great strength may be forged among them. There springs up a heightened sense of the underlying social contract which is generally diluted, confused, and obscured in the larger society. It is as though people under the pressure of adversity have written the contract anew with an acceptance that is at once open and infectious. Ancient words spring alive, almost as if at that moment the ink had just dried on the parchment: "We pledge to each other our lives, our fortunes, and our sacred honor." I felt a certain sense of joy at being "in" with the "out" group. It was a bit like a newly arrived convict being cleared ("He's okay.") by a Charles Bickford-type senior con with a well-developed and long-standing fix on the screws and perhaps, outside the walls, on the society which lies beyond.

The most logical source of funds for the film project which Rhody McCoy and I had discussed seemed to be the Ford Foundation, since it had provided the seed money to set up the experimental districts to begin with. Before writing up such a proposal, however, I felt I should have a talk with Mario Fantini, the person on the Foundation staff most responsible for its involvement in the demonstration, to see where the Foundation stood as far as the districts were concerned. The Ford Foundation, on East 42nd Street near the U.N., occupies one of the most novel, elegant, and impressive buildings in the entire city. A dozen floors tall, it is a hollow quadrangle of office space constructed around an interior garden of verdant and lovely tropical plants, flowers, trees, and shrubs. The enclosed garden flourishes in a carefully regulated, humidified environment and is bathed in daylight which streams down through a huge glass skylight extending across the top of the building above the twelfth floor to enclose and protect the core of the quadrangle. The whole structure is a marvelous midtown sanctuary symbolizing the dedication of an enormous amount of money to useful and important social purposes — blood money to a degree, acquired in more predatory manifest-destiny times, but presumably good money today.

Inside the building the office periphery was equally elegant and meticulously well appointed, completely air-conditioned with the rooms and corridors all quietly carpeted. I met Fantini in a small conference room on one of the upper floors. He was accompanied by a tall, dignified black man named Joshua Smith, also a staff member. Fantini asked me what I thought of the demonstration districts. I told him I had done quite a bit of looking about and spent a long time at it, talking to people, observing classes, getting a sense of the elements, and that I certainly believed this was the way to break the bind of failure in ghetto schools in the country. He pressed me about my own impressions, and I went into more detail about some of the things I'd seen. I felt he was searching to see if another soul in the whole world would or could confirm what he himself believed. This somewhat unnerving feeling of isolation I sensed in the man reminded me of a remark of Charles Wilson's: "They just call up from downtown on the phone . . . but no one has been to see the schools." I felt Fantini was a man under psychological siege. Sitting in the small, quiet room I also had the impression that the whole elegant building was trembling slightly, shaking with fright, despite all the money and power and elegance. I looked out the window and across the treetops stretching up from the tropical garden below. I could see a great many offices on other sides of the quadrangle and noticed all the windows were equipped with venetian blinds. Curiously, they were all raised.

"You can really look in on everyone, can't you?" I remarked.

"Yes."

"All the blinds are up."

"Yes."

"But suppose you wanted to be alone? I don't see anyone who seems to want to be alone. If I had that office over there, or this one here, and everyone else could look in, I think I would let my blind down."

"Well, that's McGeorge Bundy's office up there [pointing to a row of windows high in one corner where the president of the Foundation worked.] He has his blinds up now. So everyone knows he's in. So everyone else has their blinds up, too."

I wondered how a foundation's staff could pursue its presumed social ideals and still live with such operational shibboleths. I suppose I had expected to find idealistic, independent people here, since money can certainly buy independence in America. Not at all. From the looks of things, here was just another collection of cautious organization folks, who might give funds to a Navajo Indian project or something. God knows they need them. (And they live way out there in the southwest desert where nobody much is watching.) But to a matter of serious social concern in a teeming, articulate, and powerful place like New York City? I sensed the Foundation had gotten burned there and was recoiling docilely from its adventures with the experimental districts, particularly since it was at this time that questions were being raised in Washington as to whether foundations should not possibly be taxed — which I interpreted as a congressional reverberation resulting from the outraged reactions of various New York power brokers to a presumption of independence out in the provinces. Now, like a stranded and spineless jellyfish, the Ford Foundation was quivering timorously under a rock, except that, in this case, the "rock" happened to be one of the most highly visible mauso-

leums in the whole city, projecting an image of steadfast and
courageous social purpose, while its current tenants huddled
within.   I sensed that the whole trembling organism might
abruptly contract at any moment, only to spit out Mario Fantini
as a human sacrifice to placate the demons howling outside the
battlements. I rose to leave.

"If you think something is happening out there, are you going
to write about it?" Fantini asked. I could tell from the tone of
the question that it was a stand-in, a verbal double for his real
question which remained unexpressed: "Can I hope for some
kind of statement, even fragmentary, from someone in the outside world that it was, after all, real for a time? That it was
about something? That it was about to achieve something?"

I said I hoped so and shook his hand, his companion's as
well. I could not tell where Joshua Smith stood. He had said
almost nothing, but he struck me as intelligent, well educated,
cool, and collected. Perhaps I had expected that since he was a
black man he might have been more responsive. Perhaps that
was presuming too much.

I went home and wrote up a formal proposal to the Foundation for filming the things I had discussed with McCoy. I did
not even mention Rhody McCoy except for identification purposes. I said nothing about community control, confrontation,
or any other inflammatory issue. The proposal was strictly concerned with filming teaching situations and other specific activities so that such materials could be used in replicating these
positive approaches in other cities and in other ghettos. Since
the disaster of ghetto schools was rather well known on a na-
tional scale by now, and since there appeared to be some public
support for breaking the bind if possible, there were implications in the proposal that if the Foundation contributed to the
resolution of the problem it would, in the long run, be able to
wipe off its currently bloody nose and end up smiling — though
I did not put it in that way. I simply proposed a worthwhile un-

dertaking with no broader social connotations whatever. The lives of too many children were at stake to do otherwise.

With the film proposal launched I phoned John Vachon, and for several weeks we toured the district so he could take pictures of things I have already described. John rented a car for us, and the first few days I took an early bus into Manhattan, met John, and then drove with him to Brooklyn. We quickly realized that this arrangement put us in the thick of the rush-hour traffic, going to work in the same direction as everyone else. So I took over the car instead and picked John up at his apartment on Riverside Drive near Columbia University, where traffic was lighter. From there we headed east across the Triborough Bridge, circled in an arc around Queens, and entered Brooklyn by the back door. With this system we were traveling in the opposite direction from the flood of inbound commuter traffic and generally had rather clear sailing. After school we left Brooklyn by the same route and headed back toward Riverside Drive, now in the opposite direction from the evening traffic beginning to pour out of Manhattan. In Ocean Hill, when we were not working in the schools that lay some distance away from the district office, like the Annex and P.S. 73, I parked our car behind the portables on the P.S. 178 playground. From there we could cover that school, I.S. 55 a block away, the district office, the math lab, other activities at P.S. 144 a short way off, Eva Kerr's ladies, and the desolate, rubble-ridden terrain itself. When noontime came we usually walked down to the luncheonette on Rockaway Avenue for a sandwich, though sometimes we drove into downtown Brooklyn to a restaurant to eat.

One day I received a message from Henriette that Eva Kerr wanted to see me. I left John working away in a classroom and walked over to Eva's hut. Her ladies had tackled the problem of finding a neighborhood parent who would consent to our taking pictures of the mother and her children working in the home reading program. Eva introduced me to one of her group, an attractive young woman named Terry D'Ormond with a marked West Indian accent. Terry reported that one of her parents was willing for us to come and take pictures.

"How about this afternoon?" I asked.

"Oh, my!" Terry's hands shot up to determine the condition of her hairdo. Then she looked down. She was wearing slacks. "Oh, my!" She shook her head dubiously, distressed at the prospect of appearing in the casual clothes she was wearing, even though they made so much good sense for her travels about the district to go over homework and other school matters with neighborhood parents.

"Miss D'Ormond," I said, laughing, "we're not doing some television commercial about 'Oh, gee, my! Look how the wash comes out with new Superwhiz!' This is Ocean Hill and I think you should look just the way you look right now while you're working. You look perfectly fine to me."

"Well," Terry said, still hesitant, "okay, but I'll have to explain that to Mrs. Thompson. She might just want to go to the beauty parlor, you know."

"Please, keep her out of the beauty parlor."

"Okay, I'll try. See me this afternoon."

We all went to the building where Mrs. Thompson lived. There were railroad flats on each of the four floors, and Mrs. Thompson and her half-dozen children occupied the third-floor apartment. She proved to be a large and friendly person. John took photographs of Terry reviewing homework with her and then other pictures as Mrs. Thompson and one of her children worked on these same problems at the kitchen table. It all went off quite casually, informally, and with little effort, except perhaps on the part of John, who had to perceive these vignettes in his own way. After it was all over we chatted briefly with some of the older children. Mrs. Thompson looked at me.

"Tell me something, now that you all have taken pictures and everything. I have a Polaroid camera, and I've taken a lot of pictures of the children, but their faces all come out dead black. You can't see anything at all except their eyes."

With a mixture of mock seriousness and feigned surprise I said: "Surely, Mrs. Thompson, you know the answer to that question yourself."

The woman shook her head negatively.

"Well, that camera has an exposure meter built in, right?"

"Yes, indeed!"

"Well, it's set to take pictures of white folks, not black folks."

Everyone enjoyed the joke immensely, particularly the children.

On our way back to Manhattan John turned to me and asked in his hesitant, raspy, and very human voice:

"Robert, are you part Negro?"

The question dumbfounded me, especially since I'm about as waspish as they come — at least in physical appearance. I wasn't sure whether John was serious or whether he had some sly trap in the back of his mind into which he was trying to lead me. I thought I might as well play it straight and see what developed.

"No," I answered, "what made you ask?"

"Well, when you first called me on the phone after talking to Joe Roddy I just sort of assumed you were a black man, being so concerned about a black thing like Ocean Hill, and the way you talked about it, and how important you said it was. So when we met one another first, at the Oyster Bar in Grand Central, I guess I was looking for someone who looked sort of like a black writer. We were both standing around there looking for a long while, remember? When you finally came up to me, I guessed you must have figured I was Vachon, the white photographer. Since then I've been wondering if maybe you weren't one of those very fair one sixty-fourths like Walter White, the fellow who was head of the N.A.A.C.P. some years ago. He was so white the only reason he seemed black was because he said he was, and because he talked like a Negro. That's what made me wonder, that's all."

John put all his film in for processing, and then we spent a whole day in the photographer's lounge at *Look* going over contact sheets of the thousands of pictures he had taken to select a reasonably small number of the best ones to have enlarged for layout purposes. Though I had sensed John was a fine photographer, this was the first time I was able to see what a great eye he actually had, and how perfect had been Gordon Parks's recommendation. What impressed me most was how well John had captured the sense of life and purpose that infected those classrooms, something I felt and something John, in his own fashion, had managed to see. We had a terrible time winnowing the results down to a manageable number of prints but finally succeeded, had the story laid out, and took the results to Martin Goldman for approval so I could then write the text. Martin had a few minor suggestions, then okayed the layouts and turned to me:

"Say, Ira Mothner [a senior editor I did not know] saw 'Ocean Hill' on the story list, and he's terribly curious as to what it's all about. He sort of considers that subject his province. He did a text piece on community control about a year ago, talked to Rhody McCoy and some of those people, educators in other cities, too, so he naturally wonders who you are and what you're up to."

"Maybe I should go talk to him."

"I think that's a good idea."

"Before that, though, I'd like to read his piece so I'll know what he did."

"Fine. My secretary will find you a copy of that issue."

I read the piece, several times in fact. It was thorough and very well done. I remember one marvelous quote from a black educator: "Why should a kid read 'See Jane run' when he's already seen Jane raped?" The article was concerned with activities and ideas about community control as expressed in current fights in various cities. I saw no conflict between what Ira had done and what I was now doing. His basic concern was with who runs schools; mine was with children and the inside-the-schoolhouse side of things, though some aspects of what was happening in the classroom naturally related to the power struggle going on in the city. I dropped by his office and we chatted. Several things quickly became clear. One was that he didn't think much of the Ocean Hill schools. He had visited them a few times during the second year and came away relatively unimpressed. We compared notes on how it looked then and how it looked now. I told him about Mr. Barrett's rod program and the math lab which had only gotten off the ground in the third year and said that the same applied to other teachers and projects as well. He seemed both surprised and interested in the many things that had blossomed now that Ocean Hill was no longer "news." But he also expressed doubts about the possibility of anything significant happening in ghetto education. His wife taught in a ghetto school, thought it was appalling, and they both felt the whole thing was impossible from any practical point of view. We obviously had different attitudes toward the district, partly due to his having seen a foundation whereas I was observing a schoolhouse. But there was another difference. I now thought something was possible, so I tried my two propositions on Ira:

If something is necessary, it can't really be impossible.
If something is impossible, it can't really be necessary.

It was obvious enough which proposition Ira believed in because his only response was:
"Bang, bang — you lose."
"What do you mean, I lose?"
"You lose, that's all. You're dead."
"But suppose I'm halfway dead and I need something, man. What then?"

"You just don't get it. That's 'what then.' You're dead."

I looked at Ira presumably as one experienced reporter and writer to another with the expectation that he might have some thoughts to contribute to this contradictory impasse which would be illuminating to both of us. He looked at me as though I were some greenhorn newly arrived in the city room, an overexcited kid out of *The Front Page:*

"Look," [he might as well have said: "Look, kid . . ."], "you can spin your wheels all you want to. The Board of Education can afford to listen to your noise. They can weather it, tolerate it, wear you down, and wear you out. You know why? They sit there, year after year. Guys like you come and go and make waves. They stay."

I suspected there had been a time when Ira had come and gone and made waves. But now, like many fine reporters, he had grown cynical and for good reason. He was right. "They stay." Indeed they do. Down through the years how many a reportorial wave has been broken and fragmented into harmless spray by the granite fortress of the establishment! So the great waves of the ocean roll in and crash against a seemingly implacable shore. And yet in the course of time that shoreline becomes inexorably altered. I felt that Ira's resolution of the question was simply not acceptable. I left his office and took the elevator down to the street. Suddenly I remembered what I had said to Linda King and a new thought crossed my mind:

> They said it couldn't be done.
> So I didn't do it.

I wrote the story, made the anticipated editorial changes Martin and Bill Arthur requested, and it was accepted. This meant that John and I got paid for it, an event I would have gladly swapped for getting it published, because the question of when it would run now became a cliffhanger. I knew *Look* was in financial trouble, and I phoned Martin from time to time, as the closing of school approached, but was told that competition for space in the magazine was keen — a fact I could appreciate, but not entirely. I realized what they thought sold magazines: fashions, celebrities, strange things and places, William Manchester's mesmerizing but maudlin and mixed-up account of the Kennedy assasination. Yet I felt quite strongly that we deserved a piece of the action, too.

IV

"Something Alive to Haunt Them With"

I HEARD FROM the Ford Foundation about my film proposal. The response was so curious I realized something that had never occurred to me: a foundation, just like a person, can develop a psychosis. Though my proposal had been strictly educational and had deliberately avoided "politics" in the form of McCoy, confrontation, or anything else, the kiss-off read in part:

[We] have discussed the proposal for a film about the development of the projects, and the ensuing conflict. It is provocative, and we agree that our involvement with the ghetto schools was an invaluable experience for the Foundation. Unfortunately, we are simply not in a position to . . .

I began to consider what alternatives there might be. One was other foundations or organizations; another, wealthy individuals who might be willing to underwrite the filming out of personal interest. My connections in both areas were practically nonexistent, but I felt obliged to try.

I knew a couple of important people, and I had never presumed upon their acquaintance. One of them was Andrew Heiskell, chairman of the board of Time, Inc., and an active principal in the Urban Coalition. I had known Andrew when I was a *Life* reporter and he was the magazine's publisher. I felt the Coalition might be one route for funding. I phoned his office, identified myself to his secretary, and Andrew came on the phone immediately. After an exchange of greetings I said I would like to borrow a few minutes of his time to talk about a problem of some urgency. He consulted his calendar and suggested I drop up two days later. Up meant his spacious office on one of the top floors of the Time & Life Building. I was shown in promptly and had to look up as usual to greet my host — Andrew Heiskell stands about six feet four or so. He was lean, tanned, and handsome as ever with the same air of unpretentious informality I had known several decades earlier. His top executive position, which might have turned the heads of some people, seemed not to have changed him in the least. He welcomed me in shirtsleeves, closed the door behind us, invited me to sit down, sprawled casually in the chair behind his desk with one long leg draped over an arm of it and otherwise indicated that he was pleased to see an old colleague.

I took a chair and instantly a quite unexpected feeling came over me. I knew Andrew's welcome was both simple and genuine, yet I suddenly felt seedy and out of place. There were certain presumptions that had made this meeting possible — about identity and behavior and making out decently in the largely white world of midtown Manhattan, unwritten assumptions which provided an invisible passport to such midtown towers. It wasn't elitist or clubby or anything like that, though there was that aspect to it that some people traded on. I had done so myself years earlier, before I realized it was a lot of foolishness. Rather, it was a simple and accepted franchise to operate here, an understood social contract I had taken for granted all my life. Now I felt completely uncomfortable about those assumptions. I felt like an impostor or a displaced person whose passport to this accommodating world had been confiscated, torn up, and thrown away. All the time spent "out there" among people who were so obviously disenfranchised had led me to wonder whether the American social contract I had accepted for so long was actually valid if it could produce such inequities. That was certainly a big part of it. A carousel of disconnected images was whirling in my mind. I knew, for instance, that after our meeting I could walk into any good restaurant in the area and have lunch, and if for some reason I had forgotten to bring any money, I could easily apologize to the manager, identify myself, and sign the check with a promise to pay the bill the following day. Few of my besieged battalion in Brooklyn could have done that. If I were Bob Campbell, a Puerto Rican who spoke halting English and lived in a cheap flat above a luncheonette on Rockaway Avenue, I could not have done it. More than likely such a suggestion would have occasioned a call to the police, even if I actually did have the money at home. More likely still I would have been told all the tables in the restaurant were reserved. If I were *that* Bob Campbell and wished to buy the house we live in, I doubt it would have been possible. Many people in our country community, including some real estate brokers, have been fearful for some time about bands of blacks and Puerto Ricans from Newark or Elizabeth invading the area by the carful, particularly in the summertime, perhaps to demand reparations. Questions as to how much these imaginary marauders might fear the state and local police, or where they might find a car and the money to buy gasoline, seem not to have occurred to them.

Scattered among these swirling images were the torn-up fragments of a passport I knew was no longer humanly valid. As I settled into the comfortable chair opposite Andrew's desk, I sensed I was now looking at my old Manhattan home through the other end of the telescope. It had nothing to do with Andrew, a decent and worthy man. It was just that I had called him as the person I presumably was the last time we had talked many years ago. But I was not that person anymore.

My voice came on. It struck me as nervous and agitated, faster than it should have been, as though it might explode in a cascade of incomprehensible, high-pitched gibberish or simply fade away into an unutterable silence. I managed to control it somewhat, I thought, but after a moment I noticed Andrew had uncoiled his lanky frame and was leaning across the desk with one hand cupped to his ear. I realized I was speaking in an almost inaudible whisper. I pulled myself together and began to describe what was going on in the schools in Ocean Hill, the importance of this to other cities, and why I felt the Coalition, because of its involvement with urban affairs, might be interested in my film proposals. With a gesture that expressed concern, friendship, and patience Andrew interrupted me and called in his young executive assistant to hear what I was saying so he would know what the conversation had been about and could act as directed later on.

Our meeting led to a prompt contact with an official of the Coalition. The official asked me if I had presented my proposal to the Board of Education. I said I felt doing such a thing would be the most direct route to suicide I could imagine, that probably the Board would welcome the suggestion, take it under advisement, and tell me to come back next year after the proposal has been approved. But, of course, by that time the experiment would be dead and buried and there would be no remains to be photographed. (My conversation with Ira Mothner had not been completely unproductive.) The Coalition man said all their experience indicated that when they worked through channels they could accomplish something, but if they went outside little or nothing was ever achieved. It turned out that in any case my emergency was too immediate and their funds too committed to make anything possible on such short notice. The man was helpful in suggesting other possibilities, however.

I visited two young men at the offices of the Laurance Rockefeller Foundation on a floor of the RCA Building in Rockefeller Center. Though most floors of that building are laid out following the logic of its rectangular structure, this space had clearly been privately and elegantly planned. Corridors ran at strange angles, like a labyrinth. Original Mirós and other fine paintings hung quite casually here and there. Original sculptures perched in tastefully illuminated niches. It was terribly informally posh. I struck out again but continued searching. I discovered there were a number of small foundations in the city whose directors might be sympathetic. I spoke to one who thought he might be able to find a few thousand dollars if I could get other support elsewhere. I then went off to search, but I soon learned to my dismay that practically all local foundation directors had gone to a convention in San Francisco to compare notes about, among other things, the terrible prospect which had just arisen in Washington of taxing them. I telephoned several directors there and found them, much to their surprise. Apparently they had never been confronted with the fact that a serious reporter, if he decides to foot the bill, can use a telephone cross-country as easily as if he wanted to locate his wife at the local shopping center, just by calling around. I spoke to hotel and motel operators, ladies in charge of meetings and work sessions, ferreted the directors out, and stirred some of them up. My hope was that while they were together they might caucus among themselves and decide to underwrite my project. But despite the interest I generated, hope began to fade. Foundations, I discovered, simply cannot work that way. Basically one must go the formal grant route, submit a proposal, get it approved by the board and defined as a project for "next year" or thereafter. The difficulty was compounded by the fact that, however much I may have fancied myself as the inadvertent champion of certain social needs, I could in no way qualify as an appropriate recipient of anyone's funds. I was not a faculty member in a university department of education. I was not a graduate student seeking funds for some sociological film thesis. I was only an individual confronted by what I had decided was a crying need. I realized that the foundation route was quixotic at best.

A jet-setter could have underwritten my operation and taken a tax deduction to boot, so I shifted over to that prospect. Carter

Burden had come up, a very wealthy member of the City Council who represented the upper East Side of Manhattan, which is
a largely Puerto Rican district, and who cared about the area
and its schools, among its many other needs. I got a good reception from his press secretary, Frank McLaughlin, a former
Daily News reporter, who pressed my cause. Unfortunately just
at that time the stock market took its most disastrous plunge
since 1929. People who had $30 million were abruptly con-
fronted with the unpleasant news that they were only worth $18
million or thereabouts. That seemed fine with me, but naturally
they regarded it differently. Things were tough all over. Nevertheless Frank kept trying to put something together for me
and asked that I check in from time to time to report how I was
doing. I knew he was rooting for me, and meantime I continued my rounds hoping to come up with something. But once
again, who in hell was I?

It was now nearly the end of April. In two more months
Ocean Hill would be gone for good. My pursuit of funds
seemed increasingly hopeless. Had it been possible to think of
doing something the following school year I could have taken a
different tack, creating some organization or affiliation that
could make me legitimately eligible to receive fundings. As it
was I was simply too late and quite unaccredited — a situation
that was no one's fault. I could see no way around it. I began
to consider some sort of rock-bottom "poor boy" way of pro-
ceeding just in case something should nibble at one of the
dozens of lines I had dangling from the boat. I went to see an
old friend, Bill Donati, who had been production manager for
the Madisons and now had a small film group which he had set
up with his life savings called Donati & Friends. (For a ten-
dollar investment I had become one of the "friends.") Bill's
conception of his company was simple and idealistic. He had
quite a few acquaintances in the film and TV commercial business. His idea was to open a small office, find work, put
together whatever combination of friends was needed for the

job, and share the profits. His anchor man was Mike Konkus, another Madison alumnus who had become a really fine cameraman-director. I found that Donati & Friends was not doing very well. Bill had the bad luck of opening his shop just at the time the stock market was going to pieces. The film and TV commercial business collapsed with it. Potential clients all over town were pulling in their horns, and among the first items to feel the new austerity were advertising and promotion budgets. Bill had set up camp beside a watering hole that was rapidly drying up. I explained that I was sniffing around a pretty dry hole myself and told them what I was trying to do. Mike felt I could play the role of director since I knew the classroom situations. He could manage with one assistant which left us needing only a sound man, who would probably have to come from the union at union wages. So with a little money for film, equipment, and token salaries we could manage something, which would be preferable to standing around on one foot as we all now seemed to be doing. Thus we assembled a poverty-level film group in case its services should be required.

With this established I continued to pursue my receding expectations. I stayed on the telephone. I made my rounds. And faintheartedly I watched the calendar. Each day the countdown for Ocean Hill continued — formlessly, mindlessly, indifferently. The lifeblood of something that struck me as vital to the survival of American society, if it were to mean anything, was dripping away through some fatal defect in that institution. I would have thought that somewhere within the great, dominant white world a few voices, just a few at least, would be raised for commuting its sentence. But though I strained my ears, I could hear nothing but the deadly silence of acceptance, and always the clock, which seemed to grow a bit louder each day. Something was fundamentally out of joint with the American social contract when it led to such indifference and to the almost automatic liquidation of the rights and expectations of minorities. As I wandered about Manhattan an unexpected and disconcerting psychological shift occurred in my mind. I first noticed it on a sunny afternoon while walking west on 42nd Street past the public library. I suddenly found myself looking at white people on the street *as* white people, glowering at them with feelings of suspicion, distrust, and downright hostility.

Throughout May I continued my search as one contact led to another. Almost by accident I discovered an educational film project already in the works and, after discussing Ocean Hill with the people involved, it appeared as though some of the teaching situations I described might make worthwhile sequences for their production. But since their film was now well along and my time was running out, it was hopeless to expect them to shift gears on such short notice. When I could I took the A train to Rockaway Avenue to see what was going on and what the prospects were for a stay of execution. There didn't seem to be any. I happened by the P.S. 178 portables on Earth Day to find a young black paraprofessional and a group of kids sweeping up broken glass in the playground. It was their Earth Day project and everyone seemed to be enjoying it.

"Hey! Whatcha doing?"

"Well, I'm an assistant to an assistant in audio-visual," the young man said, obviously taken with his current project, which included shooting a few basketballs through a hoop between major sweeps. "But [sinking a tough shot with a deftness the kids admired] I do this best."

Posters had begun to appear here and there announcing a gala district fair in early June, a weekend event for children, parents, and people in the community. I bumped into Judy Frazer, Eva's assistant.

"Say," she said, "we're having this fair, you know, for the kids, and we want to give prizes for different achievements. You've got a lot of connections downtown. Do you think you could find some money somewhere we could buy prizes with?"

"I don't know. I've been looking for some money for some time now, but I don't seem to be having much luck. I'm beginning to think that finding money isn't exactly my line of work."

"But you must know some people over there who could give something."

It was a ghetto assumption made about almost any visitor from the other side of the chasm. Since there was so little out here, there must be a lot in there. And since you're from in there you must be able to touch something, get your hands on something, so why don't you do something for us while you're out here? I felt a bit put upon by these implications, since I believed I had bridged the chasm by this point. Yet there it was, a feeling and an attitude neither of us should have had to adopt. I reflected about the fair, however, for it would indeed be nice to have some awards to hand out.

"Say, I have one idea. A couple of my oldest friends run Atlantic Records. These kids would certainly dig a lot of their recording stars. I don't suppose it would do Atlantic any harm to donate some records as prizes for an Ocean Hill fair. In fact, they might like the idea."

"Cool!"

"How many records do you want?"

"Seventy-five, one hundred maybe. All you can get."

Once again I felt Judy was pushing me, getting a bit greedy, in fact. A hundred LPs was asking a lot. How many prizes could there be at the fair? Would Atlantic records end up like so many Frisbees skimming across the P.S. 178 playground? I decided to do what I could, however.

"Well, let's try right now."

We entered hut #10 and I picked up the phone, dialed PL 7-6306, and asked for Nesuhi Ertegun. Nesuhi and his brother, Ahmet, the founders of Atlantic, had been friends of mine from college days, when their father was Turkish ambassador to the United States and dean of the Washington diplomatic corps.

The brothers, educated in Europe before coming to this country, were avid jazz fans and by around 1940 had assembled one of the greatest collections of jazz records in the world — original Okeh, Brunswick, and other labels featuring King Oliver, Jelly Roll Morton, Louis Armstrong's Hot Five, Django Reinhardt, Bessie Smith, and so on. They also knew virtually all the fine jazz musicians of the day. In college Ahmet introduced me to this classic music of the 1920s and 1930s, which I might have missed otherwise, because the recordings had long been out of print and out of style and were not reissued until years later. I have been grateful to him ever since. From this basic love the two brothers built their recording company, but they had something else going for themselves as well because they were Turkish — the nonprejudiced view of the world that so astonished Malcolm X when he visited Mecca. Ahmet and Nesuhi never saw "black" or "white" and so possessed a state of mind I doubt a white American can ever acquire completely and naturally, though possibly there are some exceptions.

Nesuhi handled album production and Ahmet, who had a good ear for hits, was largely in charge of singles. He had also become a charter member of the jet set — a life-style he always loved — and was now flying at such a rarefied altitude I had virtually lost sight of him. His brother and I had maintained a closer contact. Nesuhi happened to be in Europe, but since I knew his secretary I was able to explain the favor I was asking and so inquired if anyone else might help. This quickly produced Nesuhi's assistant, Mark Schulman, whom I knew only slightly. He immediately sensed what albums would be appropriate for the occasion, but doubted they had 100 different ones and asked if a few duplicates of one or another star or group would be okay. I said I felt so and relayed the question silently to Judy, who nodded. Mark asked me to call back and confirm the arrangement later that day. I was surprised at his instant receptivity to such a large order, since we were scarcely acquainted, though I am sure the secretary had confirmed my status as an old friend. I wondered if perhaps Nesuhi had a secret file on me as one of a number of people on his "po' boy" list who should be granted reasonable favors from time to time. I told Judy I would look her up as soon as I had an answer. I dropped by the hut two days later.

"We have the records, one hundred of them."

"Great."

"There's one problem, though."

"What's that?"

"You're going to have to borrow a car and find a couple of strong Mau Mau friends like Jonathan and Robert to go get them."

"What do you mean?"

"Well, the fellow at Atlantic says he's got four twenty-pound boxes stacked on the floor beside his desk, each with twenty-five LPs in it, and when I told him a young lady named Judy Frazer would come by to pick them up he said she'd better bring along a couple of assistants."

"LPs?"

"Yes."

"A hundred LPs?"

"Yes."

"Oh my! I was just thinking of a hundred of those little forty-fives. You got us a hundred albums?"

"Yes, I thought that's what you meant."

In a "good" television drama script Judy Frazer would probably hug the white man, kick up a heel, and exclaim insipidly: "Mah goodness, that sho' was white of y'all. I mean for all the chillun." I, in turn, would look embarrassed and get my feet tangled up shuffling around like Festus and say: "Aw shucks, Miss Judy, it warn't nothin' really." But fortunately with all its trouble and misery Ocean Hill was not a place to write or to find such a script. So we settled for the material at hand — a mutual re-evaluation by two human beings who, through circumstance and race, had been frozen off from one another in an ice-locked polarity that was neither human nor useful.

The month of May trickled away.

As the school year came down to the final days, I periodically bugged Martin about running the *Look* piece, but with fading hopes because it was now virtually too late for it to have any effect on the course of events. A strange, negative, and quite alien feeling was enveloping me, a growing lethargy and listlessness. I felt helpless and ineffectual, almost as though I were becoming a nonperson, a cypher. Of all the people I had seen, called, pursued, or badgered, not one seemed to possess the human or material resources for relating to a passionate need. I began to think that Ira Mothner's somewhat cynical view of the world was perhaps the only real view after all ("Bang, bang — you're dead!"). The oppressive futility and defeatism that pervades a ghetto was beginning to rub off, to the point where I sensed a startling thing about what can happen to the soul if that well of despair grows too deep and too dark. One can begin to sink in it, to drown in it, to come to feel it is all that is real and then, quite paradoxically, begin to enjoy and revel in these negative, antihuman, and suicidal sensations, like a scuba diver who has been down too far for too long and so begins to experience the heady effects of nitrogen narcosis — the "rapture of the deep" — and as enthralled and confused as a hopeless drug addict, descends ever deeper into the abyss, never to be seen again. Isolated as I was, I began to think that perhaps I had not seen anything worthwhile after all, that maybe the whole experiment had been a chimera, a figment of my imagination.

I phoned Walter Lynch, the school community-coordinator for the district, and asked if he would be kind enough to take me on a brief driving tour of the area. Walter was a middle-aged, mild, friendly, and outgoing black man who had been an Ocean Hill resident for many years, and who managed a variety of programs to bring people and schools together. He knew Ocean Hill–Brownsville, its varying neighborhoods, and a great many residents. We met in McCoy's office.

"How's the district assassin?" I asked.

"Shoo! Isn't that something?"

There had been an article in the *New York Times* reporting that Walter and several other local people had been implicated in a plot to assassinate Albert Shanker. I had chatted with Walter on many occasions and could scarcely picture him as an underground plotter, let alone a potential assassin. He was too mild, too well known, too balanced, and too interested in continuing the life and times of Walter Lynch.

We toured the area slowly in Walter's car, and he chatted about the character of this street and that, this school or that, which helped me reaffirm in a quiet hour or so my basic impressions. We stopped briefly at I.S. 271, the other intermediate school in the district which had been the focus and the battleground for all of the confrontations, hassles, and the great teachers' strike of earlier years and even now bore the brunt of occasional eruptions in the district. Walter had an office here and wished to attend to a few things before we continued our tour. He introduced me to Bill Harris, the new black acting principal of the school whom McCoy had appointed to try and keep the lid on and who certainly appeared to be succeeding reasonably well. Unlike I.S. 55, which had been kept largely out of the political turmoil and so afforded Percy Jenkins three relatively stable years to get his teachers, kids, and programs going, this school, embroiled in strife, had had no such sustained management. Instead there had been a succession of assistant principals, of whom Bill Harris was the last, trying to hold the fort against the periodic disruptions which occurred.

Walter and I visited another intermediate school about a dozen blocks from I.S. 55, but not in McCoy's district. Like 271 it was strictly Board of Education architecture. Virtually all of its windows were broken. If 271 was only holding on by district standards (with windows intact despite that) with 55 well off the ground, then this intermediate school was no school at all by any standards. Without looking farther I knew we could find other schools in the area which were no schools either, like P.S. 158 a few blocks off in East New York. Our tour was not a detailed resurvey of things, nor was it intended to be. For me it was like a brief glance into the mirror on waking in the morning, just to make sure I was still there, that I had seen what I had seen, that I knew what I knew. It was a reaffirmation. Afterward I felt more like my usual self.

June came.

I checked around the schools to determine, amid all the confusion and uncertainty that now enveloped the district, whether any of the people and the projects might possibly remain there the following year. I knew that a great experiment sinks slowly, without all the passengers knowing it is really going down. Some state and federally funded operations might continue for a while. So might others like Jackie Rogers's program in the Annex, which had been an imported university pilot study. If some semblance of the district could survive, then I could pursue my film project without so much pressure and have the whole summer to do it. It looked as though a few elements would still be there. Percy felt his school would be intact because he had his staff ready to carry over. But at P.S. 144 I found the math lab bare, stripped of its ingeniously contrived computer, store, metric weights, and so on. The five teachers were still there, but faced with an uncertain future they had disassembled their marvelous inventions and carted them away for storage in an empty garage behind one teacher's house. Eva Kerr reported her hut was dead, to me and to the ladies as well. The Community Education Center was clearly on a list of programs to be liquidated. Considering the fact that Brooklyn Assemblyman Sam Wright, a local black political figure and a party accommodator who had quickly disowned the experiment when trouble with the power structure erupted, would probably become head of the new local school board when the larger district was established in the fall (as he did), it seemed unlikely that Eva and her rather militant and polarized ladies would be personae gratae, in any case. If Wright took over no waves, no ripples even, would ever wash out from Ocean Hill again. Doing anything next year was hopeless.

I had a sandwich at the luncheonette and walked back to the district office. Henriette handed me a note. I had received a call from the head of the educational film project I have mentioned with a message that I should call back. By this time I was quite familiar with the little labyrinth of offices off the reception room, so I looked about to see if I could find one that was unoccupied and return the call. One cell was empty. On the wall was a poster I had seen many times before, but which now struck me with a new intensity, probably because of the hopeless feeling that had overtaken me. It was a photograph of a black boy, maybe ten years old, in rather tattered clothes, with his back against a blank brick wall as he looked at the camera. He was simply staring at the photographer with a completely ambiguous expression on his face. It was not hostile, or appealing, or demanding, ingenuous or obsequious, hateful or hopeful. Rather there was a completely suspended feeling in the expression, that of a kid who was simply watching you. Not dead blank, yet not anticipating or reflecting any particular emotion either. The boy just stared as though awaiting an answer, mature in his childishness, prepared for whatever the answer might be to a question he was not asking, a plea he was not suggesting — except for the fact of being a living child, here and now, standing against this blank brick wall, and watching me. At the bottom of the poster was Langston Hughes's poem that begins: "What happens to a dream deferred?" The last three lines now took on a new meaning:

Maybe it just sags
like a heavy load.

Or does it explode?

For several years I had been living with the delusion that the
last line of this poem was the answer to the opening question.
Now I had become insidiously convinced that the two lines
preceeding it were, in fact, the real answer. I blinked at the
poster and startled myself by hearing my own voice speaking in
the little room.

"Okay, kid, let's give it one more try."

I picked up the telephone and dialed the number Henriette
had given me. To my complete astonishment I learned their
film had unexpectedly shifted its production arrangements,
which opened up the possibility for me to shoot some teaching
and learning situations in Ocean Hill in the little school time
remaining, provided this could be done via my "poor boy"
route. I believed it could.

I went to see Bill and Mike. We all agreed without much talk
that we should assemble an interracial crew, which I think we
would have felt anyway at that time even if the subject had
been something quite different from Ocean Hill. But under the
circumstances, I certainly needed Mike because I knew I could
rely completely both on his ability and his technical compe-
tence in a host of matters of which I was totally ignorant. He,
in turn, needed another Mike (Mike Martin) he knew and
trusted as his assistant, since we were going to have to move in
bare-bones fashion. He was also white. That still left options
open for a good black sound man, and Mike said he would contact the union. I phoned McCoy and told him the good news.
To my surprise he was hesitant.

"Man, it's spring out here and these schools are coming apart!
Everybody's on the street. You know. Nice weather and only

three weeks to go. Classes are coming apart at the seams. How're you going to find teachers that can hold them together for filming?"

"I'll try."

I knew he was right and that I had a serious problem. In his little office he sat like a perceptive spider at the center of his web of eight schools, sensitively detecting phenomena as they sent vibrations in over the slender fibers of the district network. I hope he will forgive me for what is aesthetically an unfortunate analogy, but I know of none better to suggest the continuous input he received, both over the telephones and from the constant flux of people in and out of his office. However, I had been in and out of the district myself long enough to establish reasonably solid relationships with the people I needed now. I was one of them as far as they were concerned. They would do their very best to pull things together when the film group showed up. Knowing how capable they were, I felt they would succeed.

On Tuesday, June 9, I circled the district to check "my people," to assess whether what I believed could be delivered was in fact possible. In the afternoon I went to McCoy's office to report the results of my soundings. He shook his head in smiling disbelief.

"You're a beautiful cat, man. You think you can do it, so go."

"I don't think I can do it all, in the time we have. But I think we can do enough of it to get a big piece of that rabbit stew I once mentioned."

"Okay, 'fore I turn you loose, though, I got to make sure it's okay with the governing board."

"How long will that take?"

"We have a meeting this evening. Call me tomorrow."

I did and learned the meeting had been put off a day. The next day the news was the same. I sensed what was happening. The district was now fighting for its life, and the crisis was extreme for all concerned. I suspected that McCoy, under all this pressure, felt that bringing me up in such a situation might appear stupefyingly frivolous:

"Say, everybody, there's this albino cat Bob Campbell, a pretty good cat, who wants to do some shooting in the district. You all seen him around." (The Reverend Oliver and Father Powis nod in a distracted way. The others look blank.) "Well . . ."

As I thought about it I doubted the board meeting had been postponed at all. Rather, I suspected it had been meeting almost around the clock. But, under the circumstances, I just didn't fit in, couldn't fit in, in McCoy's mind. On Friday of that week he said, simply, "Go ahead."

On Monday, June 15, Mike got the equipment together, and we met our "interracial" sound man, Lee. I picked up a rented car that afternoon, drove it home, and we all rendezvoused early the following morning on Dean Street in front of P.S. 178. I directed our cars into the playground behind the portables, we took the equipment into the school, and spent the day filming a long sequence on the rods with Mr. Barrett and, in the afternoon, with Jonathan and Robert teaching. So in the next days we proceeded from one to another of the classroom situations I have already mentioned.

From the first day our interracial sound man began to bug me. He was an older person, in his fifties I guess, and extremely competent. He was also foul-mouthed, speculating as to whether or not he might find some fresh nookie on the job, and commenting that if you liked to make out you couldn't drink. I began to realize that an aspect of the "professional" film business had infected our project, and I didn't like either the sight or the sound of it. Having been out on many film jobs, I knew what union people were like — electricians, sound men, grips, and so on. Not all, but many. These technicians, essential to the work, also adopted what they felt was the aura and glamor surrounding it. In many a motel room on many a location I have listened to them talking into the night about the productions they had been on, the girls they had laid, the good times they had had, emulating what they imagined the "stars" were doing. Such people reminisce about "When *I* made *High Sierra* with Humphrey," "When *I* did *Who's Coming* with Spencer and Sidney and Kate," and so on and on into the dreary drunken night, bolstering their parasitical egos, when in fact what *they* did was run a tape recorder, set mikes, or whatever. In the past I had listened briefly and then drifted away. Now that old sweet chicken had come home to roost on my own poor-boy chicken-shit production.

After the first day's filming I checked in with McCoy.

"Man, I'm getting by now six unto a dozen calls a day about what you cats are into out in the schools."

"I'm sorry. I'm trying to be as simple as I can."

"I know that, man. I'm just telling you that things are coming apart out here, and there are a lot of funny people running around asking funny questions."

"Well, I don't know what to do except to keep going until I strike out."

"I understand that, and I'll do my best to keep these cats off your back. But don't count on it."

"What are people thinking?"

"Well, like I said, there've been a lot of people in and out of here recently looking to pick up a piece of the corpse before it's buried."

"You know that's not what I'm after."

"Sure, I know that. Your teachers know it, too, from what you say. But not everybody knows it. Look, we got nice warm weather now. People are on the street, wondering about you, among other things, carting stuff in and out of the schools. It only takes a minute for a rumor to spread through this whole neighborhood, now that good weather's here, and it doesn't much matter whether the rumor's true or false. If the wrong rumor gets moving, you're dead."

That was the second time I had been told I was dead, and I didn't appreciate it much. But I knew that Rhody was right. Any elation I had felt about being able to shoot a final two weeks' worth of film in the district evaporated on the spot. We were running on borrowed time, day by day. One of the problems that had come up even before we started was the question of releases, which McCoy had turned over to Mr. Eduardo Braithwaite, his curriculum coordinator, a small and modly dressed black man who reminded me a bit of Charles Click, the library teacher in Harlem. For some reason we had not met before. In the course of working out the wording of the releases, Mr. Braithwaite told me about a pet idea of his which he had instituted in P.S. 73 called "Project Serve." In this pilot program particularly disruptive fifth graders, who were doing poorly and feeling increasingly put down and worthless, a negative psychological effect that is a major cause of bad behavior, were told they were needed to help tutor third graders who were having difficulties in reading and math. The effect on fifth graders who were tapped for "Project Serve" was, Mr. Braithwaite said, instant and practically magical, with almost no exceptions.

"That boy or girl, you know, he's going downhill fast, falling farther and farther behind to the point where things are looking pretty hopeless. Of course, the kid knows that better than anyone else and begins to believe he really will never make it. Well, if you tell a kid like that you need him to help in the school, that he has some value after all, that's like the first big breath of fresh air that kid's had for as long as he can remember. And you may not believe it, but that kid has got to do a complete about-face."

I believed it all right, to the point of scheduling "Project Serve" for the second day's shooting. I had also worked out a shooting schedule for the few remaining days in the school year so that we could film the various things we wanted in one school and then move our equipment on to the next. But after my conversation with McCoy, I scrapped good logistics and arranged to film the classes according to importance rather than convenience so we could operate on a day-by-day basis in case something unexpected developed to terminate the filming.

On the second morning we hauled our gear up to a fourth-floor classroom in P.S. 73 where Mr. Braithwaite was waiting. He introduced us to Miss Eva McEachern, a slim and attractive young lady with a stylish Afro wig who was the teacher in charge of "Project Serve." We spent the morning filming fifth graders working with their younger pupils and then, in the early part of the afternoon, shot Miss McEachern with three tutors as they prepared lessons for their third graders. With a collection of fifth graders present I decided to set up something. I asked Mr. Braithwaite to select three of them, and we would film a little discussion group with him as the moderator. Out of this I hoped to get some expression from the children themselves as to how they felt about "schools as usual" before the district took over, manifested in this case by the project they were involved in. Lee, the cynical and very professional sound man, began to bend my ear.

"You a director?"

"No."

"But you're supposed to be the director?"

"I guess so."

"Well, seems to me you're awfully casual. At CBS we'd be in, set up the lights and camera, shoot the interview, and be out of here." (Lee had been the sound man on a variety of CBS ghetto jobs.)

"Shoot *what?*" I asked.

"The kid or the teacher — doing whatever they do or are supposed to do."

"Like what? Wiggle their ears? Or roll their eyeballs and sing 'Swanee'?"

"Well, not that exactly, but they'd be efficient and prepared. They'd shoot and be out of here. They'd know what the point was."

"Well, I'm operating under a couple of handicaps. For one thing I'm not a director and am not technically qualified so I can't be all that efficient. Also, I'm not sure what the point is. The only way I can think of to get a feeling for what these kids are doing is to run a lot of film and tape and hope we end up with a few good moments that express what it's all about." (Though I did not say so I felt quite convinced, from what Lee said, that if CBS operated in the way he described then they did *not* get the point — at least, if something about children and teaching and learning was the point. In fact, they hadn't even gotten the point of the hassles, which was easier to see.) "Also," I concluded, "as far as directing you and Mike to do things, I'm used to working with people who know what they're doing to begin with."

Mike Konkus and Mr. Braithwaite had arranged a cluster of chairs for our little seminar which would involve Mr. B. as moderator and three fifth graders who were from the same class and so had a continuity of experience together. Two of our "panelists" were Puerto Rican, Jocelyn Ramirez and Carlos Otero; the third was a black youngster named Vernon Smith. I asked Mr. B. to try to draw the children out on two points: how they felt about school before the project and what their current assessment was. Here are some highlights of the seminar:

Vernon: "When I first walked into that class I cried. I didn't know what I was supposed to do."
Jocelyn: "That Mr. Johnson, he was out of his mind."
Mr. B.: "What do you mean?"
Jocelyn: "Why, he just started telling us what to do. And I didn't know what to do or how to do it. Or what he wanted. So I just sat there in my chair rocking back and forth. He was out of his mind."
Carlos: "All he give us was 'our day.' You know (in a mimicking and singsong voice), 'This — is — our — day. It — is — a — nice — day.'"

Vernon: "I used to try and make people laugh. Like I'd hide in the closet and make funny faces. Or climb on top of it. Mr. Johnson got after that, you know, threw me out of class. After that I got expelled."

Carlos: "I thought I'd never make it."

Mr. B.: "What do you mean, you thought you'd never make it?"

Carlos: " 'Cause I couldn't hardly read. Couldn't even read or spell or anything. Do math."

Mr. B.: "And now?"

Carlos: "Now I know how to do the work. I'm going to make it."

Mr. B.: "Of course, you are."

Vernon: "One day, the day before I got expelled, Mr. Johnson came after me with a ruler. And he's big, you know, with those funny kind of spread-out feet. Well, he went for me with that ruler and he stepped, got one foot in a wastebasket. And he fell right on top of Sheila!"

The three looked at each other and laughed, recollecting the scene.

Mr. B.: "Vernon, now that you are over here, how are you doing in your class?"

Vernon: "I'm getting good grades — eighty-five, sometimes even ninety. My teacher says it's good for me, being over here helping other kids to learn. And I'm learning better myself."

Mr. B.: "And how about you, Carlos. How are you doing?"

Carlos: "Well, I'm doing better, too. I understand the reading and the math better. I figure, like, if I'm over here, like if the kid don't know a word, and I don't know it either, what's the use my being over here?"

During filming there are periodic interruptions to reload cameras, check tape, and so on. I noticed that Lee was using these moments to cozy up to the attractive Miss McEachern. Earlier on he had said, in an aside to me, something about how he would like to get her wig off and get her into the sack. Now he was exchanging familiarities about how they both came from high-class families in North Carolina and proposing a date for the weekend. Though I knew Lee was married he could — he hinted to the teacher — still be conveniently "on assignment" when Saturday came around. I knew Miss McEachern had an apartment in Queens. What I did not know was whether she had a local Mau Mau boy friend, what the encroachments of this lecherous pseudosophisticate might mean, or what reverberations such a move could set in motion in the district.

After the day's shooting was over I had a talk with Mike Konkus about this and explained my worries as the pseudo-director, telling him what McCoy had said. It was evident we were into a sticky situation, and there was no clear way out of it. I could have fired Lee, though that would have been personally difficult, since I had never done such a thing before. But that would leave us with the problem of finding another sound man, something we could hardly have done overnight. The only recourse seemed to be for me to talk with him and insist that he give up his date, at least until the job was done. We met on the street as usual the next morning. I took Lee aside as unobtrusively as possible to avoid any status problem before the others and tried to explain the situation to him as I saw it — how potentially explosive a scene we were involved in, how quickly rumors could spread, true or false, that if we couldn't continue to the end of school the whole thing would be a bust. I expressed my misgivings about his forthcoming date. He shrugged his shoulders with the air of a working cynic, shrewdly wise to the ways of the world, and now confronted with some novitiate. There was an aura of moral and professional blackmail in his position which I had no defense against, apart from being the pseudodirector.

"Look," Lee said, "I know the streets out here. I know these street niggers. I was out here with CBS during all the strikes and so on. I never had any trouble. I know these 'down home' people and how to handle them."

His sense of power and contempt shook me.

"That may be," I said, "but I think you'd better call off your date. If that goes the wrong way, I'm out of business."

"Well, it's your production," meaning if the lid blew it would be my problem.

I had pushed Lee as far as I could. I knew I could not force him to scrap his date, and I regarded this as a character weakness on my part. He had expressed himself, and we left it at that. I crossed my fingers and checked my pocket to make sure my green six rod was still there. After that, though, I didn't hear any more of his usual on-the-job smutty talk. As the end of the week approached, Lee instigated various conversations with Mike and me about how he could expect to be paid for his weekly services, exactly when and where.

Toward graduation time we moved into I.S. 55 to film Becky Taylor's class plus an unexpected bonus Percy Jenkins had passed the word to me about. This was a session in "Words in Color," the verbal equivalent to the rods which he had mentioned earlier, to be impressarioed by none other than the man himself, Caleb Gattegno, who was visiting the school for a day as a consultant to demonstrate his new technique for the English teachers. We filmed a bit of his classroom demonstration and afterward an impromptu seminar featuring Gattegno, Becky Taylor, Jeff Nilson, and half a dozen other teachers. Technically this is known as "in-school training," a term which I believe actually exists in print somewhere in the New York school system's lexicon but which, so I am told, has almost never come to pass in actual fact.

One thing I wished very much to film was the graduation exercises of I.S. 55, which were to be held in a nearby church. Eddie Bonnemere, the first-rate musician who had a considerable music program going in the school, had rehearsed many numbers for the event and Percy hoped we could cover it, offering to set us up in the loft of the church for the occasion. Despite his confidence and encouragement I was afraid to appear with the crew either outside the church or in the balcony. Our established routine in the schools was tenuous enough, and so I felt obliged to decline the opportunity of filming something I wished very much could be recorded.

During these last days I had become increasingly disenchanted with *Look,* since it was now too late for the story to do any good. Though I had rewritten the text at Martin Goldman's suggestion so it could appear after the funeral, I had little confidence that the story would ever run. Besides, it was one thing to try to rescue a drowning man; I had no faith in the prospects of resurrecting a dead one. Finally I went to see Martin.

"Look," I said, "suppose you were Johnny Cash and had spent some time in Folsom Prison. Gotten to know quite a few of the inmates pretty well, you know? And suppose you'd written a song about them and a lot of them knew about it, okay? And then you take the song to your publisher, but he can't publish it for some reason or another. And, you know, you happen to believe in the song. And suppose now and then you meet a parolee on the street and he says: 'Hey, Johnny baby! How you doin'? Whatever happened to that song you wrote about us cats when you were out there in the jailhouse?' Well, Martin — I understand embarrassments. I am used to living with them. We all are. But there are certain embarrassments I can't really live with, and this is one."

"I understand," said Martin. "I think I really do understand. What do you want me to do?"

"I want you to give me my story back. I want you to release me from any obligation to *Look,* and I want you to give John Vachon his pictures back. I want to see if we have any other options at all, later on."

"That seems to me a perfectly reasonable request. I think I understand it very well. We all care about this story, but after all it's your story. So let's go talk to Bill Arthur about it right now."

We walked down the hall to the publisher's office.

"Bill," Martin said, "you remember Bob Campbell and the Ocean Hill story? It's been around a long time now. He feels it can't wait forever and wants it back."

Bill looked quizzical and a bit sad: "As I remember, everything we asked of you was done. I suppose, under the circumstances, we should release the story."

Had I known at the time how fast the magazine was dying I could have sympathized more with the heaviness and helplessness that seemed to be enveloping two decent men. All their options were going up in smoke, including the one that is the lifeblood of every good journalist — the opportunity for a head-knocking crusade in behalf of something important. It takes security to pick up that kind of option. It vanishes overnight if one is confronted with a grinding day-by-day problem of what in hell will "sell." Getting the story back was a Pyrrhic victory. Yet sometimes marching backward is better than standing still and growing numb and freezing to death. Now, as my adopted battalion marched surely into the jaws of death, I felt, should anyone happen to ask me about the story, that I ought to be able to say I had committed one last act of defiance, however negative and self-defeating, one last and futile shaking of an impotent fist at a thoughtless society now herding a large procession of children toward a gas chamber designed to asphyxiate their minds — which is what the impending destruction of the district added up to in my own mind.

One day during the last week of school an incident occurred on Dean Street in front of P.S. 178. A group of local militants ambushed Gene Aptekar. A rumor had gotten on the wire to the effect that during a bus trip with his class to Washington, D.C., Gene, who related directly and physically to his children, had coddled one girl on his lap and that an erection had resulted and been seen. That, naturally, was a very ugly story. David Lee, the Chinese principal of the school, had heard the rumor the day before and had tried to head Gene off on the way to work. The effort was unsuccessful, but he managed to contact

Gene's father-in-law. When Gene arrived a melee began. David Lee appeared promptly on the street with a blackjack to defend the teacher. At that moment Gene's father-in-law drove by in his car. Gene jumped in and was whisked out of the district. I felt extremely sorry for Gene, that a fine teacher's fine year should end on such a dreadful note. Dave Lee told me privately afterward what I knew anyway, that this was a serious charge. He added, however, something I also would have surmised, that given Gene's relationship with the parents of his class, not one of them believed any such thing had happened. Whatever event, or imagined event, had been the source of the story, they regarded it as trivial. They knew Gene and they knew their children, but none of this knowledge had any effect on the germination and ultimate eruption of a nasty and sinister rumor which led to violence.

That afternoon I went to a party. Several days before certain people had been handed, in almost surreptitious fashion, a mimeographed sheet of paper proclaiming that a "final blast" was being hosted by Wayne Barrett, one of the teachers at I.S. 55, and his wife who taught at P.S. 73. This young white couple lived in the neighborhood a few blocks away from P.S. 178. I felt rather honored at receiving an invitation because it seemed a bit like being passed a furtive message on the damp and foggy streets of Dublin in 1920 or thereabouts to attend an underground rally of the IRA. I stopped by a local liquor store, picked up a bottle of bourbon as an offering, and headed for Bergen Street. Quite a few familiar faces were there including Glendora Pender and Emma Kelly from P.S. 73 whom I was happy to see. The Gemini, Robert and Jonathan, were jiving to some phonograph music with various female teachers. Father Powis dropped in. As we were chatting one of the local militants whom I did not know approached with a look of concern on his face.

"Father, don't tell that reporter about where's the guns hid in the church!"

"Don't worry," I said. "I know the secret of the church."

"You do?" The young man looked extremely alarmed.

"Yes." I assumed an air as though I were about to produce a dramatic revelation, like "Mr. Memory" at the climax of that marvelous old film *The Thirty-Nine Steps:* "The secret of the church — is — that the C-sharp organ pipe — is — actually — a bazooka!

Everyone relaxed and laughed. Shortly afterward I went home.

For some time I had been pestering Eva Kerr, because I considered filming a working session with her ladies a matter of high priority. This had been difficult to arrange as the whole group, since it was about to be disbanded, was embroiled with problems about the future. They found the time one afternoon, however, and we moved the equipment in and set up. Practically everyone was there, including Terry and Linda. I handed Linda a release and a pen.

"You know," I said, "I can hardly think of a greater pleasure at this point than to ask Linda King for her signature."

Linda smiled, read the release quickly, and signed it without hesitation. The others did the same. We settled in for several hours of shooting as the group reviewed the year's home reading program, various aspects of the testing, and discussed a variety of things they had learned.

During that last week I was concerned with a number of details including gathering up releases from different principals as they came in from children's parents, paraprofessionals, and teachers who had been involved in the filming. So a pattern developed in which I remained in the district to attend to various chores after we wrapped up shooting in the schools at 3 P.M. This was reasonable enough since there were all kinds of tag ends to take care of. But to a degree it was also because I was simply incapable of tearing myself away. The great experiment was sinking fast now, and I felt rooted to the spot, hypnotized, like some latter-day Ishmael transfixed by the portent of these final moments. Each passing image seemed to hang suspended for a second before vanishing and so appeared larger than life and took on colorations different from the hues of everyday events. Who could foretell, at the end, what strange and cataclysmic spectacles might occur?

In the course of one of these afternoons I stopped by headquarters and poked my head into McCoy's office. He was on the phone but waved me in and indicated I should take a seat. From his telephone conversation I could tell he had just become a grandfather and that felicitations were being proffered by the party who had called him. As he hung up Mrs. Hattie Bishop walked in. She was a very large and very black woman, a long-time resident of the community, and a member of the governing board. I had met her briefly at I.S. 55, where she was frequently in evidence, for she was also in the Parents' Association of the school. Percy had introduced us one afternoon in his office, but we had never really become acquainted. Now Mrs. Bishop looked at me, still a comparative stranger, and hesitated. But on learning the news, she extended her own congratulations to McCoy.

"What are you going to do after school?" she asked.

"Mrs. Bishop, I'm going to go so far away that nobody'll be able to find me, not even the FBI. I'm tired, Mrs. Bishop, but I'll send you a postcard marked X."

Mrs. Bishop had been almost monosyllabic in my presence. I imagine she was that way around other people she scarcely knew, whites especially. But for a brief moment the veil disappeared.

"Don't leave us, Mr. McCoy. Please don't leave us."

"I'll try not to, Mrs. Bishop," McCoy said in a hesitant voice.

After that day or thereabouts the Green Hornet was not to be seen in the parking lot anymore. Though Rhody McCoy was supposed to preside at various graduation exercises, including the one for I.S. 55 in the church, he never appeared. He simply disappeared, as he had suggested to Mrs. Bishop. Many people, including myself, regarded him as a somewhat severe and demanding man, moody at times, but these attributes were certainly understandable, given his drive to build a ghetto schoolhouse. I had come to sense another side to the man as well, and now a final meaning of the small plaque on his desk came home to me. He had indeed done everything with love, insofar as was humanly possible. He had put his whole heart into the district. But in that last week the thread had snapped, so that he was now incapable of presiding over what could only be considered realistically as the final interment of what had been a grand but a fleeting dream.

School closed for good.

Two days later I drove back to Ocean Hill. Though McCoy had vanished I knew the district office would be open as well as the main offices of the schools, where a few late releases had accumulated. Driving along under the el out Atlantic Avenue I stopped for a red light. Unexpectedly I was accosted by a drunken middle-aged black man who lurched from the shadows with hand outstretched toward the open window of the car.

"I's ain't mad 'bout what your grandfather fucked my grandaddy. I's ain't mad 'bout none o' that shit. You unnerstan'?"

"I sure hope not, friend."

"Say! I's ain't mad 'bout none that shit!"

"Well, I sure hope not." I took his outstretched hand in mine and grasped it. "I hope the old days of that kind of shit are over."

A handshake was not what either of us had expected, but it was what had happened. So I continued to hold his hand. Suddenly I noticed the light had turned green and horns were blowing impatiently behind us.

"You go on take care of yourself, you hear?"

"Okay. Care of m'self."

"Okay."

"Say! Not mad 'bout that!"

"Okay. But you watch out there, now!"

As the man stood gyrating uncertainly beneath the elevated tracks, traffic began to move and accelerate around me as I pulled away slowly. I watched the man in my rearview mirror as he miraculously made his way to the sidewalk through the oncoming vehicles. Then I moved the car off and almost ran head-on into a steel stanchion supporting the el.

After picking up releases here and there I stopped by the Catholic Presentation Church over which Father Powis presided but which I had never actually visited before. It was a rather decrepit old church on a seedy side street with a dilapidated frame house next door which, I assumed, was the parish house. A faded and poorly lettered sign over the doorway proclaimed it to be a Community Center. I walked in. There was virtually no furniture on the ground floor, at least in the two rooms I could observe from the hall. The room on the left contained a couple of rickety chairs, the one on the right a battered old desk and one chair. I assumed Father Powis lived upstairs, but I found him in the right-hand room with half a dozen teenagers. They were stuffing envelopes with mimeographed notices I presumed the kids were to deliver in the neighborhood. Father Powis looked up.

"Hi."

"How are you?"

"Come in. How in the world did you find me here?" Since Father Powis spent virtually all his time on the street it was the only place I had ever seen him, except occasionally in McCoy's office.

"I'm lucky, I guess. If I weren't lucky I'd be dead." As I said it the words struck me as a bit strange, talking to a priest. Yet I felt it was true enough.

"I suppose I understand that. What's on your mind?"

"I just wanted to ask you a question."

"Fine. Just give me a few minutes, okay?" Father Powis and the boys continued with their work. One of them kept muttering at him:

"Motherfucker! Fuckin' priest or somethin'. You didn't have that phony collar turned 'round I'd bus' you right in de mout'. You some fuckin' holy man or somethin'? Shit! Cum'on, cum'on. Square off, motherfucker! Turn that collar back 'round where I can see it good! Jus' 'cause you got some motherfuckin' collar don't make you no special motherfucker to me. You hear?"

The scene struck me as reminiscent of the point where I had come in, three years or so earlier on. Father Powis and the other boys went on stuffing envelopes as though this troubled teenager were saying nothing at all. So did the challenger himself. They finished and Father Powis ushered the boys from the room.

"I have a visitor now," he said.

I felt a bit stupid about my intrusion. I reported that the *Look* story was dead and I had withdrawn it; that I was considering what other possibilities there might be for it and the pictures. I was upset because I knew quite a few people had become aware of the effort, and I felt it was personally difficult to just walk away now, after that.

"I don't think it will make any difference to people out here at all. They are used to that. They don't plan. They don't expect. They don't do or react in any way you are used to. Two days ahead is a lifetime as far as these people are concerned. What happens this afternoon is what matters. What you say or do doesn't matter at all. Not at all."

I left the rectory severely depressed. Now, finally, I had been presented with the reverse "Ira Mothner effect." Spin your wheels. It just don't matter. It just don't matter at all — motherfucker.

I got in the car and headed back toward Atlantic Avenue.

From a street corner a young Puerto Rican in his twenties hailed me, smiling. I assumed it was someone I had met casually around the schools. I stopped the car. I had been driving slowly anyway, circling like a last plaintive sea gull piping for a final handout, unwilling to admit the ship was down. The windows of the car were open. As the young man approached, I noticed he was slowly wrapping around one hand about a yard of clothes line with several feet of heavy chain attached to the end of it. This, I could easily see, would readily produce a do-it-yourself version of a massive and formidable mailed fist. The Puerto Rican came to the car door.

"Give me a ride home?"

"Sure, get in."

We drove off slowly.

"Where do you live?"

"Dean Street, just below Saratoga."

That address was, at the most, six blocks away.

"You live around here?"

"No, I've just been down at the Presentation Church talking with Father Powis."

"What about?"

"Oh, about the school district here. McCoy's schools, you know."

"Guess I heard something about that. I just got out of the army. I got wounded in that thing."

"Hope you're okay now."

"Yeah, I'm okay now I guess. But my head's a little funny sometimes."

"Which house do you live in?"

"The green one, the one right up there."

I stopped the car.

"You come out here much?"

"I been coming out quite a lot."

"Coming back sometime soon?"

"I don't know for sure."

"Well, if you get back, say on a Saturday night sometime, you know where to find me. We could go out and have a lot of fun. I don't mean spendin' your money or nothin' like that. I mean, maybe you and me could just have some fun together."

"I'd like that. Maybe we can do that sometime."

As we sat in the parked car talking the mailed fist was slowly unwound to free the human hand inside.

"Okay, man. Look me up."

"I'll do that if I can."

We shook hands. He got out of the car and vanished into the small green house on Dean Street. I knew that the young man was slightly demented. Whether this was due to the Vietnam war wound, or Brooklyn schools as usual, or something else, I could not tell. As I drove away I cursed myself. I had lied to him. He was the first human being in that whole wretched ghetto I had lied to. Not directly, perhaps. But I had dissembled, agreeing that we might get together some Saturday night and have some fun when I knew perfectly well this would never come about, never in a million years. As I drove off I gradually realized why I had lied. My hands were trembling and sweating and the steering wheel slipped a bit in my grasp. I felt cold, alone, and afraid — afraid for the first time in all those many weeks I had spent in Ocean Hill. Until that last day fear had not been permitted. I had been apprehensive at times, on the dark and lonely Rockaway Avenue subway platform or walking along some of the grimmer side streets of the ghetto. Yet I had had good reasons for being here, which I had felt would somehow bail me out should an unforeseen and dangerous situation arise. In fact, I was actually afraid of being afraid, for then I would not have been able to do what I desperately wanted to do. Now I found myself hastily rolling up the car windows, locking the doors, and moving at a speed that would prevent my being accosted by anyone on the street, leaving Ocean Hill in much the same fashion as I had entered Harlem to begin with.

I knew why. My passport was no longer valid. My franchise to operate in the district had expired along with the district itself. A unique and life-giving social contract that had been the heart of a group of experimental schools and a small ghetto community, creating an umbrella of common purpose large enough also to shelter a marginal visitor for a time, had now been brutally terminated. The hopeless, fatalistic scene in the rectory told me the consequences. This small area of Brooklyn, which for one brief moment had seen the light of hope where none had existed before, could only plunge into an even deeper gloom now, if that were possible, a darkness that could conceal unimaginably dank and mindless horrors. In that deepening gloom, that excruciating and silent twilight, I felt terribly white and terribly visible, an unjustified intruder in the new darkness. I left Ocean Hill for good.

Turning left on Atlantic Avenue I headed for the Brooklyn Bridge in the far distance. I slowed down and relaxed a bit. My mind felt leadened, almost suffocated by the sense of failure and futility, personal and otherwise, that I had been living with for so long now. In all that time I had accomplished nothing, except perhaps a strange and personal and extremely quixotic rain dance among the jungle bunnies who dance beneath the bridge that does not touch down. Some shit. Some rabbit stew. I rolled a window down as I headed up the ramp onto the bridge and passed through its classic stone arches. From time to time, as I crossed the center span, I looked down on the shimmering East River. And I looked ahead, just to make sure the old Brooklyn Bridge did, indeed, touch down as it always had. Somewhere in mid-span, with the breeze off the river blowing in, I began to feel like my old self again, though transformed perhaps. At least I had managed at the last hour to smuggle back across the chasm, across the old and magnificent Brooklyn Bridge which always did touch down, something of importance — many feet of good film, the thousands of fine photographs which John Vachon had taken, and above all a meticulously kept log of a three-year voyage: "something alive to haunt them with" as Charles Wilson had said at the end of a previous spring which now seemed long ago and very far away.